INEFFABLE

Architecture, Computation and The Inexpressible

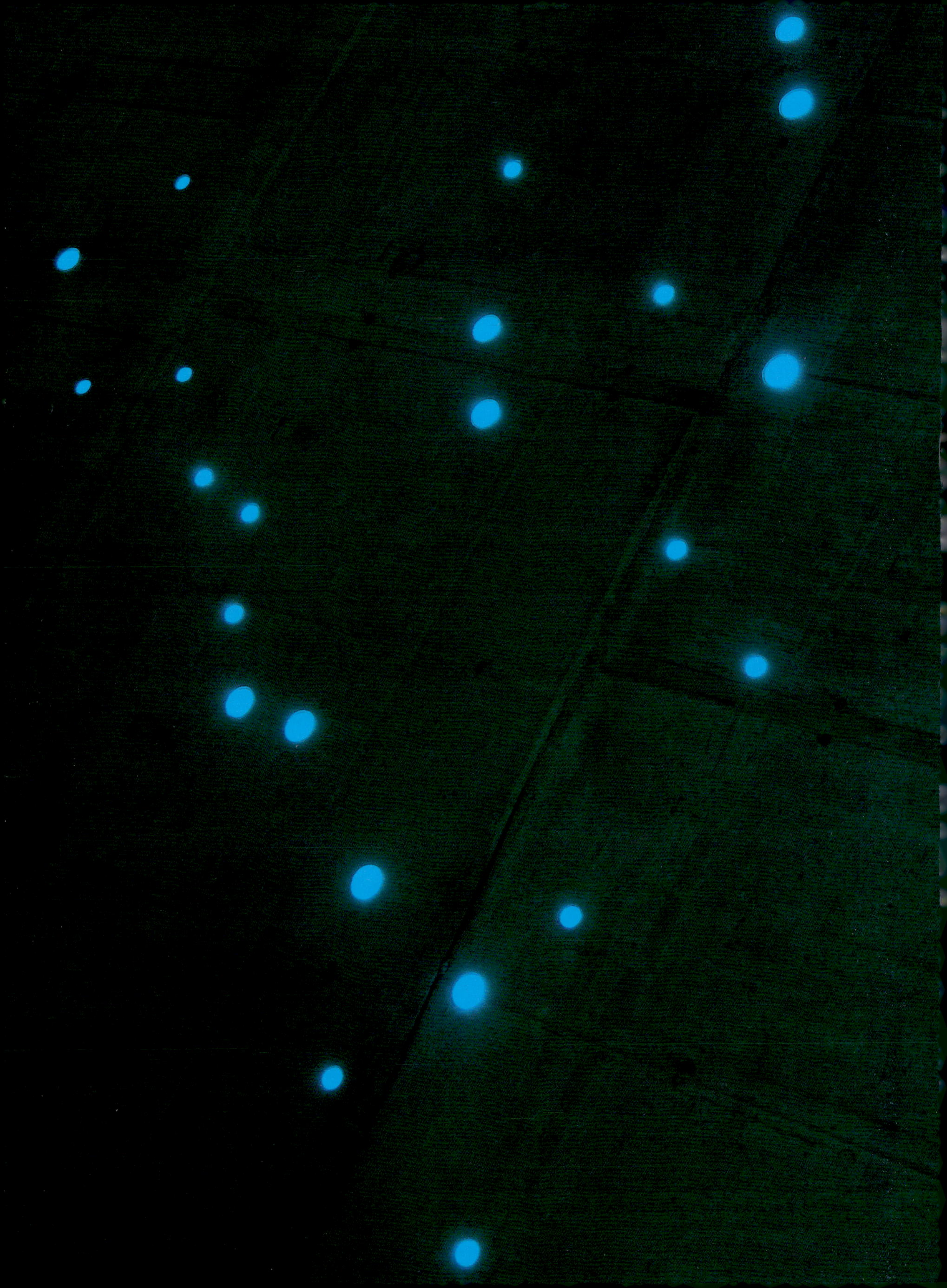

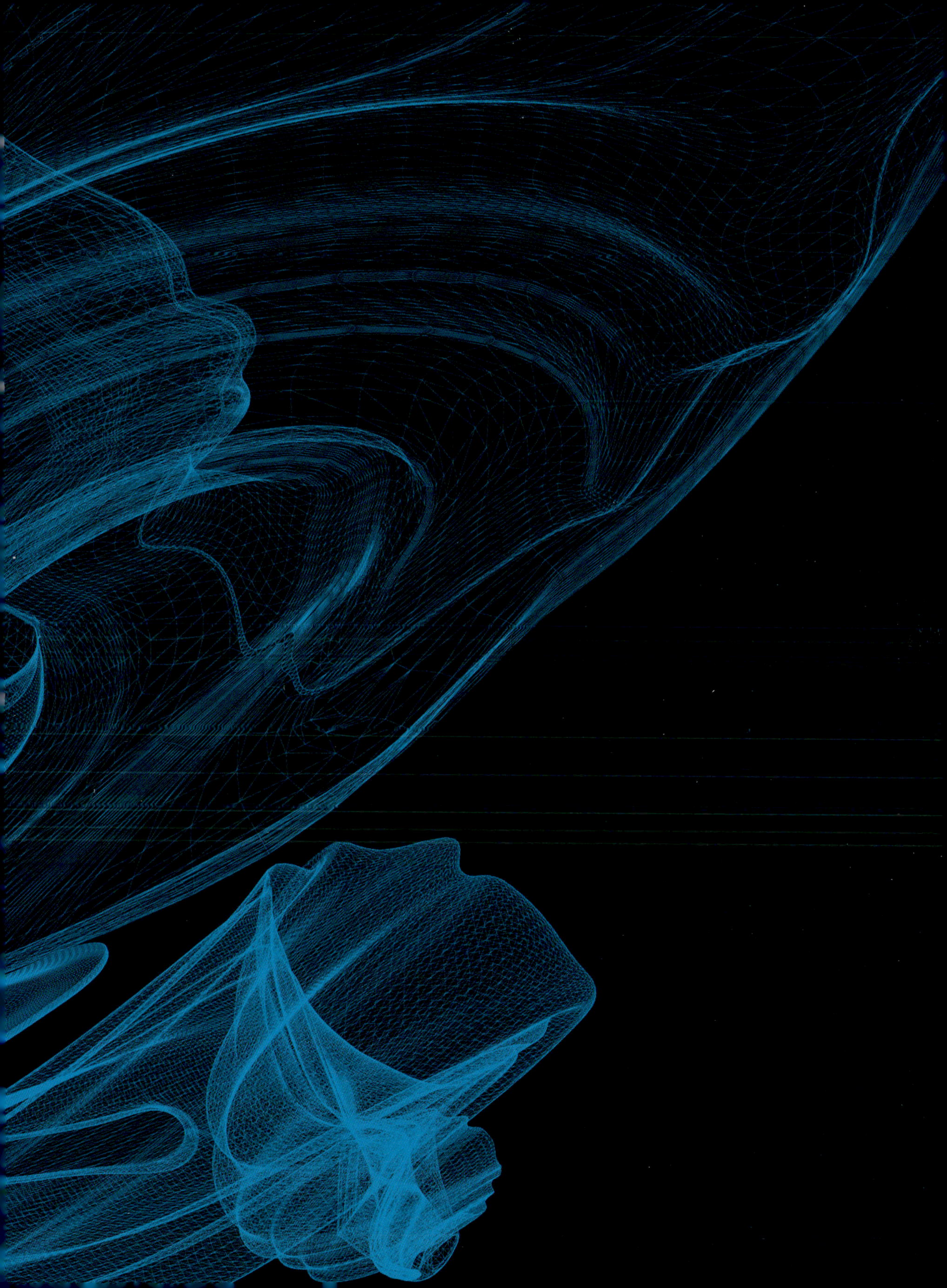

Ineffable was made possible by generous funding from
The Graham Foundation,
The Solow Foundation,
The LEF Foundation and
The City College of New York
Bernard and Anne Spitzer School of Architecture

The City College of New York CITY COLLEGE IS CUNY

INEFFABLE

Architecture, Computation and The Inexpressible

Edited by Bradley Horn

OSCAR RIERA OJEDA
PUBLISHERS

Table of

CONTENTS

Panel Three

Appendix

Acknowledgements

The Graham Foundation, The Solow Foundation, The LEF Foundation and The Bernard and Anne Spitzer School of Architecture
Whose generous support made *Ineffable* possible.

Dean George Ranalli
For his commitment to The Spitzer School of Architecture and his staunch support of its faculty.

President Williams and Provost Dagan
For recognizing the school of architecture as the unique place that we all believe it to be.

Michael Sorkin, Toshiko Mori, Danielle Smoller, Thomas Beeby, Patsy Orlofsky, and Lou Taffera
For their support.

Maria Berman
For her wisdom and advice.

Ashley Schafer
For her encouragement when this project was merely an idea.

Junko Fujimoto
For her tireless research.

Michael Silver
Whose unique imagination and Universal Machines symposium at Pratt in 2005 served as a significant inspiration.

Stephanie Smith, Camille Hall, and Kathleen Sheridan
For their intelligence and immense resourcefulness.

Brett Snyder
For a beautiful poster.

Rosa M. Santos
For the beautiful design of both conference programs and this book.

Howard Schneiderman
For his skill and endless generosity.

Hiroko Suda
For helping us to acquire copyright permission for the images in this book.

Marina Ovtchinnikova, Sheng Pu, Mojtaba Ansari, Calista Ho, David Seto, Nana Akwafi Ankamah
For their help on the day of the event.

The City College School of Music
For the venue.

Oscar Riera Ojeda
For his commitment to excellence in publishing.

Introduction

"If those arrangements were to disappear as they appeared, if some event of which we can at the moment do no more than sense the possibility – without knowing either what its form will be or what it promises – were to cause them to crumble, as the ground of Classical thought did, at the end of the eighteenth century, then one can certainly wager that man would be erased, like a face drawn in sand at the edge of the sea." [1]

While architects are notorious abusers of the term crisis, there can be little doubt that this term is an apt description of the current state of the profession. Despite the fact that our ecological predicament has inspired designers to think harder about important social and environmental issues, it has also produced a worrisome strain of pragmatism within the profession. Add to that the collapse of the financial system, and what you have is a recipe for either blatant instrumentality on one hand, or unbridled escapism on the other. Under these circumstances technology is either blamed for the damage wrought upon the environment or viewed as a cure-all for it. In the meantime we have established little ground for productive exchange regarding the relationship between technology and human agency. (So-called computational architects are rarely seen kibitzing at the water cooler with those who teach the history of the Renaissance.) Yet this conversation seems increasingly necessary if we are to reformulate the ethical implications of architecture in the twenty-first century.

It was with this in mind that fifteen distinguished architects, historians, and educators with diverse points of view were invited to The City College of New York School of Architecture, Urban Design and Landscape Architecture on November 10th, 2007 to address the ineffable. Unlike the Yale symposium *Constructing the Ineffable*, however, which took place at exactly the same time and which dealt exclusively with the problem of sacred buildings, the conference documented in this volume focused neither on the sacred nor on buildings. Instead, it addressed the cultural and philosophical implications of the recent focus on computation in design. As increasing numbers of architects begin thinking and designing directly in the language of machine code, what becomes of the less tangible, more ambiguous dimensions of human expression? Does our reliance on zeros and ones eliminate these nuances or, on the contrary, produce an even greater capacity for their materialization? In this context the term ineffable served as a provocation which pointed to the linguistic limits of the human (think Le Corbusier on the Acropolis); but also to something trans-human (think Harraway's *Cyborg Manifesto*). The former a sublime encounter which defines the boundaries of the human observer, the latter a form of distributed agency which dissolves them. In between these poles participants debated the place of the human subject in contemporary design and the role that technology plays in situating it.

Looking back on that day, many presenters saw the ineffable as related to that place in the not too-distant future where life as we know it is no longer recognizable. In his presentation Karl Chu argued that the postmodern dissolution of the first person subject paved the way for the more radical transformation of the human in what many are now controversially calling the post human era. Chu claimed that the convergence of computation and biogenetics would lead to the dissolution of the political, social, and biological prejudices of what Giorgio Agamben famously called the 'anthropological machine'; an exclusionary agent whose ontological separations have prevented the human from achieving a symbiotic correspondence with anything that exists 'outside' of it. In his presentation *Speaking with the Alien* Ed Keller conjured this 'outside' as a space of potential communication with the Other through film clips from The Andromeda Strain, The Exorcist and Fellini's 8-1/2. Keller's cinematic meditation on energy politics pointed to the irony of trying to separate what it means to be human from the new dimensions of existence which technology perpetually liberates. Instead, he argued, we should be leveraging the unavoidable exchange between energy, information, and matter as a productive means of achieving higher orders of consciousness. But what does this mean for the role of the architect in the 21st century? For Michael Silver this digital enlightenment was a way to finally escape the discord of the past hundred years of architectural theory and achieve an architecture of true empathy. In his project for a baptistery on Mont Saint-Michel a font emerged at low tide as a result of the interaction between a small platform and the sediment which organically flowed around it. A Beowulf cluster supercomputer allowed Silver to simulate the otherwise immeasurable geometry of these provisional landscapes, which completely disappeared at high tide. "In this way design transcends the distinction between building and landscape, here and there, self and world. As an infinite, non-conceptual architecture no I-dentity, I-mage or I-dea can encompass it." For Silver computation was the unavoidable next step in the evolving relationship between human beings and architecture.

It was just this kind of inevitability, however, about which many other presenters harbored suspicions. David Gersten saw the urgency underlying both Chu and Keller's reading of the future as a device for market-driven consensus-building. Drawing on David Harvey's *A Brief History of Neoliberalism*, Gersten argued that architecture's survival depended upon wresting the ethical dimension of human action back from the veil of the free market economy and the "massive computational technologies" which fuel it. In a diagram, Gersten showed the human imagination displaced by these technologies which become an all encompassing lens through which corporations and capital bring each other into mutual focus. Equally apprehensive of meta-narratives, Lebbeus Woods' slides of Bosnian families in war ravaged landscapes reminded fellow panelists of the mortal consequences of any idea of the absolute. Over and against the collective "nostalgia for the unattainable,"[2] Woods framed the ineffable as a profound expression of individual loss; a condition which disrupts the very framework through which we see the world. At a time when individual sovereignty is continually at risk, design must serve as an instrument for expanding our limits; a constant reminder of the relativity of value systems.

Does the contemporary fragmentation of history and subjectivity however, leave us without common ground for meaningful exchange?

Not according to Alberto Perez-Gomez who argued that we are capable of overcoming any "nihilism of despair" by inventing ways to renew our relationship with the pre-existing natural and cultural worlds. Drawing on Heidegger, Perez-Gomez warned of the dangers of "denying death as the positive limit and essential qualifier of life". Questioning the algorithmic architecture proposed by people like Chu, he argued that "Ethics and aesthetics reduced to rules are useless: ethical action is always singular and circumstantial, it always seems miraculous and unique, a transformative experience that is, significantly, analogous to our encounter with beauty in works of art; the arrow of eros."

As a challenge to speakers who remained doubtful that this could be achieved in today's media-saturated and technologically-immersed culture, Evan Douglis posed the concept of Digital Regionalism. For Douglis this meant "...harnessing current digital practices in favor of reaffirming cultural heterogeneity." Worried about what he called the "moralist tone" of the discussion, Douglis argued that in the hands of an enlightened author computational tools can be used to bridge ethics and aesthetics in healthy and productive ways. For speakers such as Ben Nicholson and George Ranalli however, the contemporary fixation on digital technology belied the fact that architecture is as much about feeling as it is about technique. For Nicholson, systems of measurement mirror human desire; they reveal the character of our connection to both each other and to nature. "Measurement is not only about the length of a finger," Nicholson asserted, "it is a whole cultural equation in which love is an essential part." While his presentation questioned the nature of human measurement, Ranalli's concern was with how it ultimately gets encoded into buildings in a manner which conveys both beauty and emotion. Using the drawings of John Soane, Carlo Scarpa and Louis Kahn as examples, Ranalli emphasized the importance of cultural continuity, and worried that computational tools lacked the necessary memory to achieve it.

Still others chose not to view computation as an abrupt epistemic break, and were committed to ways of bridging these opposing positions. Jason Vollen and Yael Erel, for example, argued that design was as much about objective fact as about the projection of the human imagination. In this view neither the bottom-up approach (associated with digital computation) nor the top-down approach (associated with a human author) are adequate in themselves in addressing the uncharted ethical and ecological territory the human race is now entering. Similarly, N. Katherine Hayles and Todd Gannon characterized the evolving relationship between man and computer as one of productive coupling. Answering fellow panelists who felt that the human was in peril, Hayles argued that "The term human is not a trans-historical conception but is very historically specific and culturally embedded... I wouldn't necessarily say that we are moving away from the human, I would rather say that what it means to be human is in flux as it has always been. ...in my personal opinion the most likely scenario is not that humans will continue to exist and somehow dominate machines or that machines will stamp out humans and become the dominant life form on our planet but rather what we already see at a very advanced stage, which is a symbiotic relationship between humans and machines..." The sparks of this symbiotic relationship were found in Howeler/Yoon Architects' *LowRezHiFi* installation in Washington DC where an LED screen registered the movements of pedestrians as an illuminated field of pixels. Here, according to Howeler, "...analog inputs are filtered through computation only to come out on the other end as an analog condition once again." These "digital shadows" were a suggestive counterpoint to the natural light patterns of Saint-Pierre de Firminy, recently completed by Jose Oubrerie; suggesting a shift from an analog to a digital phenomenology.

Having adapted the original design for Firminy to a wide array of construction techniques (both analog and digital), Oubrerie emphasized the relativity of heritage and fully embraced both Howeler/Yoon's and Michael Silver's research as a necessary exchange between different tools and traditions.

This sentiment was echoed by Yehuda Safran who addressed the broader discussion with a cautionary note about the role of history in contemporary discourse. Speaking out against both those who argue for an inevitable future and those who hold fast to a past idea of culture or the human, Safran maintained that historical change is the result of individual action and that freedom only comes from leveraging oneself out of a collective field of time, no matter "when" it is.

When this conference project was conceived it aimed to bridge opposing camps: those who believe that computation has fundamentally changed what architecture is; and those who believe that what is fundamental to architecture is beyond change. The former can be seen as struggling to identify a new perspective for research, practice and theory; the latter as protecting those aspects of the discipline which this perspective would threaten to eliminate. In that sense this book can be read as a collection of strategies for both crafting and addressing an architectural future, which though inevitable in its approach, is still unknown in terms of substance. We are all soothsayers. But, unlike the story of Oedipus, the outcome of the ever greater advent of technology within our lives and profession is not writ in stone. Choices and paths are many, and what participants have given us here are several possible ways forward. What they have in common is the understanding that in a time dominated by technology it becomes even more crucial to grapple with the unquantifiable.

Bradley Horn
New York, 2011

Notes:

1. Michel Foucault, *The Order of Things: An Archaeology of the Human Sciences* (Random House Vintage Books), 387
2. Jean Francois Lyotard, *The Postmodern Condition* (University of Minnesota Press, 1984), 81

Panel One

TECHNOLOGY, LANGUAGE AND TIME

Moderated by Bradley Horn

Panelists Mike Silver · David Gersten · Yehuda E. Safran · Alberto Perez-Gomez · N. Katherine Hayles & Todd Gannon

This panel examines the role of human agency in architecture against the background of a computational universe and its attendant world view. Have new technologies liberated modes of expression that were previously unavailable? How have algorithms changed the way we think about and construct literary space? Does the full spectrum of our humanity fit within the world view produced by technology? Can computation help us to overcome the narcissism of architectural theory and the tyranny of function?

(DIS)APPEARING TIME

"The Prisoner's Guide to Astral Projection" *is a small pamphlet, printed on paper coated with dark, blond threads the size of eyelashes. Through a focused series of visualizations inmates can propel themselves into a vast realm of boundless potential. Unfortunately, boredom and fear are what motivates these travelers so for them there is nowhere in the universe that is not already like a prison.*

Excerpt from "*Projects and Technologies*"
by **Mike Silver**

Mike Silver

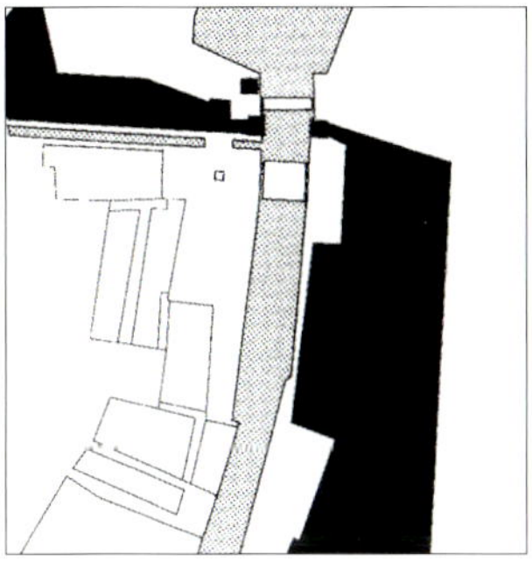

2

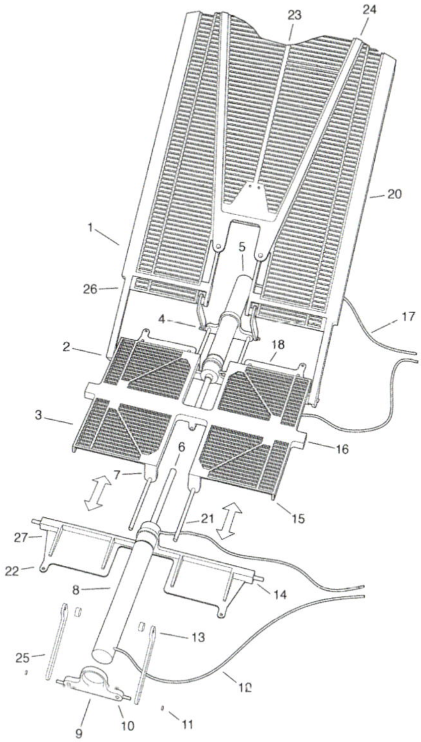

3

1. Function Follows Formlessness

"There is nothing that can be pointed to as the thing itself…despite this utter unfindableness, phenomena nonetheless exist conventionally and are able to perform functions."

Elizabeth Napper (1)

Modern Architecture was a rational, technologically inspired style influenced by Protestant values and the cultural changes brought about by the industrial revolution. The leading figures of the movement believed vehemently in the necessary correspondence between utility and form. For them function was an absolute, a self-evident truth that assured architecture's relevance and meaning.

Deconstructivist architects in the 1980s reacted against this thesis by using fragmentation as a way to disrupt the narrow, utilitarian focus of Modernism. While their highly agitated projects sought to undermine the connection between use and form they could not escape the realities of program. Thus restricted to the representation of disorder their work became increasingly iconographic…a systematic manifestation of the "Post-functional" picturesque. In order to undermine "firmitas", the Vitruvian identification of buildings with permanence and mass, sound structures were often hidden in a sea of broken surfaces, i.e. elaborate props that moved the observer's attention away from the actual facts of construction. When a column intentionally fails to meet the ground or when a motionless wall is tilted or cut to question its stability, architecture is reduced to a signifying process, an elaborate, semiotic game.

Facing page: 1. Detail of super computer sediment transport model for the Baptistry of Mont St. Michel. Simulations produced by William Deitz of Flow Analysis, Inc. **2.** Arsenal Canal site plan, Venice, Italy, 1995. **3.** Axonometric of the Drowning Bridge showing hydraulic actuators and folding deck.

4

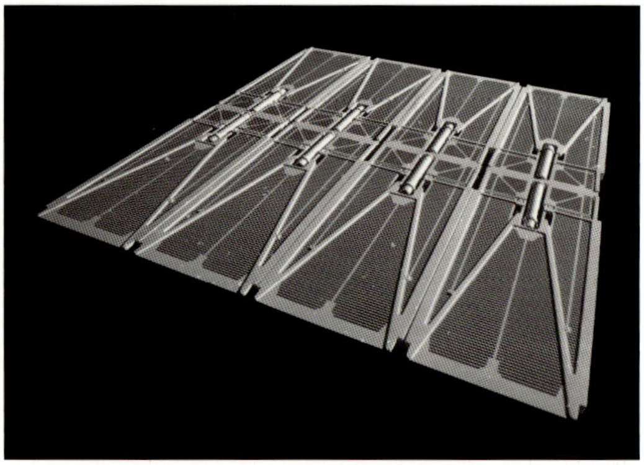

5

6

Of course, more extreme attacks on Functionalism were pursued through the demolition of existing forms. In his 1974 project "Splitting" Gordon Matta-Clark cut a house in half with a power saw. By denying use Matta-clark turned a house into a ruin and a ruin into a sculpture. From a design perspective both results are nihilistic. *More compelling would have been a work that could unbuild itself, a work that functions by disappearing.*[2] In this way architecture can occupy a middle position between the symbolic critique of function on the one hand (too little negation) and the extreme destruction of purposeful form on the other (too much negation). Instead of opposition and violence one might still imagine the deconstruction of fixed origins and absolutes as a pathway to an architecture of empathy over discord...an architecture that exceeds the symbolic, a practical architecture of openness and tranquility.

2. Drowning Bridges

Traditionally, the construction process ends with a tangible product - a presence that organizes space and consumes real estate. With the Drowning Bridge projects, the act of building worked in reverse, yielding an empty and self-effacing design (Fig. 4-8). The Drowning Bridges are located at the southern entrance of the Grand Arsenal in Venice, Italy (Fig. 2). The span of each bridge can be mechanically altered so that it sinks into the water, freeing up space for the passage of boats (Fig. 9). This arrangement takes advantage of the simple fact that the distance between the top of a boat and its waterline is more often greater than the distance between the waterline and the bottom of a boat. Given the sensitive context of the site, submerging the new structures became the least obtrusive and most efficient way of generating clearance for passing vessels.

The Drowning Bridges satisfy programmatic demands though a literal process of decomposition. The absence encountered in the project cannot absolutize use as an origin or grounding essence for design because empty space is empty! No 'thing' is useful in and for itself but also, "nothing is useful"[3] because actual voids are what

4-9. Fabrication and delivery sequence for the Drowning Bridges, Arsenal Canal, Venice, Italy. Through a process of endless negation the site is returned to conditions that existed before the project was installed.

7

support real functions. In this way a unique relationship between bridge and site is achieved through the unbuilding of the "new." What results is a radical contextualism predicated on a planned negation and on a temporary lack from which form is recovered. Here neither gain nor loss endures. *Function follows formlessness and the freedom from formlessness.*[4] Thus spared an irreversible demise the unmaking of structure remains forever unexhausted; its disappearance is not irreversible, it is endless.

8

"More compelling would have been a work that could unbuild itself, a work that functions by disappearing"

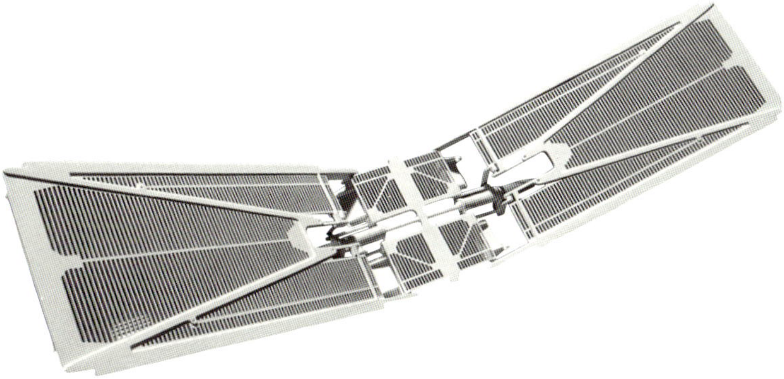

9

3. Non-Conceptual Architecture

"Disenchantment of the concept is the antidote of philosophy." [(5)]

Tidal basins are formed in coastal areas by the ebb and flow of the sea. Characterized by the intermittent presence of shallow water and traversable land, these constantly changing landscapes are traditionally considered unsuitable for the creation of viable structures. At low tide, the bay of Mont-Saint-Michel becomes open ground stretching for miles along the Normandy coast. (Fig. 11). The baptistery was designed to harness and reshape this landscape. At low tide the "font" of the project is produced by the interaction between a small platform (provided for church sponsored events) and the site's hydrodynamic forces (Fig. 12,13). Here the needs of parishioners are served by small pools of water trapped in alluvial flows of silt and gray sand.[(6)]

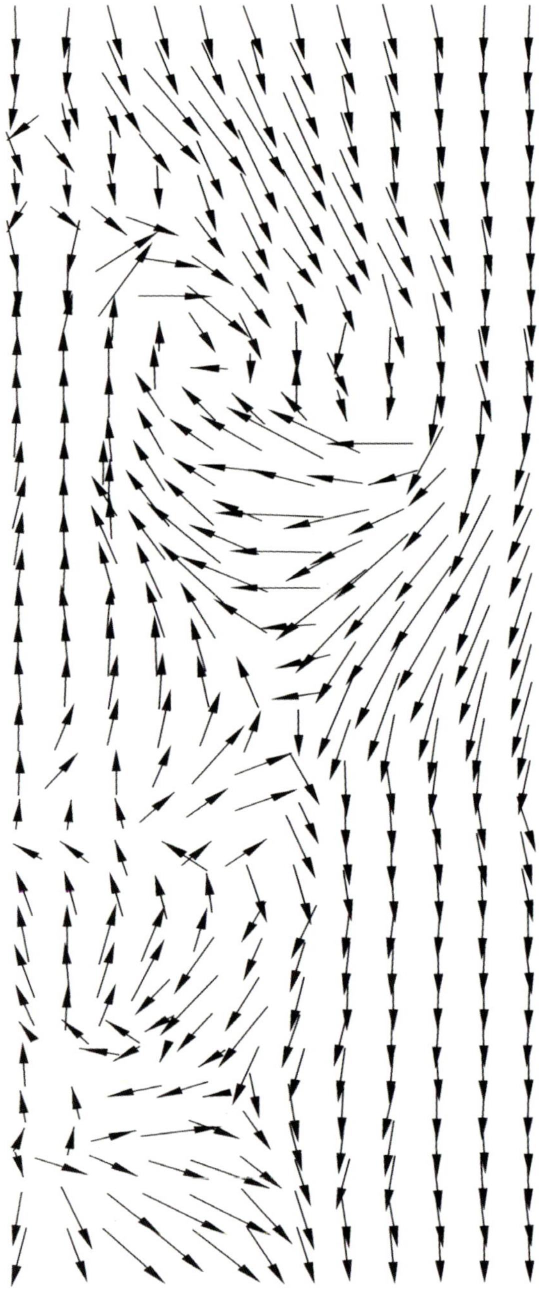

10

At high tide, the building disappears into the sea becoming a boundless font, an Architecture without architecture. In this way the baptistry both exists and does not exist. It exists because as a world without architecture it has a specified function. It does not exist because as a world without architecture its function cannot be established with absolute certainty. (The site could just as easily become a swimming pool.) While the endless reappearance of the project suggests a purpose for the entire bay there is nothing intrinsic in a place without buildings that necessarily makes it useful. Neither the lack of form nor its accessibility is ever fixed or eternal. The endless transformation of the landscape over time insures architecture's independence from both form and formlessness. In other words a great void is not more or less real than a column, a platform or some wet sand.

At high tide there is no architecture 'out there' that is different from the here and now which has no origin or center. (Everywhere in the water is functionally the same.) Space does not exist as a condition established by the distinction between near and far, inside and outside, large or small. This condition of non-duality also encompasses time since the parishioner does not experience the baptistry in the past, the present or the future. Instead, being all-pervasive and formless, *architecture is (like) the consciousness of the observer!* It is not determined by the thought of something lost because it is inescapable. It is not a desire for the yet

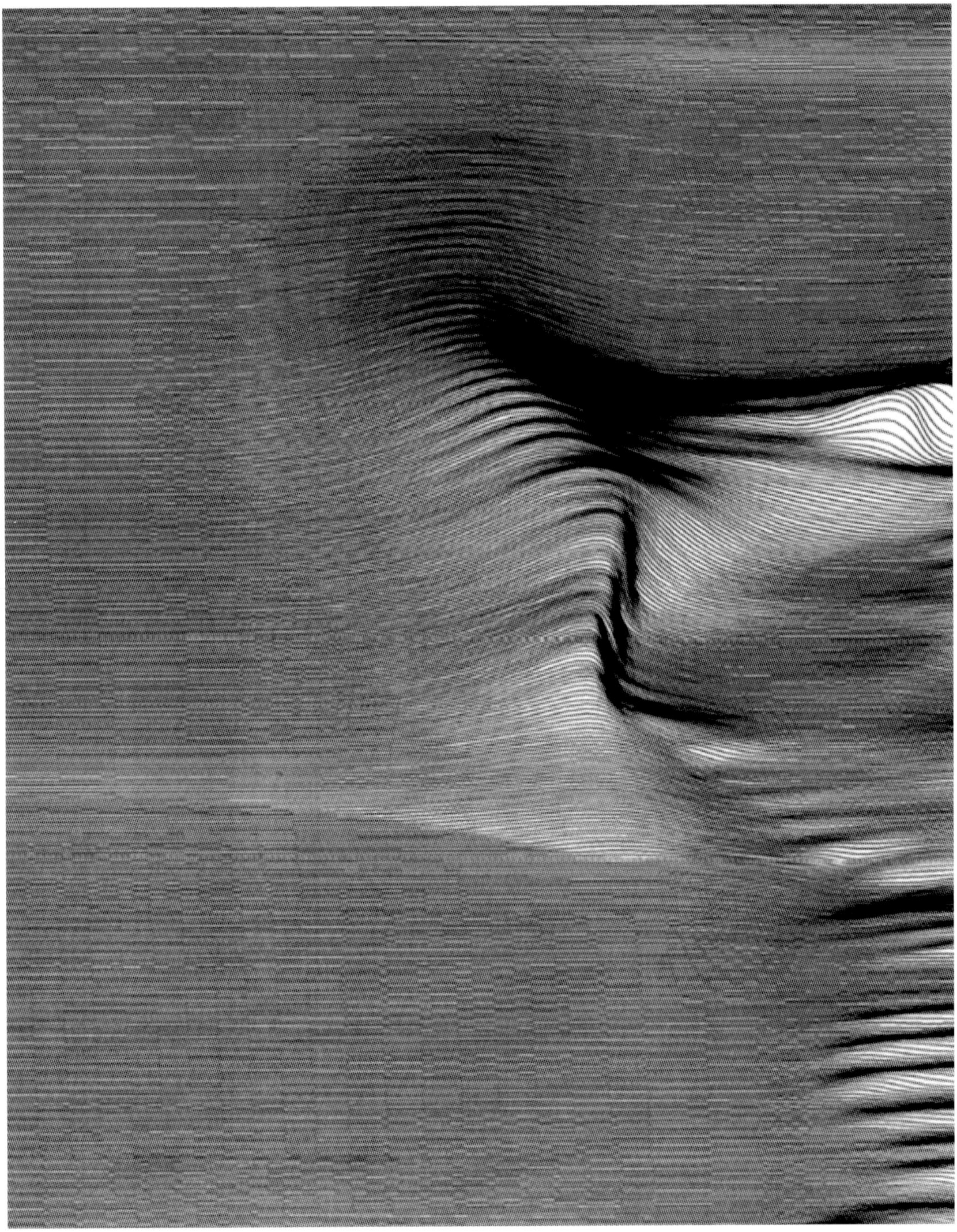

11

10-11. Sediment transport models rendered on a beowulf cluster supercomputer. High throughput machines offer new possibilities for design by manipulating large data sets in extremely fast interactive simulations of complex systems.

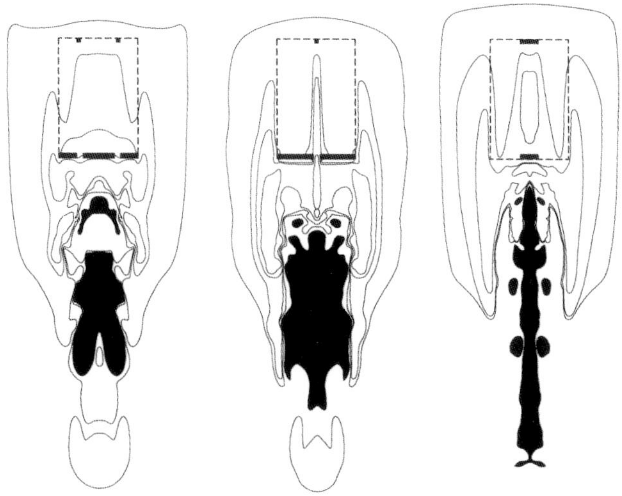

12

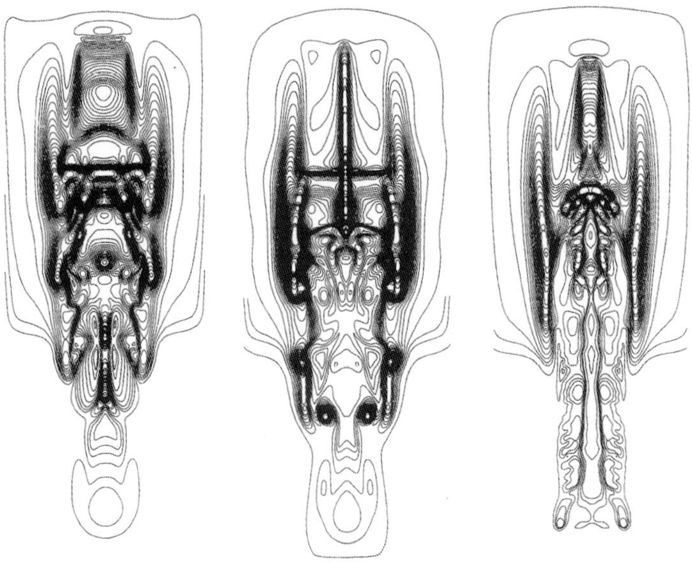

13

12-13. Three sediment transport models of the Baptistry were produced on a Beowulf cluster supercomputer. Each 2.5 D surface map was extrapolated from a voxel rendering of silt, water and wet sand. Note the variation in deck to column layouts and how they produce different landscapes. The parishioner's access to water (solid black) is best facilitated by the plan on the right.

to be realized since it has already been found. At high tide function is satisfied for free by a void no one created (Fig. 15). The baptistery is timeless and pure. Being empty its ritual is fulfilled without effort. In this way design transcends the distinction between building and landscape, here and there, self and world. As an infinite, non-conceptual architecture no I-idea, I-mage or I-dentity can encompass it.

4. Six Permutations Without Tautologies

1. Form Follows Function - Orthodox Modernism.
2. Function Follows Form - Unintended use.
3. Form follows Formlessness - The appearance of architecture.
4. Formlessness Follows Form - The disappearance of architecture.
5. Formlessness Follows Function - The selflessness of objects and persons.
6. Function Follows Formlessness - The usefulness of empty space.

A special thanks to Tam Van Tran, Bradley Horn, Alberto Perez-Gomoz, John Loboll, Joffery Kipnis and Garchen Rinpoche for philosophical clarifications, text edits, and project critiques.

14

14. Model of Baptistry at low tide. **Following pages: 15.** The Baptistry at high tide becomes the biggest building in the world.

Notes:

1. Elizabeth Napper, "*Dependent-Arising and Emptiness*", Wisdom Publications, Boston, 1989, p. 3 and p. 49.)
2.The point here is not to deny use as the driving distinction between architecture and sculpture but to show that there is nothing in a building that is intrinsically functional.
3. Lao Tsu, "*Tao Te Ching*", trans. Robert G. Hendricks, New York, Ballantine Books, 1989.
4. Formlessness is the lack of form i.e. an empty space or absence. It is not a signifier of the amorphous or curvilinear. Formlessness is 'no-thing', a space or void that becomes 'some-thing' by virtue of its perception. It is also not absolute 'nothingness' which by definition does not exist.
5.Theodor Adorno, "Infinity" from "*Negative Dialectics*", Continuum International Publishing Group, London, 1973, p. 13.
6. If inflowing water is blocked by sediment from future, costal runoff or increased because of catastrophic changes in sea level due to global climate change then the delicate balance between architecture and nature is disrupted. Both geological and man-made processes can have measurable impacts on the bay's existing ecology. Everything is interconnected.
7. While the bridge changes its use from crossing to gate through the literal disappearance of form the Baptistry's function remains constant despite normal variations in the tide.

GLOBE DOUBLE; MIMETIC CAPITAL; TECHNOLOGY

David Gersten

A number of years ago, I was speaking with an architect, who was very excited about his new project in Europe. He was telling me how he was going to do this and he was going to do that, and how the mayor said this, and the paper said that. I finally asked, "Oh, what is the program?" to which he responded, "Form Z." I hesitated, and chose to keep to myself what I had meant by "program." This, of course, could be understood as a simple misunderstanding or an architectural Freudian slip and left at that. But since that moment of exchange, I sensed it was more; that it was an expression of a deeper shift, of a new dimension in our discipline and perhaps in the world. In the years since, I have been haunted by my hesitation; I have wrestled with it, and meditated on it. Today, I would like to share with you a few pieces of what I have found. And a good place to begin is the birth of modern incorporations.

Modern incorporations were born out of ships and navigation. Individual ship owners grouped together and "incorporated" the ownership of their ships, allowing the predictable 'burden of loss' arising from the uncertainty of the long voyages to be distributed through the corporate structure. When an individual lost their ship at sea, they were sunk in business. Conversely, if twenty individuals agreed to bind together and share the ownership of their twenty ships, when one ship was lost, the incorporation remained buoyant–it still owned nineteen ships and could redistribute the load of this new value among its shareholders. These early corporations were promises about time and value. They worked because there was no one individual, but rather structures that served as a "second self" absorbing the load of losses by distributing it through the structure. This structure of risk distribution reflects the structure of the ships themselves, which can be seen as physical manifestation of the second selves of incorporation, each a set of promises made in advance from the shore; one in materials, one in words, two expressions of the same will to navigate uncertainty and conquer time. This double structure, half material (displacing water) and half temporal (displacing the individual ship owner) creates two forms of buoyancy transporting value across time.

The ships and their incorporation mirror and manifest the principles of risk management and distribution; they are the same project, the same desire to conquer time. This early mirroring of physical and mental structures to navigate uncertainty and collapse time, speaks to the larger parallel growth of capital and technology. Like gravity, capital is difficult to perceive; we can feel its pull and see its impact but not quite recognize its location or physical

Facing page: 1. Recognizing global technology as a mimetic exchange between incorporations and capital we begin to understand the profound ruptures between the globe and its double.

existence. Perhaps capital moves just outside of our perceptible spectrum and technology can be understood as visible evidence of capital offering a glimpse of its force within, or partially within, our perception.

The basic algebra of capital is grounded in the mediation of time, in the ability of currency to "defer consumption" and the ability of debt or credit to accelerate consumption or to allow us to consume that which we don't have. These two concepts of deferred consumption and debt or credit act as valves compressing or extending time and have direct impact on the ability of capital to affect our perception of time.

Modern banking has developed a complexity and intensity that has arguably positioned capital as the primary ground for our cognition of time. These tools do not remain external; they operate on an instinctual level allowing us to feel at ease, providing a sense of temporal shelter, a sense of well-being.

In providing a mental framework that aligns time and value–making their exchange possible–the monetary system functions as a time-based belief structure. It is our current temporal orthodoxy. Its forces impact upon the metabolisms of the individual, the many, and the earth itself. The early binding together of incorporations and the birth of modern banking contained the seeds of a vast calculus of time promises all of which rest on the requirement of continuous and expanding consumption (Fig. 3). The impact of these promises reverberate right up to our time. We see the ships bringing slaves to the new world. We see the slave ships stretched out to become the Mason Dixon line, and the Mason Dixon line bend and twist into the racist banking practice called 'redlining' that built the ghettos of American cities.

Today, we see redlining in the walls of a racist U.S. prison system. We see the echoes of Walls, Weapons and Debt in the dams of India and China, in the walls of Palestine, Baghdad and Cuba, in the levees of New Orleans, at the border of San Diego and Tijuana, and perhaps in the fences encircling the 'free speech zones' at demonstrations through the U.S. The tools of capital can repel violence and be violent, perhaps at the same time. While the seeds of our current knots of capital and technology lie in the early reflection of ships and their incorporation, it is clear that today we are within a new dimension.

Over the last thirty years, we have seen a dramatic acceleration in the calculus of global capital. Today, the majority of Global market trading occurs within vast frameworks of information technologies. A relatively new practice called "algorithmic trading" employs massive computational technologies emulating neural networks to monitor the markets and carry out billions of trades a day with no human knowledge of the individual positions being bought or sold. The frequency of the positions held is often in milliseconds and would not be conceivable as a human activity. In some cases, algorithmic trading employs genetic algorithms, which learn to adjust their strategy independently and in live time.

Algorithmic trading is one aspect of a new universe of global capital markets. Risk syndication, insurance raps, derivatives, interest rate derivatives, and all manner of new tools allow time to be cut, packed, broken down and reordered with the same speed and precision of particle physics.

The following is from David Harvey in *A Brief History of Neoliberalism:*
"In so far as neoliberalism values market exchange as 'an ethic in itself,' capable of acting as a guide to all human action, and substituting for all previously held ethical beliefs, it emphasizes the significance of contractual relations in the marketplace. It holds that the social good will be maximized by maximizing the reach and frequency of market transactions and it seeks to bring all human action into the domain of the market. This requires technologies of information creation and capacities to accumulate, store, transfer, analyze, and use massive database to guide decisions in the global market place. Hence neoliberalism's intense interest in and pursuit of information technologies (leading some to proclaim the emergence of a new kind of 'information society')." [1]

2. If we can recognize time and information as the two dominant forces of our current epoch, it is remarkable to me that the inverse opposite of time could be thought of as space and the inverse opposite of information could be thought of as substance. It seems that architecture with its capacity to mediate an exchange of: substance, space and life, holds a unique position in our time. **3.** The capital markets constitute a vast calculus of time promises that have become our primary mode of collective judgment. Price discovery within the bid and ask model is to a large extent the primary determinate of global resource distribution.

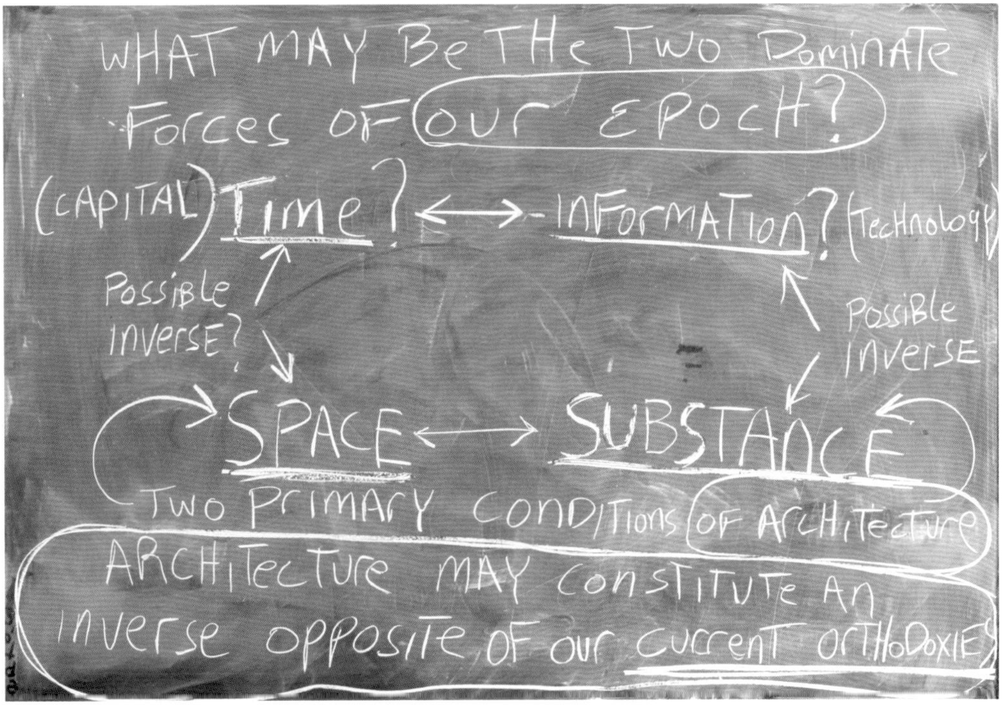
WHAT MAY BE THE TWO DOMINATE
FORCES OF OUR EPOCH?
(CAPITAL) TIME? ←→ INFORMATION? (TECHNOLOGY)
POSSIBLE INVERSE?
POSSIBLE INVERSE
SPACE ←→ SUBSTANCE
TWO PRIMARY CONDITIONS OF ARCHITECTURE
ARCHITECTURE MAY CONSTITUTE AN
INVERSE OPPOSITE OF OUR CURRENT ORTHODOXIES

2

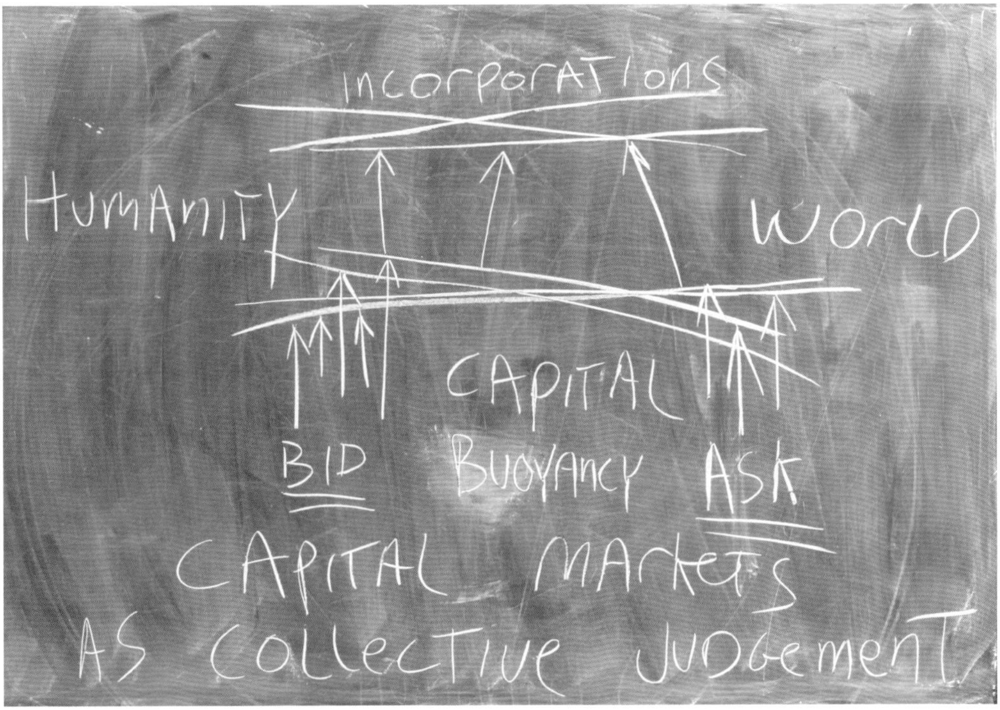
INCORPORATIONS
HUMANITY
WORLD
CAPITAL
BID
BUOYANCY
ASK
CAPITAL MARKETS
AS COLLECTIVE JUDGEMENT

3

The new ethic of global capital which seeks to "incorporate all human action" into the "market exchange," has found its ships in information technologies. Unlike the early double structure of ships and their incorporations, this double structure can be traced to a single defining event and perhaps the most seminal event of the 20th century: The Manhattan Project, or, the building of the first atomic bomb.

Linking capital, politics, technology, life and death, The Manhattan Project simultaneously produced nuclear weapons and information technologies. The mathematical demands of splitting the atom led to the birth of digital computation. The complexity of atomic catastrophe required numbers that could make numbers.

"The mathematical demands of splitting the atom led to the birth of digital computation. The complexity of atomic catastrophe required numbers that could make numbers."

Perhaps the first verifiable act of alchemy, Robert Oppenheimer's Faustian bargain of number, substance and energy launched a radically new Janus face of capital and technology. I have often thought of the odd symmetry of the sun (in the sky) being an enormous life-giving fusion event, and fragments of the sun on earth (nuclear weapons) being the direct inverse (enormous life-taking fusion events). This vast arc contains a difficult paradox when imagining the globe's resources.

To estimate the total wealth of the planet, economists must consider the planet in its entirety as a closed system with no addition or removal of any resources into or out of the system with one detectable exception: the energy of the sun. This gigantic nuclear fusion event is ultimately the only external input that continually adds to the resources of the planet. At the economy's other end is debt. The cost of debt is not a source but a sink. What I find remarkable is that the sum total of the world's debt is secured directly by nuclear fusion devices. World trade, like many forms of consensus, contains agreements that are enforceable; this means that they are maintained by force.

In a chilling symmetry to the gift of the sun, these technological fragments of the sun on earth are the collateral, at the bottom, securing every loan. The threat of total consumption is the anchor of the entire economy.

Globally, the link between nuclear weapons and debt has had important spatial and political consequences; the weapon that ultimately brought about the collapse of the Berlin Wall was debt; this debt, of course, was created by the nuclear arms race.

Following the first use of nuclear capabilities in Hiroshima and Nagasaki, Japan, where the emperor was viewed as deity, a switch to the western value and economic system occurred almost overnight. The extremely credible collateral of nuclear annihilation led to an immediate foreclosure. Japan has been the second largest economy in the world for decades.

The Manhattan Project originated both the collateral at bottom, binding together the globe's debt, and the computational ships, transporting value from computer port to computer port at the speed of light. Comprehending this new double headed mirror is assisted by looking at the most elemental definition of mimesis or "the mimetic," which to paraphrase Dalibor Vesely is "The re–enactment of the movement as significant gesture,"[2] Looking at the current horizons of technology we can identify a number of significant gestures that may be understood as re–enactments of the movement of capital. From the early mirroring of ships and incorporations to the inverse technological mirror of the sun on earth found in the collateral of nuclear weapons to the latest nonhuman, genetic time trading which are grounded in information technologies, we see the re-enactment of the movements of capital as a significant technical gesture.

It is quite possible that the construction of a technological globe that we are witnessing, or that Globalization itself, is not solely the result of a mimetic exchange between us (humans) and the world but instead between incorporations and capital; that the model which positions humans perceiving the world and engaging in a mimetic exchange (leading to an intermediary plane of making and creativity) has to a large extent been displaced by a model which positions the second selves of incorporations viewing not the world, 'per se,' but capital, and the intermediary plane of exchange is technology (Fig. 4). It is quite possible that technology is the other half of capital, allowing it to manifest its movements into the world.

The original will to overcome the unexpected by constructing entities that collapse time was certainly human. The double trajectories of incorporations and capital however, have become two picture planes facing each other, a double mirror to infinity, producing a flickering constellation of station points, focal points, foregrounds and backgrounds, a cacophony of second selves, producing in fact a second technological world (Fig. 5).

Recognizing global technology as a mimetic exchange between incorporations and capital, we begin to understand the profound ruptures between the globe and its double (Fig. 1). This leads us to ask:

Does the world fit?
Does the full spectrum of the world fit within the second technological, constructed world?
Do we fit?
Does the full spectrum of our humanity fit within the prism of capital?

The capabilities of capital and technology as modes of binding freedom are in serious doubt. This is evidenced not only by the "20th century war" continuing now into another century with no sign of slowing, but in the unprecedented inequities in resource distribution generated by the requirements of global capital. The binding together of ownerships does not insure the binding of freedom.

The navigational telescope of capital with its lens of scientific reason has its origins in the desire to objectively view the world–to see the distant shore. Today, this lens has transformed into a laser which is now cutting and shaping the world along lines of production and consumption. We are witnessing an expanded totalizing representation irrevocably altering the planet, containing all of the potential for collapse into ecological, nuclear, and human catastrophes. Perhaps the ships have expanded and are encompassing the globe.

"With its seemingly unlimited growth of material power, mankind finds itself in the situation of a skipper who has his boat built of such a heavy construction of iron and steel, that the boat's compass points constantly at herself and not north. With a boat of that kind no destination can be reached; she will go around in a circle, exposed to the hazards of the winds and the waves."[3]
Werner Heisenberg

"It is quite possible that technology is the other half of capital, allowing it to manifest its movements into the world."

To return to the initial question
What is the program?
What is the promise of architecture?
As global capital "seeks to bring all human action into the domain of the market", the profound shifts in architectural ideation that have come with information technologies must be considered within the double mirror of global capital and technology.

The rise of a neoliberal world view which equates free markets with freedom itself and the parallel ascent of information technologies have increasingly constructed an encompassing mathematical interpretation of the world, of architecture, and of life itself.

Following pages: 4. The model which positions humans perceiving the world and engaging in a mimetic exchange has to a large extent been displaced by a model which positions the second selves of incorporations viewing not the world, per se, but capital and the intermediary plane of exchange is technology.

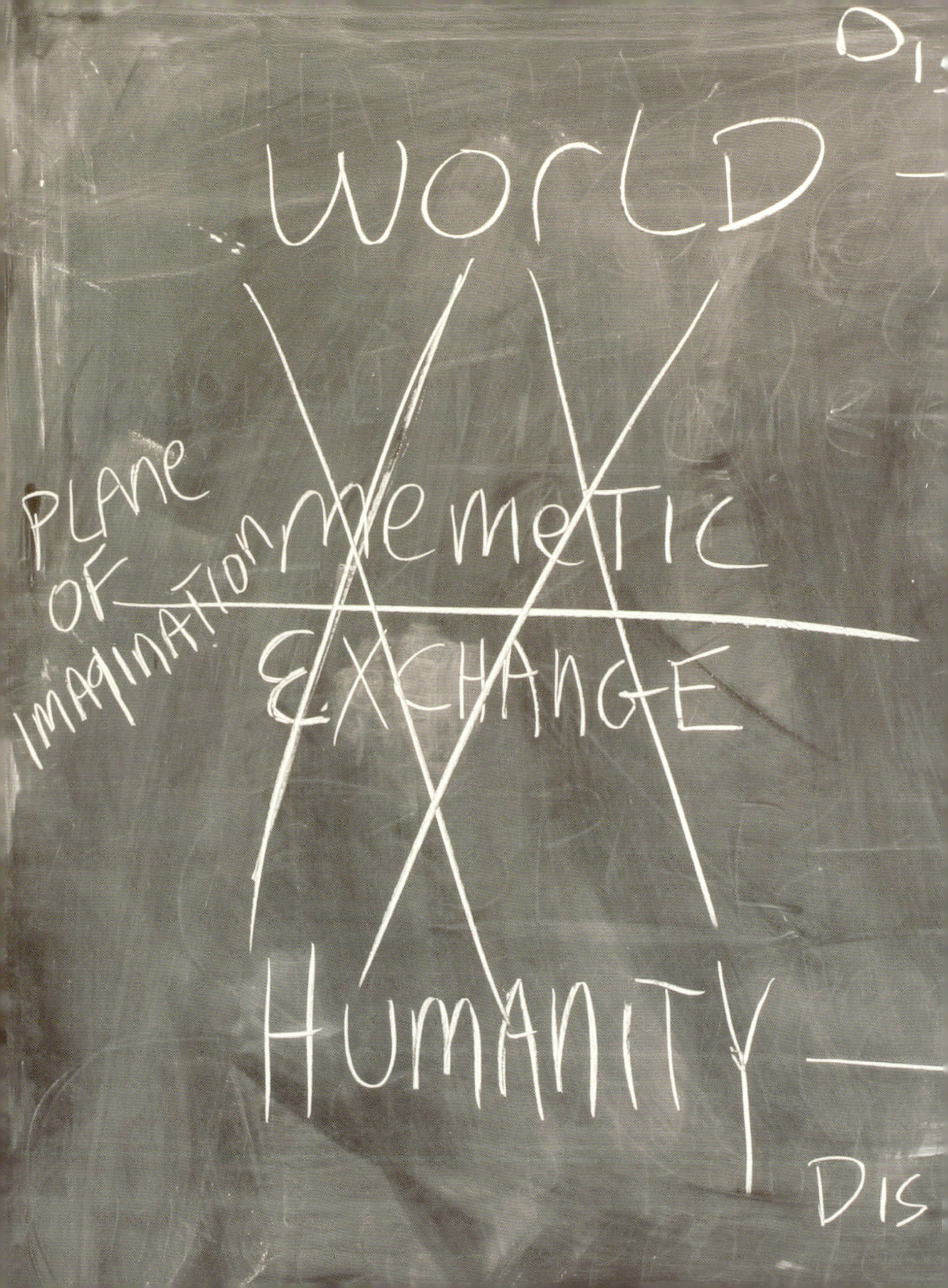

WORLD
PLANE OF IMAGINATION
MEMETIC
EXCHANGE
HUMANITY
DIS

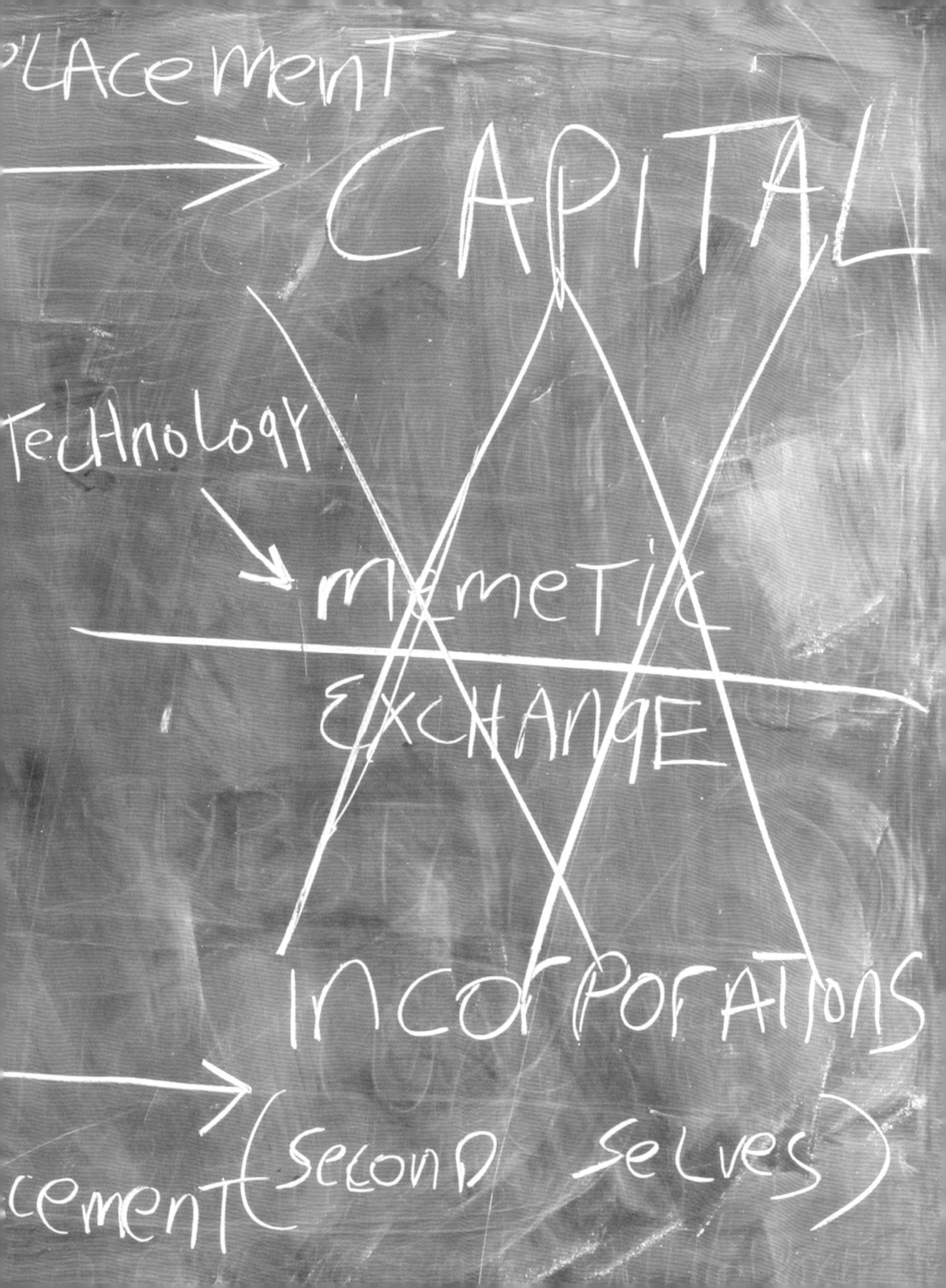
LACEMENT
CAPITAL
TECHNOLOGY
MEMETIC
EXCHANGE
INCORPORATIONS
CEMENT
(SECOND SELVES)

“Perhaps, unbeknownst to itself, architecture contains a mode of insurgency - pockets of space within the collapsed structure of capital´s hegemonic time. This may be architecture´s promise.”

Space is a participant in our thoughts and actions. It opens up the reciprocal possibility of inhabitation as a communicative exchange between our inner being and the spaces we inhabit. Our interior thoughts hold the capacity to construct literate spaces–spaces of participation inseparable from our memory, imagination and being. These exchanges may speak in whispers, telling of our fragility, embodying with great nuance the material and spatial empathy of life.

It is quite possible that space is the other half of us. As Alberto Perez Gomez has so beautifully articulated, space “completes us” and “allows us to understand ourselves and others.” Perhaps the search for what binds freedom begins with the knot of life and space as root and source; a fragile ground providing structure and, at once, binding our individual thoughts and our collective freedom.

Point to line to plane. The social contract is a form of participation and contribution among our fellow citizens, but it is also a contract with space itself, as the other half of us, a contract to embody the widest, most nuanced spectrum of what it is to be human into our reciprocal spaces. In this sense, architecture is a material imagination of the social contract. [4] Given the apocalypse of theatricalities our world is becoming, we begin to ask what spaces are completing us?

At the entrance to a memorial in Hiroshima is a sign that says “At 5000 Degrees Man Disappears”. The metabolism of the body and metabolism of the globe are linked. In fact, they are inside of each other. Perhaps at a certain degree of accelerated consumption, Architecture disappears.

Heinrich Heine once wrote, “Every epoch is a sphinx which plunges into the abyss as soon as its riddle is solved.” [5] I believe architecture contains a riddle, perhaps “our best hope of finding north.” If we can recognize time and information as the two dominant forces of our current orthodoxies, it is remarkable to me that the inverse opposite of time could be thought of as space and that the inverse opposite of information could be thought of as substance. It seems that architecture, with its capacity to articulate space and substance, holds a unique position in our time (Fig. 2). I believe that architecture contains deep within its ontological structure the seeds of an inverse perspective. Perhaps, unbeknownst to itself, architecture contains a mode of insurgency – pockets of space within the collapsed structure of capital’s hegemonic time. This may be architecture’s promise.

Architecture and humanity share the same predicament. When space breaks down into barbarism, this does not remain external; the porosity of being offers no such shelter, the plan of collective tyranny becomes a line penetrating the individual, manifesting an inner disregard of another's humanity.

As we move into the 21st century and the "reign of quantity" gathers strength and consolidates its hold over time, perhaps architecture will discover itself anew, not as a mirroring expression of the capital market exchange but as a deeply human exchange of life and space, a sheltering exchange with the capacity to imagine a social contract with all of the nuance and imagination of life itself.

In this sense, Architecture is a life-sustaining discipline; an empathetic discipline with a life of its own, reciprocal to ours–a discipline as irreducible as we are, a nuanced viscous discipline for a nuanced viscous humanity.

The poet Anne Carson says: "For a poet's despair is not just personal; he despairs of the word and that implicates all our hopes." [6] Perhaps, an architect's despair is not just personal; he despairs of space and that implicates all our hopes. If we are to address our global crisis, perhaps we must begin by recognizing that the spatial/material imagination is a dimension of human life.

It introduces a politics of slowing down, of resisting our current accelerating violence; of searching for new modes of concern for the other, new promises for distributing risk and resources, new spaces of empathy and ethics, new words for rebinding freedom.

Given the vast scope of the issues and the limited time of this presentation, I would like to conclude with a few questions: *Does space expand and compress as time does with capital?*

Does architecture have time or does it serve time? What does the ability to defer consumption mean for the consumption of architecture?

Is there a relation between the temporal shelter of deferring consumption and the spatial shelter of architecture?

Is there a distinction between the relationship of computational space and time and the relationship of space and time?

And finally, when Architecture asks, "What is the program?", does not space emphatically call us close to whisper, "The program is life itself."

5. The double trajectories of Incorporations and Capital however, have become two picture planes that are facing each other, a double mirror to infinity, producing a flickering constellation of station points, focal points, foregrounds and backgrounds, a cacophony of second selves, producing a commingled geography of algorithms and metabolisms that is infact a technological globe double.

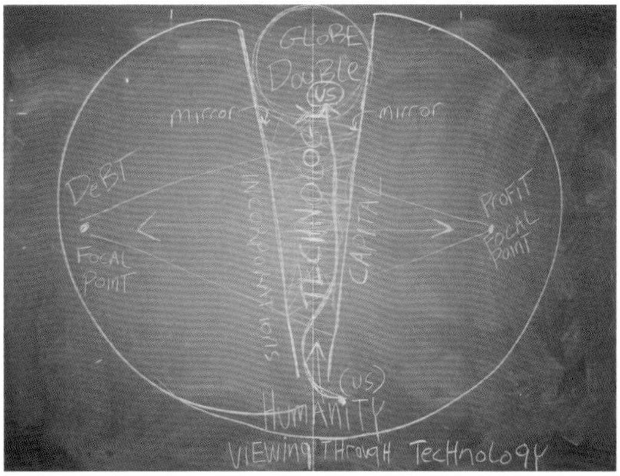

5

Notes:

1. David Harvey, *A Brief History of Neoliberalism* (New York: Oxford University Press, 2005), 3.
2. "In principle, it is possible to say that mimesis is a creative imitation in which something with the potential to exist is recognized and reenacted as a significant gesture; it may be sound, as song or music; visible reality, as image or picture; or ideas, as an articulated and structured experience." Dalibor Vesely, *Architecture in the Age of Divided* Representation (Cambridge, MA: MIT Press, 2004), 287.
3. Werner Heisenberg, "Rationality in Science and Society," in *Can We Survive Our Future? A Symposium,* ed. G. R. Urban and Misha Glenny (London: Bodely Head, 1971), 84.
4. "A Material Imagination of the Social Contract" is the title of a seminar that I have been teaching at both The Cooper Union School of Architecture and the Rhode Island School of Design's Graduate Studies Division for a number of years. I am thankful to both institutions and to the many students whose questions have made significant contributions to my thinking in this essay.
5. Heinrich Heine, *The Prose Writings of Heinrich Heine* (London: Walter Scott, 1887), 71.
6. Anne Carson, "All Candled Things," in *Economy of the Unlost: Reading Simonides of Keos with Paul Celan* (Princeton, NJ: Princeton University Press, 1999), 121.

SHALL WE BE SILENT ABOUT SOMETHING ELSE?

Yehuda E. Safran

Thank you very much for the invitation. Thanks of course to Brad for coming up with this demanding and challenging idea of inviting people to speak of that which cannot be spoken of. And as I have said on more than one occasion, it is as if one was asked to read from a white sheet of paper. And indeed it is something that we do when we write. It seems that we are tracing something that is already there except it is invisible. And so I am grateful for the invitation. And above all I want to offer certain quotes that might be worth considering in this context.

It is as if we are mere illustrations of the text: to use our words to hide our thought, to use our thought to excuse our action? There is a didactic inscription in Japanese characters in which we are told of the creatures in the garden that are affected by the ephemeral quality of the text, which at each moment matches the movements of a corresponding image. In this way they acquire the character of the surrounding circumstances. We are therefore presented not merely with a narrative, or a mere illustration of a text, but with something more like a calligraphic inscription in Japanese characters. Through this shifting medium we are told of animals in a garden whose individual songs fuse in a concert that sings of their imminent disappearance. Even if every word on the page (or is it voice in the wind?) had sung the same song before, after and around each word, monad-like, there is an infinite distance that only a leap of faith can reach.

Indeed, in *The Guide for the Perplexed*, by Maimonides, words are altogether one of the main causes of error because whatever language we employ, we find the restrictions of our expression extremely disturbing. We cannot even picture its concept by using inaccurate language. Our effort in sound and language is futile when we attempt to articulate the ineffable. Insofar as our language is concerned, it is always as if we are in a foreign land.

It is just as St. Augustine described; when a child is born it is as if he is being born with a language but the language is not of this world.

Letters are what they are; at least independently of ink, paper, or even words. 'Medaber', to speak, is the human position in which the speaker, that which makes us human, is being able to speak. In Greek the term for Word also means thing. The original unity of word and thing, which you find in the word 'davar' in Hebrew, is a different one from the discourse on truth that Greek philosophy has constructed: Logos. The word for speech in Hebrew is 'davar' or 'deber', a thing that speaks, a word and object are intimately connected. It is of the same

Facing page: 1. Micha Ullman, *Bibliothek*, 1994.

root as the word 'midbar', which means desert, The Ten Commandments: 'Aseret hdibrot' also belongs to the same semantic field. 'Deber', which means speech and 'midbar' – the desert where, these commandments were presented. They were presented, the text in Kings 19:12 states; in, 'dmama daka' which means a 'thin still voice', a thin still voice, nobody knows exactly what that means but it implies the presence of a very fine silence. One thing leads to the opposite and being able to listen to 'batkol', which means the 'daughter' of sound, the daughter of voice, is the precondition for human beings to listen to themselves, their thoughts, their consciousness. Indeed there is a passage in Edmond Jabes in which he speaks precisely of that experience of being at a loss. I will contrast it with an image that I would like to show you.

It is a monument to the books which were burnt on the fire. The work of Micha Ullman; a monument to the event that took place in front of the Berlin Opera in May 1933, 75 years ago (Fig. 1,2). I was thinking of the letters that are not written, that are not made, that are not to be found anywhere, I was also thinking of the letters that have in German been *verlust*, lost, but they are not lost because nothing is lost in the world as David so eloquently described. So where are they? The difficulty lies in being able to listen, being able to hear and in this monument by Micha Ullman, the sculptor, you can see, I think, among other things, you can find the most important characteristic of every work of art, which is miniaturization.

It encourages you to reflect on the fact that the promise to show, the promise to utter the inutterable is doomed to remain unachievable; and the work of art will show this impossibility. I think it is particularly poignant in this monument. Perhaps the noise of too much information is the noise that prevents us from listening, prevents us from hearing, prevents us from hearing the silence, thoughts, to listen to our own consciousness, to be able to hear the sound over the noise, the sound of that which is significant, because it is the sound in its silence. Saints, sages, mystics and philosophers invite us to listen to silence in what they leave unsaid, unwritten, making themselves clear only through silence. The silence of arrogance and silence of fear define the silence of the divine. After the publication of *Tractatus Logico Philosophicus*, Wittgenstein said in a letter to Paul Engelmann that that which he did not write was even more important than that which he did.[1] Not surprisingly he felt that of the most important things one cannot speak, and that which one can show, one cannot say.

So in this constellation of words like stillness, muteness, schweigen, silence, stille, stillness, sprachlosigkeit, speechlessness, the silence. 'Dumiyah' (stillness in Hebrew) also has the first letter for blood, 'Dam' and 'shtika' which is quietness and often appears as 'sha, aha'. All of which Arnold Schoenberg eloquently expressed, when he sung of the inexpressible in his opera Moses und Aaron, identifying himself with a law giver and with an image maker; Aaron as Arnold. There he gave shape to the sound of the 'The inconceivable God!/Inexpressible, many-sided idea.' As you recall Moses was supposed to be a man who could not speak, who stuttered. It was his brother in law Aaron who was supposed to be able to speak. In the entire Opera which was relatively late and remained unfinished, Schoenberg is inverting that impossibility to such an extent that he invented a new form of singing; 'Sprechgesang' (speechsong), and through this medium Moses addresses us more immediately.

This created difficulties. Some poets such as Stefan George allowed his poems to be set to music by Schoenberg at first but then denied this right later on because he felt that the music mixed with the sound of the words would interfere with the poem, he felt the poem would be disturbed by the musical dimension. In other words he felt that the words that he was able to put together were in themselves speaking of something that could not be heard otherwise. Vienna at the beginning of the 20th century was a world obsessed with the paradox of language in which the higher function consisted of leading us to a perfect understanding of spiritual oneness with the divine that is to be only experienced through silence. It is not for nothing that when the members of the newly formed Vienna Circle came to visit Wittgenstein, he in response, did nothing else but read to them from the short stories by Tolstoy.

Jacques Lacan spoke of the word as making the world: *le monde des mots qui cree le monde des choses*, things which are confused in the hic et nunc of things *tout en devenir...* Man speaks therefore, but it is because the symbol has made him a man. Symbols in fact envelop the life of man in a network so total that they join together, before he comes into the world, those who are going to engender him... so total that they bring to his birth, along with the gifts of the stars, if not with the gifts of the fairy spirits, the design of his destiny; so total that they give the words which will make him faithful or renegade, the law of the acts which will follow him right to the very place where he is not yet and beyond his death itself. So the oneness of silence becomes the multiplicity of words or things which is referred to as 'dvarim', the plural of 'davar' in Hebrew which is the thing and the word at the same time, once the well of the silence is plumbed, the gush of dvarim, of constant creation through language never ceases. My old professor Richard Wollheim, the philosopher, used to say that there is nothing that man creates which he does not rehearse first in his mouth. Were this divine law of speech to be halted even for an instant some say that the entire cosmos would return to nothingness. So perhaps to teach mankind that life and death are in the hands of the lungs, the tongue, ('halashon' in Hebrew) is the same as words in other languages are for language itself. Life and death lie at the tip of the tongue.

Indeed, at the beginning of the last century, again in Vienna, Hugo von Hofmannsthal created the figure of Lord Chandos, a person who so despaired of words that he abandoned them altogether and completely resigned himself to silence. Perhaps this is the opposite silence to the Ineffable since it is predicated on the inability to speak rather than the inability to reproduce in speech that which is heard outwardly or inwardly. Perhaps nowhere else were voices heard against the background of silence and heard more dramatically, as in Vienna at the beginning of the twentieth century. As Karl Kraus said, it became the laboratory for the destruction of the world. There were dozens of languages spoken in the city at the time. As Mauthner observed, every Jew was certainly a born linguist. Against this background Wittgenstein formed his conviction that, on the most important things in life, we must remain silent. Calvino, in his libretto for Luciano Berio's *Un Re non Ascolto* gave this predicament its operatic form. If you remember, in that opera he described the king that does not hear, who cannot listen; here, we have the embodiment of this predicament written more recently.

Perhaps this is the significance of the Tower of Babel story. The confusion of tongues was inflicted not to prevent the building of the tower but as the expression of its ultimate impossible object, and so instills in mankind its creative urge.

The Greek labyrinth is the Hellenic material equivalent. Exile, cunning, and silence is the advice of James Joyce in *A Portrait of the Artist as a Young Man* for Daedalus. Catching the passing light during the ineffable. What is true and divine does not rely on being recognized directly, we discern it in the reflection of kindred appearances. We are made aware of how incomprehensible life is, yet we cannot renounce our desire to comprehend it during our brief time of passage on Earth. Whatever colors are, they are the action and suffering of light as Goethe observed; yet who can act and suffer if not a human being? The quan-

"Perhaps, the noise of too much information is the noise that prevents us from listening, prevents us from hearing, prevents us from hearing the silence, thoughts, to listen to our own consciousness, to be able to hear the sound over the noise, the sound of that which is significant, because it is the sound in its silence."

tum of light, a collection of independent particles of energy or any other understanding which will catch the passing light; what is true and divine does not allow itself to be recognized, the offer of "divine" or "necessary" causes will not do away with the bending of light according to the principle of least time.

If Pascal thought that a man was a thinking reed, slowly learning to appreciate our condition, one finds oneself a mere optical reed or a hearing reed for whom the minute particularities of place and time are obviously embodied in a crucial quality of light and sound which determine the totality of our lives. To be occupied with the intersection point of time always and time now as T.S. Eliot wrote, was the occupation of a saint. Perhaps if the poet was more familiar with architecture, he could understand that the architect is not a saint, yet architects preoccupied among others, are embracing, they seem to believe and behave as if there were mystery in one afternoon shadow than in all the religions of the world. Could we not imagine mutatis mutandis that what is true of light is true of sound? I believe that this task is still ahead of us or in the words of Mandelstam, who wrote a text under the title Musica Mira, 'The Sound of the World'. So what is the sound of the world? The sound of the world is being heard precisely when one enters into that kind of silence of which Cage so eloquently spoke when he introduced his 4 minutes 30 seconds piece. One could play a paradoxical and provocative game, and list the words for silence ad alta voce.

Muteness
Schweigen (silence)
Stille (stillness)
Schprachlosigkeit (speechlessness)
Sheket (silence)
Dumiyah (stillness)
Sh'tikah (quietness)
Unaussprechbar, Unaussprechlicher (inexpressible)

Arnold Schoenberg in Moses and Aaron introduced Unaussprechbar which is then uttered in the Sprechgsung.

So if I had to sum up what I have just said, I could sum it up with poem by Georg Trakl called "Nachtlied" in which he used the noun *schweigen*, the adverb *sprachlos* and the adjective *stillen* in that order in the three stanzas of his poem. Of course German has a sound pattern that is hardly reproducible but I will read it to you in English.

"Breath of the Motionless. An animal face
stiffens with blueness, its sacredness.
Mighty is the silence in stone;

the mask of a night bird. A soft triad
fades to a tone. Elai! Your visage
bends mutely over the azure water.

O! You still mirrors of truth.
On the solitary one ivory temple
gleams the reflection of a fallen angel."

"Des Unbewegten Odem. Ein Tiergesicht
Erstarrt vor Bläue, ihrer Heiligkeit.
Gewaltig ist das Schweigen im Stein;

Die Maske eines nächtlichen Vogels. Sanfter Dreiklang
Verklingt in einem. Elai! dein Antlitz
Beugt sich sprachlos über bläuliche Wasser.

O! ihr stillen Spiegel der Wahrheit.
An des Einsamen elfenbeinerner Schläfe
Erscheint der Abglanz gefallener Engel."

Trakl died of an overdose in a hospital. Wittgenstein, who as you know gave up all his inheritance in favor of his sister, left a modest portion of his great fortune in order to support artists and writers, young Austrian writers. In this context he also met Adolph Loos and through him Paul Engelman. Wittgenstein also tried to reach Georg Trakl in the hospital but when he arrived there Trakl was already dead. Dead, because I believe that the suffering was too great for him. So I think that perhaps in the words of Georg Trakl there is a more precise section of our life, a profile of our predicament vis a vis the ineffable than in any other words.

Thank you.

Facing page: 2. Micha Ullman, *Bibliothek*, 1994.

ARCHITECTURE, ETHICS, & TECHNOLOGY

Alberto Pérez-Gómez

During the last fifteen years the design professions have increasingly recognized the importance of ethical questions at multiple levels, ranging from issues of sustainability to politics. It is perhaps a good thing that numerous books and conferences have been devoted to the topic, even if, often, issues concerning the common good are engaged only through other technical questions that tend to leave the crucial problems untouched. Furthermore, it must be recognized that a concern for ethics still sounds hollow in the context of a contemporary practice dominated by a concern for novel marketable images, economic benefits, or coercive political forces. When understood as a question of the personal responsibility of a design professional's imagination, ethical issues may also appear unfashionable for a poststructuralist critical discourse that claims the deconstruction of the first person as a primary agent.

In a recent book I have tried to demonstrate how the common good has always been a primary concern in architecture, never at odds with its quest for beauty. This was evident in the writings of Vitruvius and many other writers who over the centuries attempted to elucidate the meaning of architectural praxis (practice in its full political sense). If this ethical concern is difficult to recognize, it is because it is internal to the practice of architecture rather than an external adjunct to some formalistic or technical activity. Because of their irrepressible desire to disclose a meaningful order, architects have traditionally sought to provide individual existence with a built world that reflects the purpose of social institutions and of life in general. Human thoughts and actions, ranging from myth and religion to science and art, have been responses in different times and different places to fundamental questions that have remained essentially unchanged. Far from being merely an aesthetic or technical concern, architecture seeks to set human action within an "appropriate" formal and spatial context, fulfilling this reconciliatory role despite modern humanity's tendency to control and dominate fellow human beings and the environment.

Facing page: **1. Philips Galle,** ".003:3 *Cain Leaving the Presence of God*," from the Story of Cain and Abel, c. 1565. The Illustrated Bartsch, vol. 56, p. 12.

Today we may finally realize that the reduction of architecture to an inconsequential aesthetic formalism is not an absolute paradigm but rather a historical event related to the glorification of scientific reason during the eighteenth century, and to the association of architecture with the so-called Fine Arts. Believing that positive science is capable of disclosing absolute truth–a belief whose roots grew out of theological speculation–the rationalists implicitly relegated art (and "non-scientific" architecture) to a marginal, somewhat illegitimate zone. Architectural practice then began to be defined by two assumptions: 1) That architecture is differentiated from other building practices by its interest in aesthetic manipulations; and 2) That architecture must adequately resolve the internal conditions generated by a "program," one that is external to the architect's discipline.

Imbued with the same scientific logic, ethics was assumed to be autonomous, external to the formal concerns of "ornamental builders;" believed to be almost totally subsumed by the paradigmatic technological values of efficiency and economy. Is there anything else for an architect to be concerned with than to design the most efficient building possible and to spend as little as possible in achieving that goal, adding ornament to the equation whenever possible?

The polarization of ethics and aesthetics has been exacerbated by the confusing nihilism of our culture, the Babel of specialized disciplines and interests, and the overwhelming power of technology and simulation. Often, ethics is still regarded as external to architecture (and to the other design disciplines) as ultimately subjective and therefore inconsequential in our pluralist world. And yet, can it not be simply argued that the long-term cultural relevance of architecture is ultimately related to its capacity to embody, in its very nature as *project*, a vision for the common good?

It is perhaps obvious that human desire has shaped the built environment, sometimes in ways that today we may judge as unsuitable for the common good. Impressive buildings were constructed to fulfill spiritual needs that seem almost absurd from a late-modern perspective, totally "impractical" edifices such as magnificent funerary monuments to commemorate the dead, and temples to celebrate strange divinities. Buildings have also been objects possessed by the wealthy and powerful, symbols of decadent consumption and the means for an elite to exert control over the masses. Representing ideologies and institutions like false idols, they have often contributed to repressive environments.

Modernity has rightly judged this sort of building practice faulty and dangerous. As a pragmatic alternative it has proposed that buildings should fulfill the wishes of individuals in a democratic society: a desire for shelter and protection from the elements, for a home and a place to work where humans may live their lives in as pleasurable a way as possible. In the wake of God's demise it is arguable that nothing else may be necessary. More recently, under the rubric "sustainable development," these aims have been interwoven with a sense of responsibility for the environment and the well-being of humanity at large. A meaningful architecture would efficiently fulfill humanity's material needs, while at the same time remaining mindful of the world's resources in order to perpetuate of human civilization.

If architects are to play a role in the complex world of the twenty-first century–a world more conscious of environmental limits and cultural differences while civilization continues to embrace the goal of technological globalization–they must ponder strategies to disclose their discipline's potential for embodying an ethical intentionality. In my recent book, I have argued that the materialistic and technological alternatives for architecture, however sophisticated and justifiable they may be in view of our historical failures, do not satisfactorily answer the complex desire that defines humanity. Man's greatest gift is love, and he is invariably called to respond to it. Despite our suspicions, architecture has been, and must continue to be built upon love. While recognizing the dangers of traditional religions, moral dogmas and ideologies, true architecture is concerned with far more than fashionable form, affordable homes and sustainable development; it responds to a desire for an eloquent place to dwell, one that lovingly provides a sense of order resonant with our dreams, a gift contributing to our self-understanding as humans inhabiting a mortal world.

The sense of order provided by architecture is not one that speaks primarily to the intellect. Indeed, the inherent ambivalence and opacity of architecture as a poetic universe of discourse speaks directly to humanity's perceptual and imaginative understanding and must be embraced as an asset rather than lamented as a limitation. While affirming the necessary conditions of contemporary architecture as a discipline that is both functional and conventional, grounded in use–value but also able to acknowledge the crucial role of its syntax in the potential generation of poetic metaphors, I argue for the possibility to see beyond mere formal, stylistic relativism and pragmatic professionalism. Grounded upon our historical traditions, we can indeed contemplate architecture as a non–discursive embodiment of knowledge born from a concern with the other. There are and have been exemplary works that demonstrate the points of contact between poetics and ethics: between the architect's wish to design a beautiful world and architecture's imperative to provide a better place for society. In my historical work I have sought the origins of architectural meaning beyond the traditional, often polarized understanding of aesthetics as an eighteenth century science of beauty, and ethics as a collection of normative rules, clarifying architecture's quest for beauty and the common good. Ethics and aesthetics reduced to rules are useless: ethical action is always singular and circumstantial, it always seems miraculous and unique, a transformative experience that is, significantly, analogous to our encounter with beauty in works of art; the arrow of eros.

Despite this realization that necessarily occurs in our experience of meaningful architecture, skepticism remains the norm in critical discourse, one that stems from modernity's chronic distrust of perception and unqualified valorization of mathematical logic. Well-meaning cultural critics, seeking to deconstruct oppressive power structures from our tradition and to empower the free individual, have at the same time proclaimed the self-referentiality of art–the postmodern labyrinth of mirrors and relative values–implying that the personal imagination, and with it the very possibility of ethical action, may be an illusion.

Declaring the fallacy of an absolute, ontological ground, however, need not lead to the absolute self-referentiality of language and art. Critics with diverse pursuits such as Paul Ricoeur, Jean-François Lyotard, Richard Kearney, and Julia Kristeva, among others, have emphasized, each in his or her own way, an alternative to the traditional mimetic imagination–the Aristotelian concept presupposing an intersubjective cosmos that stands for all and need only be "imitated" and to the Romantic egocentric imagination presupposing the possibility of creation *ex nihilo*. While acknowledging the inevitability of "intertextuality" and convention–taking to heart Rimbaud's discovery of the ultimate autonomy of poetic language–these writers can imagine the possibility of an embodied imagination that still speaks about something other than itself, about a possibly different future founded on values gleaned from the traces of history. The potential integration of ethical and aesthetic concerns has profound consequences for architectural practice. Indeed, it pertains to the issue of form generation at its inception.

Recent post-critical discourse (particularly in North America) has expressed a deep dissatisfaction with formalist and "hard" computer-generated architectures as being unable to respond to the expectations of cultures in the early third millennium. For over two centuries, architects, critics and theoreticians have been arguing functionalist and formalist positions, opposing art to social interests, ethics to poetic expression. Architectural writing ranging from popular professional journals to sophisticated theoretical books perpetuates this polarization that diminishes architecture's capacity to embody beauty and to promote social development. In stepping away from these prevalent oppositions, the aim of my historical work has been to uncover the deep connections between ethical and poetic values in the primary tradition of our discipline.

Elsewhere I have ventured to describe how architecture may contribute to our self-understanding. Most crucial is not its capacity to communicate a particular meaning, but rather the possibility of *recognizing* ourselves as complete, in order to dwell poetically on earth and thus be wholly human. In the Western tradition, the products of architecture have ranged from the *daidala* of classical antiquity (objects such as ships, temples and deceptive war machines, all put together from small parts through carefully crafted joints), to the sundials, machines, and buildings that Vitruvius named as the three manifestations of the discipline. Architecture, in this sense, includes the gardens and ephemeral architecture of the Baroque period and the built and unbuilt "architecture of resistance" of modernity such as Le Corbusier's La Tourette, (Fig. 2) Gaudi's Casa Batlo, (Fig. 3) or Hejduk's "masques." This *recognition* of wholeness is not merely one of semantic equivalence, rather it occurs in experience, and as in a poem, its "meaning" is inseparable from the experience of the poem itself. Its meaning cannot be reduced to concepts that can be paraphrased. The moment of recognition is embedded in culture, it is playful by definition, and is always circumstantial. These artifacts, which the Greeks qualified as *thaumata*, convey wonder, a form of beauty grounded in eros *(Venus-tas)*. This was still clearly understood during the Renaissance by the likes of Marsilio Ficino and Francesco Colonna; a quality altogether different from "formal composition" in the sense of modern aesthetics. Architectural beauty, like erotic love, burns itself into our soul, it inspires fear and reverence through a "poetic image." It affects us primarily through our vision, and

"Contemporary practices are rather myopic when it comes to history, tending to squander the unfathomable wealth of our heritage and substituting it for the latest scientific theories extrapolated into design."

yet is fully sensuous, synaesthetic: it is thus capable of seducing and elevating us to understand our embodied soul's participation in wholeness. What differentiates architecture from other artistic products is its vocation to frame significant human action, traditionally ritual.

Unlike most buildings in post-industrial cities, architecture offers societies a place for existential orientation. Architecture is the embodiment of a radical orientation. When successful, architecture allows for *participation* in meaningful action, conveying to the participant an understanding of his or her place in the world. (Vitruv. Greek theatre). In other words, it opens up a clearing for the individual's experience of purpose through participation in cultural institutions. When successful, architecture *plays* with power. It is, however, not possible to paraphrase the order it conveys. It is radical orientation in experience, beyond words. So, while its theory might have been rooted in mythic or poetic stories, philosophy, theology or science at different times in its history, architecture is none of these; it is an event. Its disclosure of beauty and meaning is ephemeral, yet it has the capacity of changing one's life in the vivid present–exactly like magic, or an erotic encounter. Like falling in love, it strikes a blow that reveals reality as it is (Socrates). Thus, it can be said to embody knowledge, but rather than clear logic, it is knowledge understood in the Biblical sense: a carnal, fully sexual and therefore opaque experience of truth. For this reason its "meaning" can never be objectified, reduced to functions, ideological programs, formal or stylistic formulas. Indeed, particularly for modernity, it seems that whenever buildings become "idols" (or signposts–trying to circumscribe a precise meaning) they lose their capacity for edification: as Jean-Luc Marion has suggested, we must search for "icons" that allow us to see through to meaning precisely by not restricting it, in themselves meaning no single thing. From this it follows that architecture may include artifacts from diverse media that make possible human dwelling and which by definition stand "at the limits of language," establishing the boundaries of human cultures within which other more properly linguistic forms of expression may take place.

But a more detailed historical outlook is out of the question here. Perhaps it would be more fruitful to devote the few remaining minutes of my presentation to characterize the dominant technological character of our world culture. This is the unavoidable context of our building practices, one that has to be considered thoroughly since architectural meanings depend on participation–they are never mere acts of creation of some solitary genius. As I have suggested, genuine architecture constructs a space of appearance, and in this sense it is public by definition. It is within a technological world that the architect must work. Technology is far more than a question of machines or computers; it is more than just one of many determinants of our culture. It has become clear that there is an intimate link between the nature of technology and a number of cultural and now global traits that define both modernity and postmodernity. Technology, especially after the Industrial Revolution, opened up the possibility of a human world that is fully constructed. Unlike traditional techniques that always acknowledged the primary reality of the natural world, functioning like a bridge between humans and the environment, high modern technology acts rather as a wall between man and nature. This is a metaphor used by Octavio Paz to describe our predicament. Our consciousness is now quite radically separated from external reality, one that we have not created and which in the last instance constitutes the hidden ground for human meanings. Let me emphasize: the question is not simply one of scale, or types of tools. There is clearly a chasm between high modern technology and the traditional techniques of pre-industrial cultures. A fundamental question of intentionality is at stake: this is what

"As it became clear that neither God nor man was at the centre of the world, technology became a morally justifiable response to the inveterate human lack in the face of the cosmos."

Facing page: 2. Le Corbusier, *Sainte Marie de La Tourette*, Chapel, Eveux, France.

Nietzsche has defined as will to power. While a sailboat acknowledges in its design the presence of the elements and its vulnerability, the sea and the sky, human frailty and the unpredictability of both the elements and our moods (what Heidegger calls the gods), the Titanic simply does not. Both may sink, of course, but that is hardly the issue.

Most importantly, and this is a question directly pertinent to architectural production, technology substitutes a "picture" for the world of our primary embodied experience. However mutable and historically determined this world of primary experience may be, phenomenology discloses it as one where the universal and the specific are given *simultaneously* in the mystery of perception, in the space *between* Being and Becoming. The technological substitution of a picture creates the condition that Marin Heidegger has called "enframing" *(Ge-stell)*. While seeking to answer the same inveterate questions about the measure of man and his place amidst the immeasurable and alien, technology opts for control and domination, for arrogant and efficient action upon the reduced picture. Success within this instrumental mode of action has led to an affirmation of man's quasi-divine ambitions in the face of a universe that, he may suspect with the insight of post-humanism, has not been made only for him, but may nevertheless be exploited for all its resources. This all-encompassing technology has been intimately bound up with architectural ideation and practice since the early nineteenth century. Despite considerable resistance, architectural theory was quick to adopt the productive models of applied science. Architecture, the art of mediation *par excellence*, has tended to become a tool for controlling the environment and producing efficient building. After many failures and dead ends, it is not surprising that today we may seek a reformulation of technology and yet, paradoxically, remain consumed by civilization's obsession for the digital, often allowing the basic issues to fall by the wayside. A true critical understanding would question fundamental assumptions that are usually taken for granted, it may reveal technology (with Heidegger and Vattimo) as a "weak truth" with mysterious origins, and would have repercussions on architectural representation, the production of architecture, the role of scientific models, and the use of language to articulate design intentions.

"Desire is associated with our inherent lack in the face of nature. Unlike other animals, humans have a very limited capacity to adapt to the environment and instead developed poetic and magical techniques."

These aspects of architectural ideation should be major concerns for theoreticians of architecture as well as for its practitioners. The cultural and political relevance of the architectural profession in the twenty-first century hinges upon these questions. Issues arising from the relationship between architecture and the technological world are the crucial theoretical problems for an ethical practice and it is insufficient, let me repeat, to simply accept technology as our inevitable destiny. The implications of that relationship are far more important than the dazzle of digital innovation and the superficial stylistic distinctions that consume a great proportion of contemporary architectural debates.

Technology cannot be simply dismissed or criticized from the point of view of traditional art, metaphysics, or humanism. It would be difficult to deny that the thrust behind its accomplishments and failures is indeed the human thirst for transcendence, especially after the epistemological turning point signaled by the works of Copernicus and Galileo. As it became clear that neither God nor man was at the centre of the world, technology became a morally justifiable response to the inveterate human lack in the face of the cosmos. The quest of technology is related to the age-old intention of European man to inhabit a space of ontological continuity, to dwell poetically upon the earth. Was this quest abandoned in favor of a "false" alternative that would appear to be true only in the absence of God? Obsessed by the accomplishments of instrumentality and its own assertive will to power, technology has led humanity into a gnostic trap in which the existing "world out there" is forgotten. Today, we are often controlled by forces that we thought we are capable of mastering. The environmental crisis and the dilemmas created by genetic engineering are two prime examples.

However, as Heidegger pointed out in his essay on technology, there are dangers present in the technological world that are more subtle but yet more serious than humanity's potential for self destruction and the threat of ecological disaster. The denial of death as a positive limit and essential qualifier of life may indeed end up jeopardizing the possibility that human existence can remain open to meaning and thus perpetuate civilization through its cultural institutions and symbols. And once again, this observation evokes an architectural mission: to reveal to humanity its limits, rather than provide a sense of endless gratification.

It is abundantly obvious that a nihilism of despair may become a powerfully destructive force, impossible to control, capable of overriding the necessary affirmative nihilism that we must embrace with Nietzsche. While questioning the absolute truth of western metaphysics as something outside experience (the Platonic "truth as correspondence"), Nietzsche's affirmative nihilism enables humanity to remain open to the powerful silence of art and architecture, to the dark radiance of light, as it maintains its sensitivity to the vibrations of the quiet footsteps of the gods that may come dancing by. The problem is, finally, to diagnose the power of the technological enframing, to understand that while we may be "enframed," technology itself may be "weak," that while God and man as a self-coincident ego may be irretrievable, the planet Earth (and the sky) are present as a central ground for our full embodied experience, one through which we are now capable of questioning the hegemony of abstract, theoretical constructs. ... Paradoxically, this realization becomes stronger as we can now observe Earth as a unique oasis of life in the desert of outer space...

In architecture, the dangers of technology are directly associated with reductive representation, cultural homogenization, and the death of the city as a place for public interaction. That the architect must become nostalgic to escape from the discourse of technology, is overly simplistic. The way out may then be sought by acknowledging the mysterious origins and historical transformations of technology itself. We may be called to question our often arrogant, instrumental relationship with the external world and to explore other options, including a strategy to destructure the languages of science and technology through a poetic vision. Eventually, a different relationship may emerge between practice and the cultural artifacts that make up our architectural tradition.

Modern Western civilization takes for granted a quest to pursue individual happiness and freedom. It is driven by what it perceives as a "natural" right to seek pleasure and avoid pain, a fundamental accomplishment of democracy brought about by the political revolutions at the end of the eighteenth century.

For a hedonistic culture, architecture's vocation is to ensure the greatest pleasure and least pain for each individual. Our technological building practices, even when mindful of ecological responsibility or claiming high artistic aspirations, still pursue a functionalist utopia to fulfill all desires through material means, eliminating all irritants and always aiming at greater economy and comfort: maximum efficiency, economy, commodity and entertaining value. Consumption and possession prevail as the bastard aims of desire. Their overwhelming presence in contemporary life enhance our propensity to forget that we are our mortal bodies whose very flesh is also that of the world, a common element which grants the light of reason and immortal thoughts, while pulling us down into the darkness of the earth. We forget that love and death, pleasure and pain, are inextricably linked through our embodied consciousness. We go even further and tend to deny the very existence of love (as technology may wish to deny the existence of death). Fragmented into multiple emotions in our materialistic culture, the cynic and intellectual alike have trouble acknowledging love in view of our modern difficulty to grasp it as a gift, often contradictory since it is *beyond* the rules of economic transactions. The wager of my latest book, following in the footsteps of José Ortega y Gasset and Jean-Luc Marion, is that love not only exists, but is crucial to our humanity; that despite its contradictions it is of a piece, and can indeed be spoken about.

Built upon love, architecture engages the inhabitant as a true *participant*, unlike the remote spectator of the modernist work of art or the consumer of fashionable buildings *cum* images. If this is not obvious, it is partly because architectural meaning has been "explained" through a deceptively simple assumption that confuses our human quest for happiness with hedonism. Love, in its multiple incarnations as desire, is as open-ended as life itself and remains the ground of meaning even in times of obsessive materialism. According to Plato, this erotic principle is operative not only among human souls, but also ev-

Following pages: 3. Living Room ceiling, detail. Casa Batlló, Barcelona, Spain, 1904-1906. Architect: Antoni Gaudi.

CASA BATLLÓ

erywhere in the universe. Yet, love and our transcultural quest for beauty will never be reduced to a mere pursuit of pleasure. A poor understanding of this issue is evident in recent writings foregrounding the interest in algorithms to generate novel architectural forms, in critical practices that stress the social history of architecture, emphasizing political correctness and a critique of "authorship," and even in architecture driven by well-meaning ecological concerns. A partial or total ignorance of the deep relationship between love and architectural meanings has dire consequences, perpetuating the modern epidemic of empty formalism and banal functionalism, condemning architecture to passing fashion or consumable commodity, and the cultures it frames to their present dangerous pathologies. We must, perhaps inevitably, acknowledge a hope in human ingenuity to solve the well-publicized problems of starvation, lack of drinking water, pollution, global warming, housing, and renewable energy for six billion people in our planet. And yet, to think of design as merely more sophisticated planning, solving with technology technological problems, will never be enough, and it misses the point in the "here and now". The appropriate engagement of desire through the articulation of ethical and political positions in the form of seductive projects is the fundamental responsibility of architecture.

Eloquent myths, poems, stories, and philosophical accounts from multiple traditions, have described the nature of human space as the space of desire. Regardless of culture, age, wealth and social status, humans suffer a *lack*, which is also a gift. Unlike other animals on our planet, our essentially linguistic being keeps us "apart" from the world. Throughout our lives we constantly look for "something," something that is missing and that might complete us, be it the physical presence of another, the acquisition of knowledge, or the experience of art and architecture. This lack is always present. It does not disappear with the fulfillment of practical needs or with the possession of goods. Despite its paradoxical nature it is perhaps the most obvious manifestation of our spiritual specificity. Christians have identified this lack with a longing for God, its satisfaction the state of grace reserved for the just in the after-life. Buddhist teachers, on the other hand, identify the illusory nature of this lack as the source of unhappiness and insist on the dangers of those desires to which we are unduly attached, leading us to forget the ephemeral nature of all things human and creating perpetual frustration by denying us the possibility of living fully in the present. While a simple answer for the spiritually aware might be asceticism, prince Siddharta himself soon discovered that this was not the solution. His enlightenment led him to the realization that we must accept desire (and suffering) as fundamental to the human condition and engage it as a vehicle for knowledge, always remembering its deceitful power of attachment.

Desire is associated with our inherent lack in the face of nature. Unlike other animals, humans have a very limited capacity to adapt to the environment and instead developed poetic and magical techniques. Animals possess a remarkable ability to communicate and construct, often far more sophisticated than man's natural capacities. Termites, for example, can communicate across a two-inch steel plate and still build a perfectly symmetrical nest. The structure they construct, however, is always the same nest.(1) Humans faced with the analogous problem of building across a divided habitat would either build completely different structures on either side of the plate, running the risk of failure and extinction for lacking some particular expertise, or else develop a technique to perforate the plate in order to communicate and build a polity, one that depends on linguistic translation and will every time be a *different* city. This activity was named poiesis by the Greeks, signifying the sort of technical making proper to humans; a poetic making in the sense that it always aimed at more than preserving life.

Even for the most sophisticated apes, desire is externally motivated and can be understood as a closed structure, a kind of complex mechanism: hunger is physiological while sexual behavior is seasonal. For humans, on the other hand, desire is experienced as an open horizon. The erotic "phenomenon" is, according to Marion, primary in all things human. It is possessed of a rationality that flies in the face of logic and encompasses experiences as diverse as charity and lust. Just as the behavior of apes around dead fellow creatures indicates indifference, the burial of corpses in primitive humanoid societies seems to have a

4. Masaccio, *Expulsion from Paradise.* Brancacci Chapel, S. Maria del Carmine, Florence, Italy.

4

"The appropriate engagement of desire through the articulation of ethical and political positions in the form of seductive projects is the fundamental responsability of architecture."

5

5. Peter Paul Rubens, *Prometheus Bound,* begun c. 1611-12, completed by 1618.

relationship with the awareness of sexual desire, and its obscure coincidence with an awareness of death as the limit of life. The many artifacts and mythical narratives of various cultures that express the need to propitiate or change external reality convey a sense of transgression: shame or guilt. Adam and Eve are punished with eventual death for their knowledge of love (Fig. 4). Prometheus is punished for steeling the fire of the Gods, (Fig. 5) and Cain is condemned to toil the earth and build cities. (Fig. 1) In mythical cultures, sacrifice usually accompanied technical works and deeds in the hope of renewing a sense of reconciliation with the more-than-human world.

This brief characterization of *techne-poiesis* should help elucidate the challenges to be faced by architecture when operating within a technological world: sacrifice is out of the question, as are cosmological referents. Yet, reconciliation with the pre-existing natural and cultural worlds is crucial. True human creativity is the revelation of something that is already there, and yet appears as new and wondrous. Unlike traditional periods, what characterizes our own modernity after the 18th Century is the possession of history; we have instead the richness of historical precedent that allows us to construct our traditions through narratives. Contemporary practices are rather myopic when it comes to history, tending to squander the unfathomable wealth of our heritage and substituting it for the latest scientific theories extrapolated into design. History as interpretation allows us to articulate positions, a politics and an ethics, it is not a "thing of the past" but rather, when approached properly, a source of true creativity and relevant innovation. As both an impression of personal imagination and a political and social activity, architecture is profoundly affected by the crises and pathologies of our technological world. However, when understood as a discipline within the humanities, with deep, often misunderstood historical roots, it is wonderfully positioned to take advantage of any possibilities that may emerge from a greater and more universal human compassion, from an increasing awareness of the limits that make human life possible, and from a new sense of human identity that respects cultural distinctiveness. Faced by the challenge of acknowledging the specificities of culture and site as well as the universalities of technology and space, the architect may still become a crucial figure in the making of an order for humanity beyond tyranny and anarchy – an order predicated on a wholly new relationship between thought and action.

Note:

1. This story was told by Juhani Pallasmaa at an exhibition on animal architecture that he curated for the Finnish Museum of Architecture.

VIRTUAL, ACTUAL, INEFFABLE: ARCHITECTURE & MEDIA IN THE AGE OF COMPUTATION

N. Katherine Hayles and Todd Gannon

With the advent of technical media, the production of written documents has increasingly been permeated by algorithmic processes. Although the use of algorithms to produce creative literature pre-dates the advent of the personal computer by centuries, the era of computation has increased the intensity and pervasiveness of these practices. Digital processes have also become increasingly important to buildings. We propose to regard both documents and buildings as "actual media"–that is, physical objects that exist in the world. Our interest lies in understanding the interactions between digital environments, especially databases, actual media, and the discipline of architecture.

The growing importance of databases has, as Lev Manovich observes, introduced a disruptive inversion into the linear sequentiality intrinsic to language and (occasionally) to buildings.[1] Employing Saussurian terminology, Manovich posits language, especially narrative, as syntagmatic, that is, as an actual linear sequence, and database as paradigmatic, a virtual set of possible manifestations. Such a conceptual structure can be seen in architecture in the relationship of paradigmatic treatises and manifestoes–from Vignola's *Canon* to Le Corbusier's Five Points–to specific syntagmatic works such as the Villas Farnese or Savoye. In digital environments, however, this syntagm/paradigm relationship is reversed. As Manovich explains, "a [hypertext] narrative is just a set of links; the elements themselves remain stored in the database. Thus the narrative is more virtual than the database itself." [2]

Virtuality, then, is deeply imbricated with the rising importance of databases and the synchronic paths traced through databases as elements are variously concatenated to produce a reading path or sequence of traversal. In turn, databases, although pre-dating digital media by centuries, became, with the advent of computers, the fast, fluid, and globally pervasive forms of knowledge construction that they are in the contemporary period. The implications of these developments for architecture and language point in similar directions. For architecture, databases and their companion technology, algorithms, have introduced the possibility of manufacturing individualized components that allow unprecedented flexibility in the customization of architectural forms. For literary forms, they have created narratives that exist as billions of possibilities, only a few of which will be actualized through a reader's choice as she navigates a synchronic pathway through the work.

To explore the implications of how virtuality interacts with actual media, our essay juxtaposes two bodies of work, one positioned at the beginning of the Age of Computation (which we date from the 1960s), the other at the contemporary moment when digital computation pervades virtually every aspect of social, personal, economic and political life in our globalized culture. The first point of comparison is drawn from the *Archigrams*, published from 1961-1970 in nine and one half issues that projected alternative visions for the future of architecture and of society as a whole. Focused on issues

2

3

of program, technology, and social transformation, these unorthodox pamphlets adopted the narrative syntax of comics, film, and other media not simply to document these transformations but rather to perform them through graphic techniques and algorithmic methodologies akin to concurrent advances in information science. The *Archigrams* reconceived architectural discourse as a constantly expanding pre-digital database from which to conjure the feeling of a future society of the information age. Nudging the discipline away from passive representation toward the design of active, evolving systems, the group advanced complex feedback loops between architects, architecture, and users that aggressively challenged preexisting notions of disciplinarity.

The second point of comparison is taken from the writing, installation art work, and architecture of Arakawa and Gins, particularly their vision of architecture as a habitat for nomadic subjectivities requiring virtualized spaces that are ever-shifting and constantly evolving. (Fig. 1) Calling architecture a "built discourse," this collaborative team of a poet and architect explores possibilities for a mode of discourse and a style of building that subordinates space to time, linearity to multiple pathways, stable structures to emergent possibilities. If a pathway through a building can be considered a narrative, their project replaces the linearity of traditional narrative with a manifold of hypertextual virtualities realized as actualities through the choices and actions of mobile and fluid subjects.

Architecture and virtuality have long been perceived as being at odds with each other. And for good reason–the "mother of the arts" has traditionally stood for solidity and

Previous page: 1. Arakawa + Gins, *Study for Reversible Destiny House*, 1992. **2.** *Archigram Magazine*, issue number 1, 1961: main sheet. **3.** *Archigram Magazine*, issue number 3, 1963 : page 2.

"Architecture is not building itself, but, as the dictionary tells us, a particular "art," "science," or "manner" of building – that is, architecture is not *what* one does, but *how* one does it."

permanence in a fleeting world, while one of virtuality's few stable traits is its commitment to ephemerality and change. Yet through the 1960s avant-garde practitioners embraced exactly these tenets of virtuality to mount a concerted attack on architecture's allegiance to static monumentality. Through a series of overlapping dissipations perpetrated by such diverse practices as *Archigram*, COOP Himmelb(l)au, Superstudio, and others, architecture was pixellated into new media, as buildings became tents, travesties, and, in the case of *Archigram*, telegrams.

Recast as telegrams, architecture as portrayed in *Archigram* took an unabashed step into the virtual. In the highly reconfigurable space of the printed page spread, Archigram was able to manipulate forms, juxtapose elements, and orchestrate combinations that would have been impossible in another medium. In each of the nine issues, individual projects by Archigram members, their cronies (Cedric Price, Steve Osgood, etc.), and their heroes (Buckminster Fuller, NASA) stand alongside contemporary products and comic book images and are blurred together by shaped texts and captions that run with abandon across the pages. Narrative and graphic techniques normally outside the purview of architecture proper–the telltale shaped texts, comic book sequences, editorial commentaries, and collagist juxtapositions–are combined with traditional architectural representations (plans, sections, elevations, perspectives) to produce architectural effects too ambitious to build but too important to ignore. These techniques effectively erase hierarchical and chronological differences between these diverse elements, encapsulated in the Archigram mantra first voiced in issue 3: "It's all the same." (Fig. 3)

In some ways, *Archigram* acts in the manner of the Renaissance treatise, in which an encyclopedic collection of architectural possibilities is brought together and intended for recombination and modification in future built work. Yet unlike Vignola or Durand, *Archigram* does not offer a simple kit of virtual parts to be recombined and reified as actual buildings. Rather, *Archigram* reifies the field itself. In its pages, paradigmatic possibilities are actualized not in constructed buildings but rather in exquisite drawings, provocative collages, and the dynamic play of text and image in the magazines to produce a still expanding database of architectural possibility. The syntagms–discrete proposals such as Plug-In City or the Suitaloon–are realized in the actuality of documents rather than buildings. This movement into mobile and reconfigurable media, epitomized by the telegram's speed and succinctness, allowed the *Archigram* phenomenon to infiltrate and influence a much broader array of media with architectural thinking. At the same time, these means enabled Archigram to inject the immediacy we associate with digital media–what they termed a "zoom boost"–into architecture, imbuing a historically sluggish discipline with the fluidity and flexibility that today we are apt to associate with digitality.

These techniques can be seen in every issue of the magazine. In the first issue of 1961, textual information is employed not to describe architectural objects, but rather to loosen architectural possibility from built form. Throughout the sheet, a multiplicity of lettering styles and overlapping strings of text suggest myriad pathways along which the eye may traverse the material (Fig. 2). Though relying on textual information as much as graphic imagery to make its point, no single narrative is privileged; the reader must construct her own path. Cook's handwritten captions follow and peel away from the contours of projects by Mike Webb, Timothy Tinker, David Greene and others, in some cases the words written across the buildings in a form of editorial graffiti. As such, *Archigram* differs radically from traditional architectural publications. In its pages, the aim is never simply to document projects. Rather, *Archigram* endeavored to transform projects and products into an alternative milieu, a virtual presentation of a future world fundamentally different from the present one.

The nature of Archigram's imagined future is explicitly narrated in *Archigram 4*, the famous *Zoom Issue* of 1964 (Fig. 5). Here, in the group's trademark comic book style, futuristic cities provide the backdrop for the adventures of Cartol Zena against a malevolent "brain." (Fig. 7) In keeping with the group's aversion to single linear narratives, SPACE COMIC is not one story but many. Citing both sci-fi comics and Roy Lichtenstein as sources, the strip intricately layers multiple narrative and graphic threads in a syncopated rhythm of the dialog - rich plot, critical exegesis from comely female commentators, and captionless futuristic skylines. The interruptions of the female commentators (themselves avatars of contributing Archigrammers) are presented in typeset thought bubbles that contrast with the hand - lettered plot line and link SPACE COMIC back to contemporary architectural discourse: "Close examination of SPACE COMIC material reveals a two - way exchange between space comic imagery and the more advanced 'real' concepts and prophesies – Geodesic nets, pneumatic tubes, plastic domes and bubbles – the worlds of the thinks–balloon and the inventors pad overlap." [4] (Figs. 6-9).

Other issues push the magazine further from linear narrative and into an unconstrained "open field" of page spaces treated as a series of two - dimensional planes, a possibility not available to contemporary construction. By *Archigram 6*, the linear sequence of traditional print media is undermined by a clever choreography of multiple narrative threads starting from both front and back covers as well as in a third section of smaller pages bound within. From Issue 7 onward, *Archigram* dispenses with binding alto-

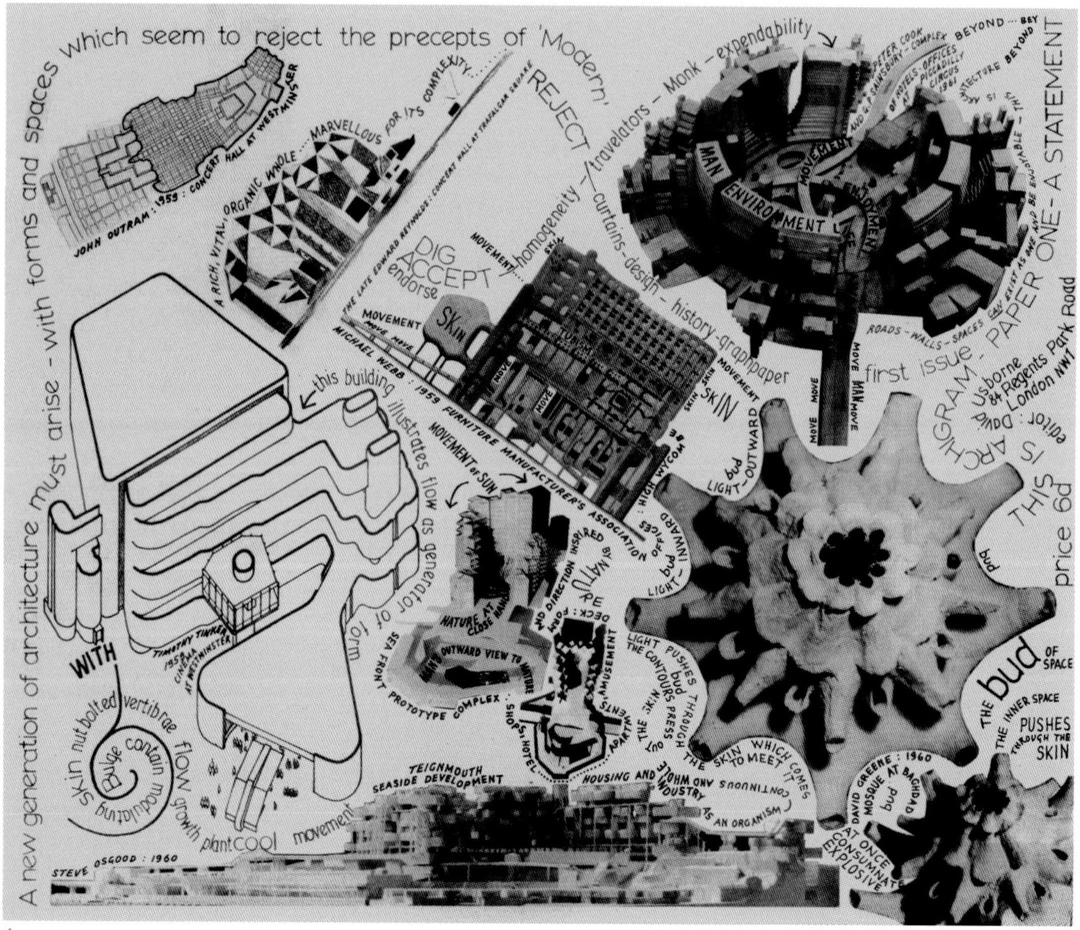

4

4. *Archigram Magazine,* issue number 3, 1963: page 5. **Facing page:** 5. *Archigram Magazine,* issue number 4, 1964, *Zoom Issue:* front cover designed by Warren Chalk.

AMAZING ARCHIGRAM 4
2/-
ZOOM
ISSUE

gether, and with it, the fixed narrative sequence of print media. In later issues, unbound sheets of varying sizes are grouped together to present built architectural works alongside unrealizable architectural speculations, consumer products, serious editorial commentary and tongue-in-cheek captions in a horizontal, dense, non - hierarchal field of possibility (Fig. 10).

As linear narrative is left behind in the magazine, important projects by Archigram members all but abandon traditional architectural form. Peter Cook's "Metamorphosis of an English Village" offers "ARCHITECTURE AS AN OPTIONAL EXTRA amongst many things…" In contrast to Le Corbusier's dire modernist mantra - cum - threat "Architecture or Revolution," Cook succumbs to a revolution in which architecture relinquishes its presumed authority over the built environment, instead taking its place alongside alternative technologies as one option for constructing a future.

Cook's collage "Metamorphosis: Sequence of Domestic Change" chronicles a further dissolution of architecture from "Straight Bits" in 1960 to "Becoming Almost Ethereal" by 1985. Architecture as a static form imbued with representational meaning vanishes and is replaced with an ever–updated kit of gadgetry that actively performs to enhance human life.

Other Archigram members push this transformative agenda even further. Mike Webb's Suit–a–loon, Chalk and Greene's Electronic Tomato, (Fig. 11) and Warren Chalk's Bathamatic all similarly abandon architecture as a representational vehicle and instead provide representations of architectural performance.

Here electronically charged forms work not to ennoble the urban landscape with monumental form but rather to stimulate the human body with interactive performance.

1.

6

2.

7

6-9. Original page collages by Warren Chalk to illustrate his essay discussing the relationship between comics, science fact, science fiction and current architecture. These were reproduced in monochrome in *Archigram Magazine,* issue number 4, 1964: page 1 to 4.

Yet as *Archigram* moved toward its swan song, the unconstrained optimism of their technological utopia began to show signs of weakness. David Greene's "Popular Pak," featured in *Archigram 8*, moves beyond the liberating dissolution of architecture to hint at the precarious possibility of the dissolution of autonomous human subjects into technologically enhanced cyborgs. Displaying the growing cynicism that pervades the later issues of the magazine, Greene writes, "The organic birth–death–life–earth–heaven–God is no longer valid. ... You merely: take it away, eat it, drive it, fuck it. ... Plug in to any or all. Switch on and be serviced. Finished, full, switch off–doesn't matter because: 2. It's all the same. ... The pill and the plastic liver have ended the concern that we are all part of some wonderful inevitable natural process."[(5)] For Greene, "It's all the same" has come full circle. No longer the liberating slogan of a fully interchangeable, technological utopia, the flattening of hierarchy into unbridled recombinatory potential reveals its side effects. In sweeping away time-honored differences–between architecture and media, between vacuum cleaners and space capsules, between the actual and the virtual– *Archigram* opens the possibility of eradicating the differences between the human and non-human. Their bold step into a future risks a fundamental transformation of human subjectivity.

A similar dynamic is evident in the work of Arakawa and Gins. As they moved from visionary art installations to visionary buildings, the ends that Arakawa and Gins sought advanced from a transformation of perception–their relatively early goal in the paper media that was their primary outlet before the microcomputer came of age–to a complete transformation of embodied existence and its relationship to the environment. In the same way that databases now are actual and narratives are virtual, so the built structures that Arakawa and Gins envision have moved from architectural

3.

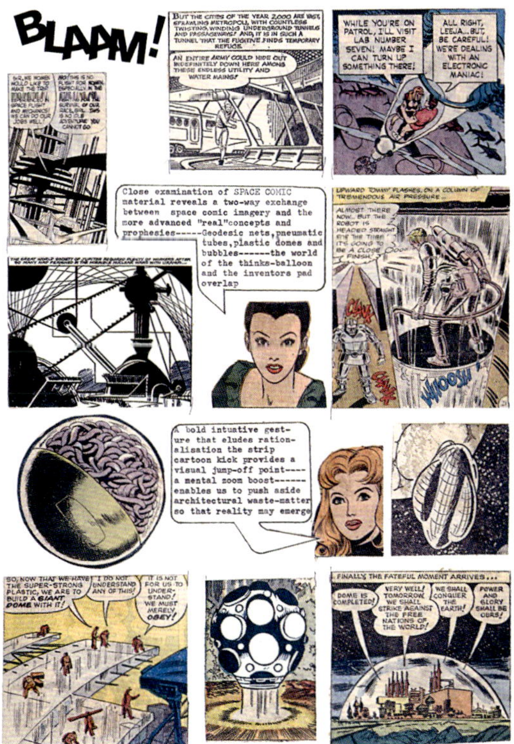

4.

8

9

forms with defined boundaries to fluid environments capable of constantly mutating and rearranging their relationships to the bodies within, which likewise have transformed from pre-given biological entities to embodied temporalities with infinite potential for rearrangement and mutation. Thus bodies, buildings, language, and media co-evolve together in trajectories that arc from durable impress and linear sequence to mutable transformations and combinatorics generating infinite virtual forms.

In *Mechanism of Meaning*, originally published in 1971 and revised in 1988, the authors proclaim that their original formulation of transforming a "model of thought" is no longer adequate. [6] Now, they state, "it is the entire situation, everything a person has at his/her disposal, that we want to build, and so we must think in terms of nothing less than a model or field of sensibility." [7] One technique is to create oxymorons that derail thought from its customary tracks. A diagram, for example, shows a series of triangles and circles, some inscribed with "THIS CIRCLE [OR TRIANGLE] IS BLANK," while the unlabeled ones are blank. A block below shows a single dot in the middle of a blank field, with an inscription below proclaiming "THESE ARE TWO OR MORE DOTS WHICH WERE UNABLE TO BE SEPARATED. (THIS IS TWO OR MORE DOTS WHICH COULD NOT BE SEPARATED)." [8] (Fig. 12)

Another diagram shows "Mistake" scribbled across equations fundamental to the scientific understanding of the world, while a cryptic graphic above has the title, "A CARD BECOMES A FOOT," [9] perhaps alluding to a counter-trajectory that arcs from scientific abstraction back to physical object (Fig. 13). Other techniques aim to expose preconceptions so that they can be challenged and displaced. A wall installation showing a slanting diagonal line assigns various titles to it, including "tornado · the shovel · vagina · length," while below is a large black cloth with the inscription, "BEFORE LIFTING THIS DECIDE WHETHER/YOU HAVE EVER SEEN WHAT IS UNDERNEATH." [10] (Fig. 14).

These strategies take architectural form in the mesh "bridge" proposed for spanning the Moselle River at Epinal, France (Fig. 15). Composed of multiple sections, each with an intricate deceptive geometry designed at once to entice perception and defeat its reification, the architectures range from "rooms" whose four walls all stand at different angles and heights from one another, to an enclosure replete with mirror symmetries and doublings, both right to left and floor to ceiling, with a second mirror-inverted enclosure looming on top of the first separated by an intervening space measuring the same twelve-foot height as the enclosures. The "three players" that Awarkawa and Gins evoke to explain the purpose of such geometries are "fiction of place, blank or forming blank, and space or forming spacetime," [11] all of which they intend to put into dynamic interactions so that the subject (or rather, post-subject) becomes a "container (or generator) of a completely new area of 'consciousness'." [12]

The mesh that is the primary architecture material for the Moselle bridge can stand as an apt transition to the later vi-

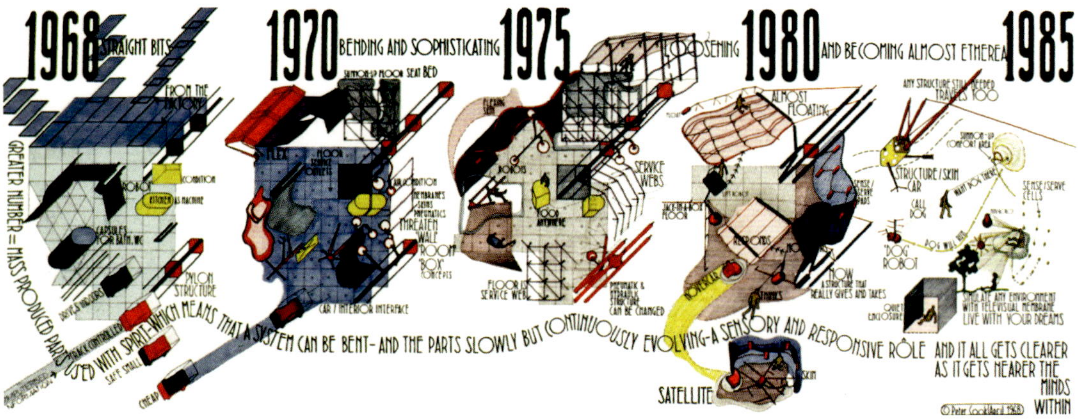

10

10. Peter Cook, *Control and Choice*, 1968. This was reproduced in monochrome in *Archigram Magazine*, issue number 8, 1968, *Milanogram*: page 3. **Facing page: 11.** Warren Chalk and David Greene, *The Electronic Tomato*, 1969.

the electronic tomato
WARREN CHALK + DAVID GREENE 1969

sion of *Architectural Body*.[13] Combining empty space with steel grids, the mesh, less solid than bricks and moveable to a small extent, is still very limited in its range of possible deformations. In a chapter of *Architectural Body* entitled "Architecture as Hypothesis," the authors proclaim "what architecture means to us: a tentative constructing toward a holding in place."[14] The self-conscious replacement of nouns by present participles anticipates the nature of the building: a flexible fabric-like structure that exists as embodied potentiality until it is entered, at which point it takes shape according to the person's movement within it. The chapter, written in part as a dialogue between Arakawa and Gins and students they are taking on a tour, shows the students progressing from their initial incredulity, when they see the un-entered house as a giant "shower cap" resembling the surrounding shrubbery more than a built structure, to their growing fascination with the rooms that shape themselves as they enter. Arakawa and Gins explain what happens once a form is initiated by entering a room:

Arakawa: . . . other spines within the surrounding material will kick in and take over . . . for ten minutes at a time.
Gins: Of course, it would really get going and open up if we had the house on one of its higher settings–one that engages the whole set of spine-deploying mechanisms embedded in the fabric. . .
Arakawa: This house is a tool, a procedural one.
Gins: A functional tool, whether it be a hammer, a telephone, or a telescope, extends the sense, but a procedural tool examines and reorders the sensorium."[15]

The use of "procedural" here recalls the digital algorithms that presumably play a major role in the mechanisms that deploy and adjust the spines; indeed, such an architecture would be virtually inconceivable, much less unbuildable, without digital technologies.

In an intervening narrative section, the authors comment: "Architecture as hypothesis plays off of the long-short history of architecture as non-hypothesis. Constructed to exist in the tense of *what if*, it presents itself as intentionally provisional, replacing definite form with tentative form, the notion of a lasting structure with an adaptive one."[16] The goal is not just to experiment with architectural form but ex-

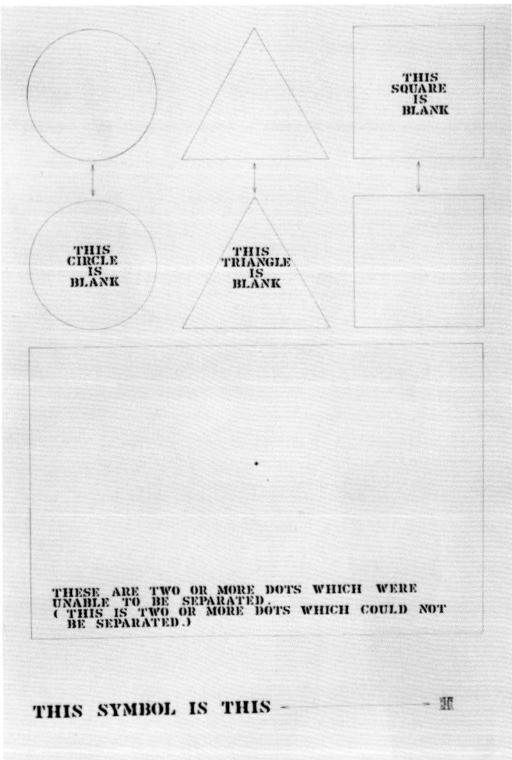

12

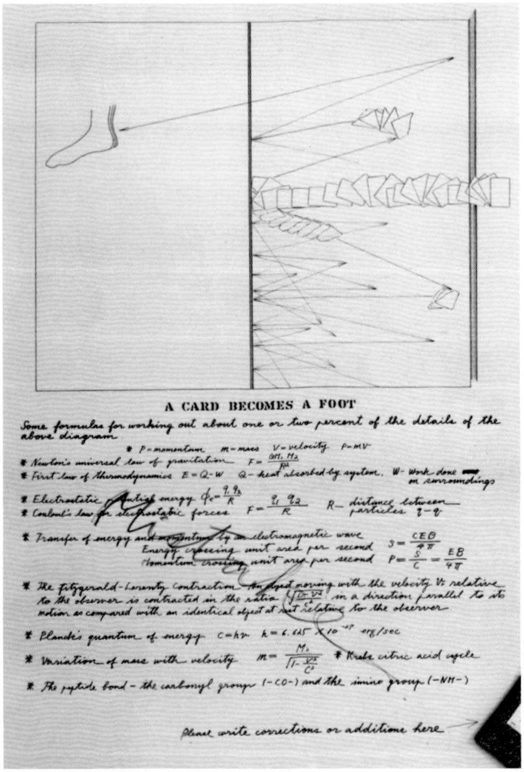

13

plicitly to generate a new kind of subjectivity and a different sense of embodied possibilities. Gins says to one of the students who asks if people can actually live in the house, "Of course. I was hoping you'd want to." Arakawa adds, "Live here and do daily research." When the student bites, asking "Research into what?" Arakawa answers, "Into what goes into being a person. This place can help you do that." [17]

The kind of person they clearly envision co-evolving with the procedural, adaptive house is one who, as they put in it in a book title, has decided not to die (Fig. 16). "Architecture is the greatest tool available to our species," they write in the introduction, "both for figuring itself out and for constructing itself differently ... the body, a complex organism that is always in the process of reading surroundings, needs to be defined together with that within which it moves; peering at it from the other way around, the surroundings need to be defined together with the bodies moving within them." [18] Alluding to their earlier oxymoronic formulation three decades ago of reversible destiny, they ask, "What if it turned out that to be mortal was not an essential condition for our species? To repeat in a slightly different way that people are so unused to hearing: What if it turned out that members of our species were not forever slated to be mortal?" [19] They see themselves issuing "an open challenge to our species to reinvent itself and to desist from foreclosing on any possibility, even those our contemporaries judge to be impossible." [20]

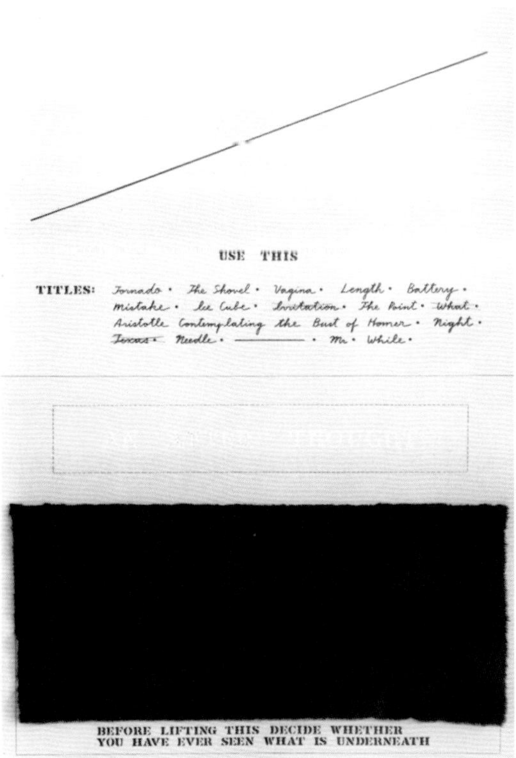

14

Scary stuff, this. The kind of stuff that has led many commentators to posit that *Archigram* and Arakawa and Gins are fringe players with little stake in 'real' architecture, that in their virtuality they pose no real threat to the discipline, that their radical proposals to engineer human subjectivity stand as mere science fiction provocations, ghost stories to tell each other at cocktail parties. We propose this to be patently incorrect. Rather, we would like to close by offering the hypothesis that architecture is inherently virtual.

Architecture, we propose, is not building, nor is it some privileged subset of building. Rather we posit architecture as an emergent property of actual media, particularly buildings and documents. It is that which imbues the physicality of actual media with an excess–especially an excess of meaning. Architecture is not building itself, but, as the dictionary tells us, a particular "art," "science," or "manner" of building–that is, architecture is not *what* one does, but *how* one does it. Similarly, architecture is in dynamic interaction with embodied discourse, that is, discourse instantiated in written documents. "Document," as the term is used in textual studies, is distinct from "text" or "work" because it implies the existence of a physical object. Just as all buildings hold within them the potential of dynamic interaction with the field of architecture, so the documents that precede, surround, and follow buildings also have the potential for such interaction. Embodied buildings and embodied documents are the physical objects providing evidence of architectural acts, but architecture itself can never be reduced solely to these objects. Rather, architecture partakes fundamentally of the virtual, in the Deleuzian sense; it is a nimbus of possibilities dynamically interacting with the actuality of buildings and documents. Both the virtuality of architecture and the physicality of documents and buildings are real. Whereas documents and buildings are location-specific and comprised of myriad individual instances, however, architecture is malleable, dispersed, always in flux. The collective labor of the discipline acts as a midwife to architecture, guiding the emergence of archi-

12. Arakawa + Gins, *The Mechanism of Meaning, Localization and Transference*, 1963-73. **13.** Arakawa + Gins, *The Mechanism of Meaning, The Energy of Meaning* (Biochemical, Physical, and Psychophysical Aspects), 1963-73. **14.** Arakawa + Gins, *The Mechanism of Meaning, Degrees of Meaning*, 1963-73.

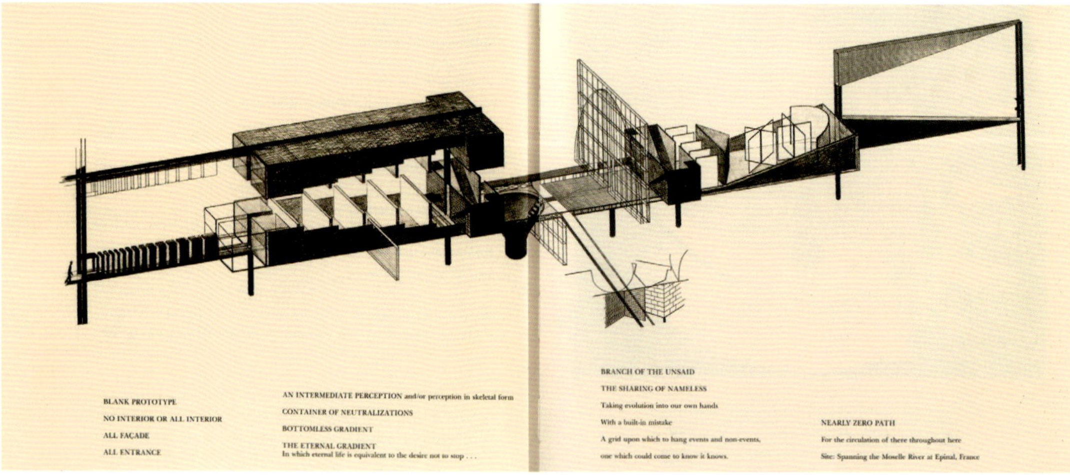

15

tecture's virtuality into the actuality of things we can read, touch, and traverse. Architecture *as such* remains ineffable, however, for as soon as it is written or built, it moves from the virtual to the actual.

An important implication that follows from this view is the impact of media on architecture. As media change – for example, from print-based documents to digital files – the dynamic between architecture's virtuality and the medium's actuality changes accordingly, often with dramatic effects. Another major implication is that virtual architecture (architecture as such), whether that gestured toward by the paper media of *Archigram* or the digitally produced diagrams of Arakawa and Gins, is not a pseudo-architecture suffering from a lack of physicality, but rather an essential architecture unencumbered by physicality. Virtual architecture does not operate outside the pale of the discipline in a lesser realm of the unbuilt, as many detractors have insisted. Rather, architecture, by virtue of its dynamic interaction with the actual media of buildings and documents, infuses their physicality with the inexhaustible potential of the virtual. Inhering in the very heart of the discipline, architecture's ineffability, unspeakable as such, is the reservoir that renews the discipline and makes innovation possible.

"In sweeping away time-honored differences – between architecture and media, between vacuum cleaners and space capsules, between the actual and the virtual – *Archigram* opens the possibility of eradicating the differences between the human and non-human. Their bold step into a future risks a fundamental transformation of human subjectivity."

15. Arakawa + Gins, *The Process in Question*, drawing of the Bridge of Reversible Destiny, Epinal, France, 1972. **16.** Catalogue of the Arakawa + Gins Guggenheim Exhibition, cover, 1997.

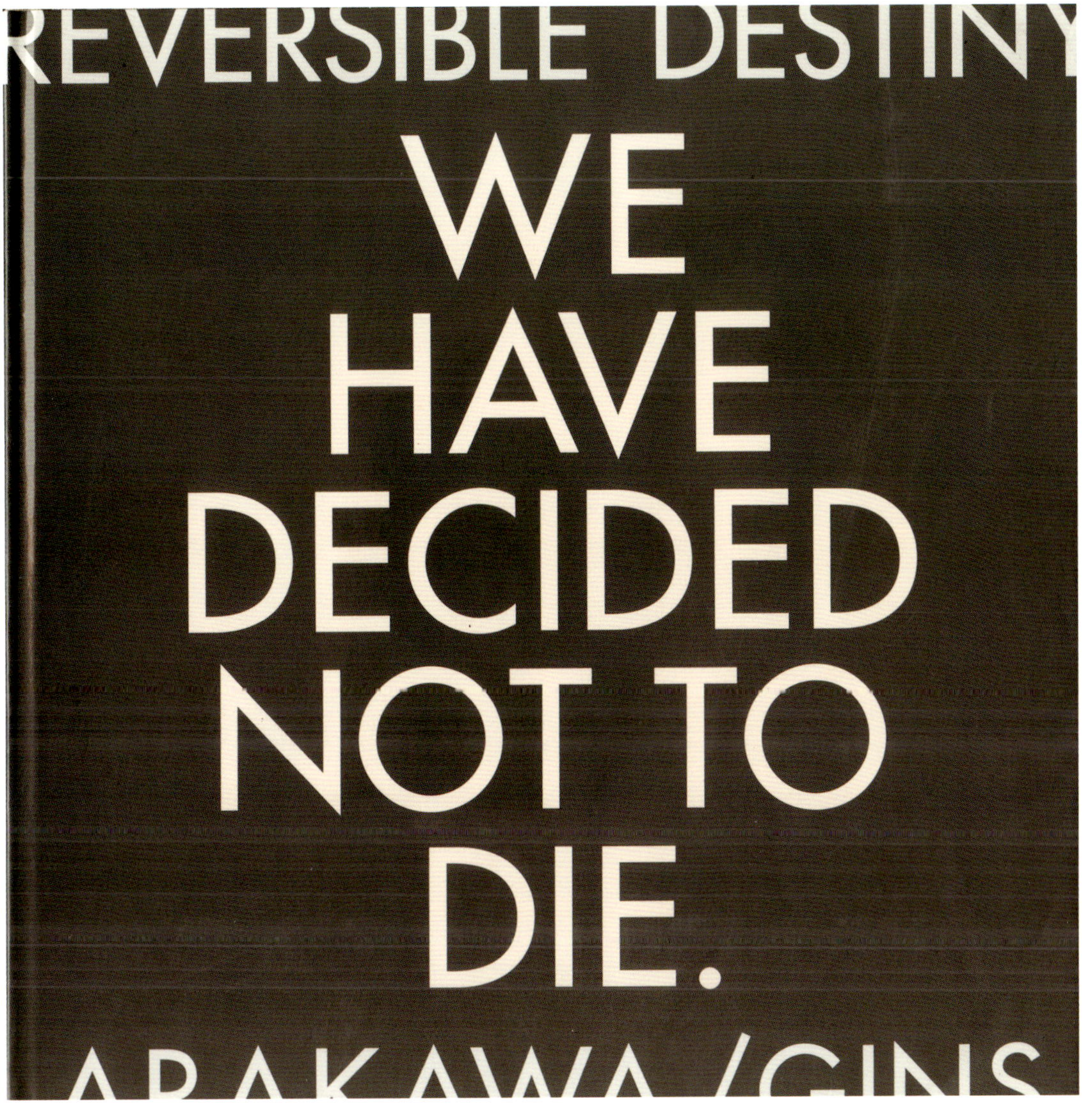

16

Notes:

1. Lev Manovich, *The Language of New Media* (Cambridge: MIT Press, 2001).

2. Manovich, 231.

3. *Archigram 3 "Expendability"* (Autumn 1963): np.

4. *Archigram 4 "The Zoom Issue"* (Spring/Summer 1964): 4.

5. David Greene, "*Popular Pak*," *Archigram 8* (1968): np.

6. Arakawa and Madeline H. Gins, *The Mechanism of Meaning: Work in Progress* (1963-71, 1978) based on *the Method of Arakawa* (New York: Harry N. Abrams, 1979).

7. Arakawa and Gins, 6.

8. Arakawa and Gins, 17.

9. Arakawa and Gins, 26.

10. Arakawa and Gins, 33.

11. Arakawa and Gins, 103.

12. Arakawa and Gins, 103.

13. Madeline Gins and Arakawa, *Architectural Body* (Tuscaloosa: University of Alabama Press, 2002).

14. Gins and Arakawa, 23.

15. Gins and Arakawa, 30.

16. Gins and Arakawa, 29.

17. Gins and Arakawa, 29.

18. Gins and Arakawa, XX.

19. Gins and Arakawa, XVII.

20. Gins and Arakawa, XVII.

Panel One

DISCUSSION

Moderated by Bradley Horn

Panelists Mike Silver · David Gersten · Yehuda E. Safran · Alberto Perez-Gomez · N. Katherine Hayles & Todd Gannon

BH: There is a reason why Michael and Katherine are the book-ends of the table. Their work each, in its own way, bridges many of the issues raised here today. Because Katherine is the outsider here, so to speak, I have extracted some fragments from some of her work as a provocation for the panel: I would like to begin with a quote from a book in which Katherine has invested a lot of her creative energies, Maturana and Varela's *Autopoiesis and Cognition:*

"Let us suppose that we want to build two houses. For such a purpose we hire two groups of thirteen workers each. We name one of the workers of the first group as the group leader and give him a book which contains all the plans of the house showing in a standard way the layout of walls, water pipes, electric connections, windows, etc., plus several views in perspective of the finished house, approximating continuously the final state prescribed by the description. In the second group we do not name a leader; we only arrange the workers in a starting line in the field and give each of them a book, the same book for all, containing only neighborhood instructions. These instructions do not contain words such as house, pipes, or windows, nor do they contain drawings or plans of the house to be constructed, they contain only instructions of what a worker should do in the different positions and in the different relations in which he finds himself as his position and relations change. Although these books are all identical the workers read and apply different instructions because they start from different positions and follow different paths of change. The end result in both cases is the same, namely, a house."

For Alberto and David the absence of teleology in the second group I gather is viewed as problematic whereas for Michael the teleonomic aspects are seen as desirable. Katherine, I wonder if you might begin by describing how this became important to you in your research.

KH: This passage in particular foregrounds the issue of cognition; where cognition is located; how cognition operates in relation to its environment and so forth. And of course the position that Maturana and Varela are pushing in their book *Autopoeisis and Cognition* has two fundamental parts; the first is that cognition is distributed and the second is that all cognition emerges from a kind of circular recursive process which generates organization as its result and it is this organization which is in communication with the environment, not any idea of disembodied information. So in a digital context what this translates to are questions about distributed cognition when cognition is distributed between human and non-human agents, where cognition is located in the body, that is, are we to associate cognition only with consciousness or is it a full body process including subconscious and non-conscious processes and then finally what is the distribution of cognition between the human agent and the environment? Where would an insistence on love fit into such a picture, and how does one talk about ethics if these processes and cognition are distributed? Todd's and my emphasis on media attempts to advance in architectural discussions a topic that's already well advanced in a field like literary studies and that is the importance of media on cognitive possibilities and seeing work within any medium, whether it's a paper medium or a digital medium as part of what is generating these recursive processes and having a profound effect on the emerging result.

YS: Could you elaborate on what you meant by distributed?

KH: To take the phrase I was using, 'distributed cognition'; distributed cognition would want to insist that cognition is not coexistent with consciousness but is a much broader function that includes subconscious and non-conscious processes, cellular processes, greater than cellular processes, sub-cellular processes and so forth and that consciousness is in fact the emergent result of all of these processes. All of these processes have a contribution to rationality so for example I'm thinking of Tony Debrassio's argument that emotion centered in the viscera and the deep senses of the body is an essential part of rationality. So it's a move that wants to uncouple consciousness and cognition and think about cognition as a much fuller distributed process.

TG: I think it's important to add the role of inanimate objects in that. There's a fantastic book called *Cognition in the Wild* by Edwin Hutchins where he describes the navigation of a large ship on the sea; that ship navigation in large scale military craft is impossible without multiple brains and also the objects that are used to track their position. I think this is completely relevant to architecture in the increased attention to the feedback loop between the things that we make and the things that we build and the people that use them whether they are reading or inhabiting; those kinds of feedback loops have always been there but have become more of an acute problem to think about.

DG: One of the things that due to time I sort of skipped is the counterpoint to large western ship building; western ship building having to do essentially with the summation of existing knowledge being put into a structure, in advance, from the shore; and of course primarily deep-cutting large vessels that in some sense attempt to mute the storm, mute the forces, cut through. The other position is the Polynesian island catamarans which of course are on the surface. They do obviously involve knots and bindings and some form of pre-existing knowledge but what makes them I think unique is that the knowledge that is key to survival is actually with the pilot as they're moving; it's held in the body. Of course western nautical history denies that for twenty thousand years Polynesian island ship builders have been crossing the seas because they can't conceive of how these frail things could do it and of course they did. And the remarkable thing is that when an enormous storm that would destroy possibly the Titanic would come up the pilot themselves would contain the knowledge to understand how to use its wind to outrun it because they have that set of imaginative skills that were human and were with them and were not in the structure of the vessel. The pilot in a western ship basically has been reduced to "Well, hopefully he doesn't get drunk and you're not going to crash" he's merely a cog. Whereas the pilot in the Polynesian islands contains the navigational knowledge as part of his own being.

APG: There is this old story about Tecton being both a ship builder and a pilot. There is a connection between shipbuilding and architecture as well. So there is this architectural wisdom that reaches beyond cognitive theory, identified with prudence, with phronesis, which is why I would hope that both groups of builders of houses in this original example that Brad was quoting might draw from their own natural languages. For me this is much more important; the wisdom that is contained in the natural languages which we actually speak everyday, the stories that we tell, that's the source of real knowledge, of a wisdom that may ground ethical action. I don't think it comes from the top; I don't think it can be reduced to one language that will be a magical solution to all our differences but rather, and here I agree with George Steiner, I would actually argue that real knowledge hinges on our capacity to preserve our very many and diverse human languages, that keep vanishing everyday and we must preserve, like endangered species. Our diverse languages allow us to articulate the poetics of the world and then translate them from one language to another; and that's where we get our wisdom. I think we get too caught up with this obsession with transparency; with one language.

DG: I think it goes back to the issue of distributed cognition or distributed agency. I think that part of the enigma or paradox that that question of cognition as a sort of distributed condition raises is how you identify the necessary. Most of the discussion is about what's possible and what's not possible. These sets of circumstances open up these possibilities and this is impossible but it probably will be and how do you get to the necessary without the ethical dimension of human language or human life and that exchange between life and structure? I know we can include silicon based life forms as the genetic algorithm of the future. How do we in that context ask what is necessary?

YS: One of the answers is song and dance because just in thinking about the Polynesians they embody these kind of energies by singing and certain kind of rhythmic movements and song that enable them to navigate. The memory and the understanding of the situation is embodied in a series of songs and dances and movements and rhythms and body contact. In fact there is a way in which one kind of boat has almost a hole in the bottom which is then filled with a soft material so you have immediate contact between the body of the pilot and the water and the ability to sense through his own contact which direction, which stream, which force, which movement, which speed etc. That combination where the boat is itself used in that way.

BH: I'd like to throw it back to Katherine. In *My Mother Was a Computer* you talked about emergence as an ethical condition. How can emergence be ethical?

KH: Well the very idea of emergence as you know is something where you have some kind of system bound together by complex dynamics and the emergent phenomenon is the result of the interaction of the components of that system in a dynamic and unpredictable way. So the idea that one could allow the play of chance and also the interactions between these components to generate possibilities that were perhaps not even envisioned if you thought of a system that was planned and designed entirely in advance opens the possibility for new kinds of creations, new kinds of innovations that couldn't be thought of by rational projection alone. But I'd like to say about these questions of how you design systems, how systems work, what their relation to the complex process of cognition is are really to my mind all tied to the crucial question that David Gersten just asked; "what is necessary?" and to that I would want to add immediately a second question; "necessary for what?" and if you attempt to ask that question which to my mind is a preceding question before you get to what is necessary you are immediately drawn into a discussion of what human future we envision for ourselves in this era of intense computation and intelligent machines. And that's of course a very wide ranging discussion but I think a very healthy and necessary discussion for where our culture is in this contemporary moment.

DG: I have to say that I couldn't agree more and that really is the question. It isn't some sci-fi movie it is about the fact that capital has a metabolism and technology has a metabolism and they're all very real. Constructed doesn't mean it's not real. I think that the earth has one and we of course have one and the question of the conflicts between them is increasing. I don't think that those metabolisms are in harmony and I think that the enormous inequities of resource distribution (I'm talking about the three billion people who live on less than two dollars a day) is an indication of the question of whether capital has the capacity to bind freedom or bring humans toward a future that is anything other than apocalyptic. Technology has similar kinds of problems all around so when one asks necessary for what or for whom either we say ok there's a silicon based life form that will transcend us or you ask what is humanity and what is its voice? Whether it is silence or the wisdom of song or language and the words we share. What is the voice of humanity?

APG: I agree of course that these questions are open but what worries me is that in the discussion there is a kind of a profound Gnosticism in the sense that we only look at our own condition and we fail to recognize the traits of our own humanity in our heritage. We are not just where we are right now; we have been doing this for millennia. So we may be able to decide, I want to become immortal even if poor people will have to die, OK, we can decide that, but that is a ridiculous framework if we close ourselves in and we don't realize what the nature of human existence is; what makes us human, why is it possible for us to be happy at some point or to recognize our purpose?

YS: So if we give up our mortality we are in a completely different world, we become like fish in a big tank just waiting for things to happen. These are the nightmares that Baudrillard has described so well. With historical knowledge of human cultures I would not be convinced even if I could have it for six billion people that this is the way you go. But of course the conversation is open. History, as Shakespeare told us, is a story told by an idiot as you know very well. As the Greek historians already told us, the poets had a much better grasp of human experience than the historians could actually offer us. I think that we seldom realize how much of history was invented. It was created, it was not necessarily causality. In the big debate between Thomas Moore and the other advisors of Henry VIII there was no a priori reason why Thomas Moore lost his head and Henry VIII expanded his economic power, it could have been otherwise. If Thomas Moore had won the day it would have meant that Europe and England would have developed more like China in the sense of tying the potential and the possibilities to a book! I think that *Don Quixote* is not about Medieval law, it's about the Bible, about the impossibility of living according to a book. Now capitalism is not a natural phenomenon, we all agree. It's not part of evolution. It was invented at a certain point for good reasons. For good or bad reasons, it was invented. Now sure enough, in order to replace an invention one has to invent something else. And that is likely to be the task of the next generation. When I look at my students I hope not that they will make capitalism work better because there is a limit, but that they will invent something better. Unfortunately the dreams of the industrial planned economy were run down simply because there was no cognitive model, distributed or otherwise, to account for the possibility of a sustained planet. It just was too primitive cognitively. The potential is there. We live in a culture in which everyone knows WHY something happened either in the past or in the present. In reality things happen because somebody wants them to happen. As Joyce's hero Daedalus says "Why is it important? Because I say so."

APG: I understand very well the Aristotelian distinction between history and poetry; but one has to understand the distinctions in those concepts emerging in Western technological culture after the eighteenth century; after the possibility of human generated change becomes self-conscious. We now make history which is very different from what Herodotus was thinking about which were narrative chronicles. Now we have to be responsible for what we have made because we have to be responsible for what we do. This is a condition that is not universal to all world cultures. I mean we invented history in the sense that we became suddenly aware that what we do and what we make actually changes the world. Prior to the 18th century no one would have actually believed that human generated change is self-evident. In view of that, I agree with Agamben here: our only possibilities are actually to revisit that which we have made in order to rewrite the traditions that may make a thread to where we are now. Of course these are inventions, they are poetic inventions, there are affinities between the poetic imagination, poetic narrative and historical narrative but at the same time our history must be particularly responsible and generous to the genuine concern for meaning that our ancestors have had in the products that they have produced and that we have inherited. And that's I think the real history; it's a revisiting of these phenomena that we first perceive as significant and transformative, in order to be able to provide ourselves with narratives that allow us to work toward a better future.

YS: I'm sorry in my view there is no real history and you should not forget that history as we use it first was invented by the prophet Daniel in the late book of the Bible. For the Greeks the word istoria meant simply an inquiry; they had no projection and no linear thinking. It was an inquiry about things that happened or did not happen. Daniel in a moment of great despair, being in exile in Babylon invented this idea of universal history in order to say "look, things are bad now but they won't go on being bad, there will be another empire and yet another..." it was an expression of hope that after certain events there will be a chance to return to the homeland. The Renaissance that you are of course so proud of as we all are would have been impossible without the identification of the past being contemporaneous with the present. This possibility was lost as a result of the Renaissance. And the sense of history that we are using now is the invention of Vico in a great book called *The New Science*. At the beginning of the eighteenth century he invents history in the sense in which we are using it. I am writing a piece right now called Against Meaning not because there is no meaning but because meaning is invented, meaning is created; meaning is put there by whoever puts it there. There is a beautiful story by a great writer Agnon about a man who dreamt of a great treasure somewhere and goes to cross seven mountains and seven caves and in the last cave there is a stone and he lifts the stone and there is a piece of paper there that said "Have you left something behind here that you needed to come back to look for it?"

BH: Michael, how does your work respond to this question of history?

MS: The idea that critique is really essential and instead of applying it to old paradigms or even history itself we need to apply it to new paradigms that are coming up. That's why I have been interested in engaging in a critique of technology, not in some old notion of foundations and buildings and walls but I would say that freedom is inseparable from empathy because really what we are trying to get at here in this creation of this new future is a destruction of the absolutism of the me. This is what I think the discussion of ethics was getting towards, that critique is a way of peeling away a focus on the self and this moment of selflessness is when you begin to engage in a distributed consciousness; that was how I took the term distributed. In a sense it's not really becoming more human but really going beyond the human. I'll just end by saying that I'm not sure we're actually not already immortal in the sense that maybe we're just incurable amnesiacs; nothing doesn't exist so you're not going to disappear into it. So I think we are here forever together, we've probably been having this conversation a million times throughout the eons except maybe I've been in the audience and the speakers have been on the podium so maybe ethics isn't really in the form but in the architect and the user.

Audience: There seems to be an unbridgeable chasm between these two groups. Katherine on one hand and Alberto on the other. So how to we bridge that gap?

KH: I don't really see this as an unbridgeable gap at all. I'm really interested in how things can be brought together rather than posited as binaries. And I would just make a gesture toward how this gap might be traversed in both directions: two small observations: one is that the term human is not a trans-historical conception but is very historically specific and culturally embedded. And it certainly has had a myriad of different meanings over time and perhaps never has been more in flux than it is at present. I wouldn't necessarily say that we're moving away from the human I would rather say what it means to be human is in flux as it has always been. The second observation I would make is that Edwin Hutchins (who incidentally has a really interesting discussion of Polynesian navigation and uses it to come to the opposite conclusion that David just articulated for us) also emphasizes cognition as a function that is supported and extended by our built environment and of course humans have been doing this ever since they invented tools. So that way of looking at distributed cognition makes it not a phenomenon unique to the late twentieth and twenty-first century but a really essential activity that humans have always engaged in. And it's true that we've now built more cognitively intensive environments than ever existed before but the idea that human cognition has always been supported and extended by artificial means is I think a fundamental notion. So it makes what's happening in the present not an apocalyptic break but rather an extension of very, very long evolutionary and historical trends. In my personal opinion the most likely scenario is not that humans will continue to exist and somehow dominate machines or that machines will stamp out humans and become the dominant life form on our planet but rather what we already see at a very advanced stage which is a symbiotic relationship between humans and machines; and we know we already advanced far into that and that will undoubtedly be likely to continue and intensify in the foreseeable future.

DG: I think you are right but the question is: are the lenses focused? I think that there are some fairly unique ruptures in that sort of smooth extension of us into tools. In relation to the idea that debt and equity is tension and compression, the specific invention of compound interest, the specific ability to write more receipts than gold has lead to a very clear required expansion of massively expanding consumption and frequency of exchange in order to make that time promise. In order to keep the promise of compound interest we need expansion. The movements of global populations are part of feeding that promise. The question is what happens to the earth because it can't grow. At a certain point the ecological ruptures that we are witnessing are not about good corporate governance or bad corporate governance it's about the requirements of capital in terms of its consumption and I think that that filters through almost the entire discussion; it filters through language, it filters through stories, it filters through how we share words, it filters through how capital writes, how the state writes; how all of that kind of authorship and authority happens is really in some sense an earlier version of the Manhattan Project; an earlier splitting of time using compound interest.

TG: Whether we take this continuum as ruptured or smooth and whether we are on the side of capital or whether we are resistant to capital and want to find new ways out, in any one of those situations what we need are new concepts, we need innovations. So how do we take some of this discussion and really start to apply it to architectural practice; how do these thoughts make it into the office when I go back tomorrow night? How do you imbue the architectural object with this capacity for change, interaction, etc? One of the things that I really enjoy about Michael's work is that the projects always incorporate radical change. The disappearing bridge in Venice or the baptismal font in Mont St. Michel both have an interactive mutability. Every architectural experiment I don't think is going to result in a new concept which will get us out of the morass we find ourselves in but I think it's important for us always to be innovative and looking for the possibilities to emerge in the way that evolution does.

DG: Two responses: The inevitability of an instrumental future may not be so inevitable. Secondly, for me personally practice and the implementation of a radical idea has to do with the idea that literature is freedom; it has to do with programmatic invention. The realization of the literary dimension of life and the programmatic invention relative to the social contract and the question of ethics has a far more radical future than instrumentality as the so called new. Given the global crisis that humanity is facing, the new is in the literary dimension of how we understand our lives, how we exchange words; how we think about language and space.

TG: And that's where the question becomes so profound. For 500 years we've had media, print media which are permanent things whose logic and permanence had come to underwrite not only literature in the form of published authentic copy but also architecture as an unchangeable built thing. As some of the technological questions which are the basis of this discussion bring into our world changeable media and changeable architecture the kind of flux that had been so resistant in the objects that we make has made these questions clear, and that for me is the core of this.

DG: The poet Muriel Rukeyser wrote that "The universe is made of stories, not of atoms."

Panel Two

PEDAGOGY, TECHNIQUE AND THE TRANSMISSIBLE

Moderated by Maria Berman
Panelists: Ed Keller · Jason Vollen · George Ranalli · Karl Chu · Yael Erel

This panel examines the way that technology has affected what is pedagogically transmissible. How has technology expanded the domain of architectural education? Has computation made it possible for students to access dimensions of architectural insight that would have been otherwise out of reach? How can the design studio be used as a research laboratory? What role should history play in the design curriculum? Should we teach design as a top-down, authored process, or a bottom-up, emergent one?

SPEAKING WITH THE ALIEN: AGENTS OF REVOLUTIONARY TIME

Ed Keller

Thank you Maria. Thank you Brad and The City College for the event. I want to read a quote that came to mind while Yehuda Safran was speaking earlier. This is apropos the theme of invention; I quote from Julio Cortázar's novel *Hopscotch*.[1]

"Yes, but who will cure us of the dull fire, the colorless fire that at nightfall runs along the rue de la Hutchette, emerging from the crumbling doorways ... to burn like this without surcease, to bear the inner burning coming on like fruit's quick ripening, to be the pulse of a bonfire in this thicket of endless stone, walking through the nights of our life, obedient as blood in its blind circuit ... it would seem that a choice cannot be dialectical, that the fact of bringing it up impoverishes it. ... Everything is writing, that is to say, a fable. But what good can we get from the truth that pacifies an honest property owner? Our possible truth must be an invention, that is to say, scripture, literature, picture, sculpture, agriculture, pisciculture, all the tures in the world. Values, tures, sainthood, a ture, society, a ture, love, pure ture, beauty, a ture of tures. ... Why surrender to Great Habit? One can choose his ture, his invention, that is to say, the screw or the toy car. That is how Paris destroys us slowly, delightfully, tearing us apart among old flowers and paper tablecloths stained with wine, with its colorless fire that comes running out of crumbling doorways at nightfall. An invented fire burns in us, an incandescent ture, a whatsis of the race, a city that is the Great Screw, the horrible needle with its night eye through which the Seine thread runs, a torture machine like a board of nails, agony in a cage crowded with infuriated swallows. We burn within our work, fabulous mortal honor, high challenge of the Phoenix. No one will cure us of the dull fire, the colorless fire that at nightfall runs along the Rue de la Huchette. Incurable, perfectly incurable, we select the Great Screw as a ture, we lean towards it, we enter it, we invent it again every day, with every wine stain on the tablecloth, with every kiss of mold in the dawns of the Cour de Rohan, we invent our conflagration, we burn outwardly from within, maybe that is the choice, maybe words envelop it the way a napkin does a loaf of bread and maybe the fragrance is inside, the flour puffing up, the yes without the no, or the no without the yes, the day without manes, without Ormuz or Ariman, once and for all and in peace and enough."

Facing page: 1. Dr. Jeremy Stone (Arthur Hill), Dr. Charles Dutton (David Wayne) & Dr. Ruth Leavitt (Kate Reid). *The Andromeda Strain* (1971).

Regarding the issue of invention and the question of intentionality, of choice, I'm going to let that quote hover in the air for just a second.

There are two other themes that came up earlier today. One investigated the mechanism of capital. I am very interested in the idea that the mechanism of capital is not necessarily something invented by humans (although I have just read this beautiful quote about invention) but perhaps is embedded or immanent in the world, outside the anthropocentric; there was a concept that David Gersten mentioned: that the original will to create entities that collapse time was human.

I thought that was fantastic, the idea of collapsing time, the original will, the notion of bodies that could do something to time. But I also would like to raise the question of whether this agency is human or non–human. I am talking about aliens today, so I am going to try and unpack that for a few minutes.

As well, the question of shelter came up; I believe David argued that "The porosity of *being* authors no such a shelter." I would like to leave that as an open question to see if some of the examples I will show can help us to rethink the concept of shelter through a redefinition of communication.

My title, "Speaking with the Alien: Agents of Revolutionary Time," brings a question: what is the alien? What does it mean to speak with it? And what is revolutionary time? Technology, concepts of measurement, control, communication, translation, the pedagogical uses of models in general, noise, agency and thought itself; all these are themes that come to my mind in relation to the Ineffable. They have a crucial relationship to it and of course the Ineffable by definition seems to be something that exists outside of language and outside of measure. I would like to cite another quote–this from Nietzsche's *Birth of Tragedy*–to deal with this question of the alien, of speaking with the alien.

"At bottom the aesthetic phenomenon is simple; one need only have the ability to see continually a living play and to live perpetually surrounded by hosts of spirits, and one is a poet; one need only feel the drive to alter oneself (sich selbst zu verwandeln) and to speak out of alien bodies and souls, and one is a dramatist. Dionysian excitation is capable of communicating to a whole multitude this artistic power to feel oneself surrounded by such a host of spirits, with whom one knows oneself to be inwardly one. This process (Prozeß) of the tragic chorus is the originary dramatic phenomenon: seeing oneself altered before one's very eyes (sich selbst vor sich verwandelt zu sehen) and now acting, as though one had really entered into another body, another character. This process stands at the beginning of the development of drama. ... Here already the individual gives himself up by entering into an alien nature. And what is more, this phenomenon arises epidemically: a whole crowd feels itself enchanted in this way."

3

Facing page: 2. Photomontage created for a special issue of the Italian magazine *Quadrante* No. 35/36 dedicated to the Casa del Fascio by Giuseppe Terragni (1932-36). **3.** East and West Berlin celebrating New Year together.

4

So I am interested in this idea of the host of spirits and the consciousness which arises when an individual becomes aware that they are part of that multifarious body. To explore this idea, I will be showing you scenes from three films. Each provides contrasting examples of communication with the alien. Nietzsche's 'host of spirits' plays a key role as well, but in each case with a radically different set of consequences. So I ask you as you watch these examples to question who or what is communicating, and with whom? Where is the alien?

I am showing you these clips in advance of talking about them so that you have a moment to be exposed with some degree of innocence.

First: a 'B film,' *The Andromeda Strain*, 1969 (Fig. 1). A dangerous alien life form has arrived on earth and scientists are struggling against time to prevent a global outbreak. There is a question of what is transmissible and what is translatable here. This is the question that is at stake in this example, the point of view of the 'alien', of the infection, the crystal, the non–human–whatever it is–this green stuff–is as important as the point of view of the human.

The scientists understand this; they are sensitive to the energetic "needs" of the alien crystal, if you want to look at it that way, they are looking for the way that it might affect human bodies. But of course something else is at stake; it is not just a game because people are being killed by the crystal. They can't speak with it, as it is an almost abstract system–but they have to come up with some way of communicating with it.

So this raises an issue pertaining to the function of a concept model or abstract model; *Andromeda Strain* is an illustration of the contemporary debate that surrounds the use of models, and how they can be leveraged to both analyze and produce architecture.

Every model attempts to establish an epistemological horizon, so we can 'see' systems that are either invisible or outside our realms of perception. But don't get me wrong, I am fascinated with models of performance and of design, yet "the morphological variations are endless" [2] and therefore any use of conceptual or technical models can only be a provisional practice of controlled folly: any advance in technology is merely one move among many to aid in the transfer of information from archive to archive or in the conversion of matter to energy, energy to information. The question is: where is the locus of that possibility of conversion? This returns us to the question of capital that inspired the morning session: where is the possibility for information to become energy, or matter to become energy, and then become information…? Is that protocol literally imbricated in the fabric of the reality that we live in? If so how can we take advantage of it? If so how are other bodies taking advantage of it? The theme of distributed cognition that came up this morning finds ways to channel itself through global systems of capital, to take advantage of that deployment.

Technology is always going to liberate modes of expression, just as language does. This question is about the nature of our world: is the very fabric of our being imbued with potential expressivity and forms of communication? This is how language and the gesture, indeed any idea of communication, are put at stake.

'We can communicate with others only through what in us–as much as in others–has remained potential, and any communication [as Benjamin perceives for language] is first of all communication not of something in common, but of communicability itself.' [3]

This passage from Agamben is relevant to the problem as he essentially makes the point that communication is not about the faithful transmission of a message from a sender to a receiver, it's actually about the notion that communication is being attempted. He is making an argument that that is the heart or the value of communication: not the transmission of information, but the becoming aware that the transmission is happening or that an attempt at communication is taking place. Once again: I am very fascinated with models; I work a lot with models pedagogically, but for the sake of this discussion I am more interested in the concept of transmission or the transmissibility itself rather than in pursuing specific technical models.

Agamben suggests that "The gesture... opens the sphere of ethos as the more proper sphere of that which is human... [and] is communication of a communicability." Any language, according to this idea, is more important in how it can show an intent on the part of the voices–the transmitters and the receivers–than in how accurately it can transmit a message.

In *The Andromeda Strain* the exchange of information between humans and aliens, and to each other, allows both parties to discover themselves connected to an interruption of signal–a noise: it's the outside, it's the open, it's the unknown, it's a parasite, it's a danger. This idea of danger, which can get scaled up to a geopolitical and a trans-historical level, brings us to the next example that I'd like to show you. Here are a couple of clips from a 70s horror thriller. I will tell you the title after I show you the clips. (Fig. 5-8)

Now think about the landscape that is being shown here. There is time embedded with this landscape; it is compartmentalized, it is speciated. The bodies that are negotiating with it have a range of techniques by which to extract *meaning* out of the landscape; by meaning, I imply the artifacts that have been buried, lost, hidden and imprisoned there, and the networks of relations that surround those bodies.

There is a cultural narrative going on as well. Max von Sydow's character, Father Merrin, is from the west and he is in a contested land–Northern Iraq. Maybe you thought it was a documentary I was showing you…

No, it's actually *The Exorcist* [1973]. In the opening scene from *The Exorcist*, Merrin is seeking for something that has been hidden. He is uncovering lost time, he is uncovering a body which has concentrated so much power in itself that it had to be buried, hidden–not unlike oil underneath the desert which is as well a concentration of millions of years of processes.

It's a conversion of energy and matter from one form to another. And it has the potential to liberate that energy and that matter when it gets released. There is something else fabulous that goes on in the beginning of this film.

"Thought takes place when systems become aware that they are formed by and communicating with agents that can only provisionally speak their language; yet nevertheless, the desire to communicate is set in motion. Only when we intend to communicate, knowing it is impossible and knowing that noise could interrupt – only then is thought more than repetition."

The question of temporal reversibility and irreversibility comes up immediately.

The demon who was imprisoned in the tomb and has just been exhumed has alternate time structures embedded within. By *its nature–it is noise*. The relationship noise has to transmission of information is inherently temporal, since signal to noise relationships can change outcomes, in the way that information flow through a system determines its future or gives it access to its past.

4. Hans Namuth, *Jackson Pollock*, 1950.

The pendulum stops swinging; the question of reversibility and irreversibility is posed here acutely in relationship to a whole series of geopolitical acts, tensions of will and intention and so forth. It's a thriller, it's a horror film, it's a geopolitical allegory.

And you'll recall that the little girl who gets possessed later in the film is living in a suburb of Washington DC. She's being raised by a single mom who acts as an actress in films about political protest. The film is laced through with subnarratives of the punished insurgent. This opening sequence is the real *Exorcist*. Usually when one is thinking about *The Exorcist* one thinks about a B horror film, but this is something else entirely.

So, noise. Noise is the demonic, it is demonic time, the multiple, the radically multiple as legion, a byproduct of the contact between non-human time and human time. The movement from one landscape to another, from one scale to another.

There is a relationship between Merrin and this demon; Merrin has almost got a love relationship with the demon, a very special kind obviously, a kind of tension. We can also think of other demons who ask if we will say yes to a question of repetition, if we will say yes to a question of affirmation:
"What, if some day or night a demon were to steal after you into your loneliest loneliness and say to you: 'This life as you now live it and have lived it, you will have to live once more and innumerable times more.' Would you not throw yourself down and gnash your teeth and curse the demon who spoke thus? Or have you once experienced a tremendous moment when you would have answered him: 'You are a god and never have I heard anything more divine.'[4]

The Exorcist positions the possession by a demon as a threat, as something that is mortally harmful to the human. The human is colonized by this radical multiplicity. The human is put at risk. And this is a key question that came up in the earlier debate about capital: to what degree can we ground the question in the anthropocentric; in any global system, any kind of intelligent system, be it architecture, urbanism, the flow of energy across the surface of the planet; to what degree does capital, as a multifarious overlap of times, pose a hazard to that environment which is human? This is a question of intentionality and again of controlled folly.

There is also an issue of pedagogy here: the relationship between noise and signal, the transmitter and the receiver. I would say that any kind of pedagogy is nothing more than

THE EXORCIST ©Warner Bros. Inc. and Hoya Productions, Inc. All Rights Reserved.
5

To what degree can we ground the question in the anthropocentric? In any global system, any kind of intelligent system, be it architecture, urbanism, the flow of energy across the surface of the planet; to what degree does capital, as a multifarious overlap of times, pose a hazard to that environment which is human? This is a question of intentionality and again of controlled folly."

6

a protocol for the transmission of information... a kind of forcible possession by a host of spirits; teaching, like any event, is an act of violence.

How do we defuse the violence? How do we make sure that it doesn't end up nasty like *The Exorcist*...? There is the need for a careful, intentional production of critical 'deviance' [thought], that leads to a position that could assert that all ethics need to be constantly questioned.

Looking sideways to one of the other themes of the conference, to the contemporary technology question, I would take this opportunity to define computation as the processing of information and energy, such that those flows can be chained to external systems, some of which are reversible, others irreversible. Again, the processing of signal and message. Computation is what happens when you feed energy or information into a system, and then extract a result. Meaning emerges when that result is plugged into another computational chain. That's the birth of language, which Michel Serres has written about very beautifully in his essay *The Origin of Language: Biology, Information Theory, & Thermodynamics*.[5]

So we have to ask what the full range of substrates for communication are: material communication as well as informational... immanent computation in matter itself or in flows of information. We have to ask about the political aspect vis a vis agency. This was my interest in showing *The Exorcist*, not really in that a hapless girl was possessed by a demon, as I argue that's not what the film is most concerned with. The film is about a very wide set of relations within which some bodies move and within which some bodies get caught: the effects that are produced when those bodies come into unexpected contact with one another.

5-6, **Following pages:** 7. *THE EXORCIST (1973).*

THE EXORCIST ©Warner Bros. Inc. and Hoya Productions, Inc. All Rights Reserved.
8

The last example I'll show you, deals with the host of spirits once again. Of course the host of spirits from my first example, *The Andromeda Strain*, was purely abstract–it was a possession by something that wasn't even biological but just a crystal. The second example, *The Exorcist*, was a host which wasn't biological either but at least was anthropocentrically recognizable as the multitude of souls trapped within a demon taking over a body.

This shot is from Fellini's *8 ½* (Figs. 9, 11-15). It's the final scene in film. The main character, Guido [who is having trouble making a film] is played by Marcello Mastroianni, and is an obvious stand in for Fellini. So this is a film about making films. It's a meta-narrative, a very carefully constructed meta-narrative.

The last scene is a fantasy circus within which all the people he has ever known, including his own childhood identities, can gather together and play roles; all of them are present.

"Noise is the demonic, it is demonic time, the multiple, the radically multiple as legion, a byproduct of the contact between non-human time and human time. The movement from one landscape to another, from one scale to another."

8. *The Exorcist* (1973). **9.** Federico Fellini, *8 1/2*, 1963.

9

Throughout the film he slips between memory, fantasy and reality, and the film itself is an incredible masterpiece of self reflexive and embedded structure, which many viewers miss as on the surface, it seems to be a narrative about a director who can't quite manage to make a film. But in fact it is a nested layering of formal structure. The final shot summarizes not just his life and the film itself, but also the most basic nature of communication through recursion, bootstrapping and a range of specific cinematic techniques that index, reveal, embed and develop communication channels. The host of spirits, again. But in this case gentle and emanicipatory. Fellini collects everyone, brings them together, and allows them to join voices in a joyous Babel, a festival of souls.

So I will close by asking again what it means to be an agent of revolutionary time. I hope that some of these examples have got us closer to a definition. How can we invoke the host of spirits? What will we do if they come when we call?

Ultimately this recalls the problem of information theory and the relation between forms of entropy and information flow. Weaver, a collaborator with Claude Shannon, wrote that: "Information in communication theory relates not so much to what you do say, as to what you could say. The amount of information is directly proportional to the number of possibilities available in a given transmission system before a message is transmitted."[6]

So a question remains whether interiority and exteriority can ever truly trade messages through the gauntlet of noise and the parasite: can a body, a monad, ever connect to systems outside itself (and I think here of *The Crying of Lot 49*, Pynchon; or *The Invention of Morel*, Bioy Casares); or if immersed in an already given situation, can a body somehow bootstrap into the 'yet to come'?

'Thought is form-of-life, life that cannot be segregated from its form; and anywhere the intimacy of this insep-

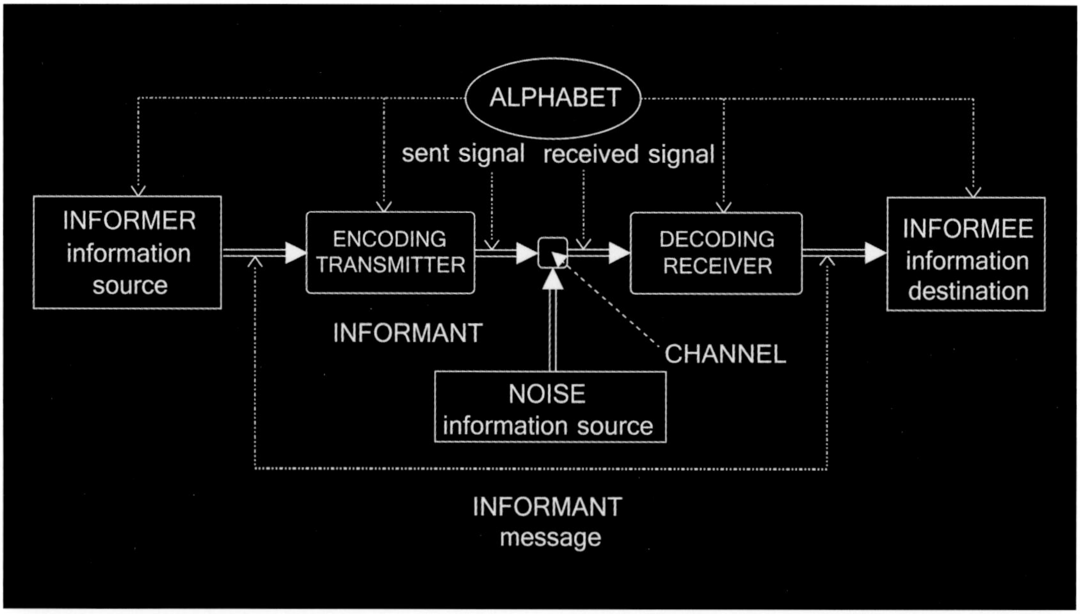

10

11

10. Communication model, adapted from Shannon and Weaver (1949). **11.** Federico Fellini, *8 1/2*, 1963.

able life appears, in the materiality of corporeal processes and of habitual ways of life no less than in theory, there and only there is there thought. And it is this thought, this form-of-life, that...must become the guiding concept and the unitary center of the coming politics.'[7]

Thought. The problematizing of information and language suggests that the very substrate of thought is in these questions. Thought takes place when systems become aware that they are formed by and communicating with agents that can only provisionally speak their language, yet nevertheless, the desire to communicate is set in motion. Only when we intend to communicate, knowing it is impossible, and knowing *that noise could interrupt–only then is thought more than repetition*. The ringing in our ears is a kind of noise, but it is also a kind of productive intelligence.

Notes:

1. Julio Cortazar, *Hopscotch* (New York: Pantheon Books, 1987), excerpts from chap. 73, 383-85.

2. Bernard Tschumi, *Architecture and Disjunction* (Cambridge, MA: MIT Press, 1996), 154-55.

3. Giorgio Agamben, "Form-of-Life," in *Means without End: Notes on Politics*, trans. Vincenzo Binetti and Cesare Casarino (Minneapolis: University of Minnesota Press, 2000), 9-10.

4. Friedrich Wilhelm Nietzsche, sec. 341 in "The Gay Science," in *The Nietzsche Reader*, ed. Keith Ansell Pearson and Duncan Large (Malden, MA: Blackwell Publishing, 2006), 236.

5. Michel Serres, *Hermes: Literature, Science, Philosophy*, ed. Josué V. Harari and David F. Bell (Baltimore: Johns Hopkins University Press, 1982).

6. Claude Elwood Shannon and Warren Weaver, *The Mathematical Theory of Communication* (Urbana: University of Illinois Press, 1959), 99-100.

7. Agamben, 11-12.

12

13

12-15. Federico Fellini, *8 1/2,* 1963.

4

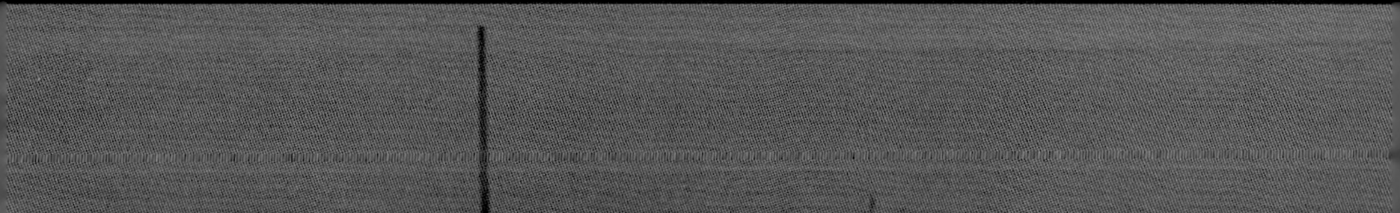

5

LABORATORY

Jason Vollen

In metallurgy, it is 'the space between the fire and flue-bridges of a reverberatory furnace in which the work is performed; also called the kitchen and the hearth' from the *Raymond Mining Glossary*, 1881. [1] Emerging Material Technologies in 7 parts.

1. Charting The Undevelopable Surface

In 1419 Prince Henry left the courts of Lisbon for Sagres and the rocky point known as Cabo de Sao Vicente where the body of Saint Vincent [patron saint of seafarers and vine - growers] had washed ashore 200 years earlier. It was here that Prince Henry, third child of King John I of Portugal, transformed into Henry the Navigator. Instrument makers, cartographers and shipwrights from all known lands followed Prince Henry's invitation to Sagres establishing the first School for Oceanic Navigation. They invented techniques and navigational instruments and the Caravel, a new ship capable of traveling farther and faster. Until his death in 1460 Henry the Navigator directed explorations from Sagres seeking new trade routes to India. His early Captains knew only that over the horizon past Cape Bojodor lay the end of the earth known as The Green Sea of Darkness, so close to the sun that ships burst into flame and whose residents included only sea demons and death, yet they willingly went forth. Some 12 years and 14 voyages later the equator was reached and over the next 30 years Henry the Navigator's captains continued to return from the Green Sea, methodically charting most of West Africa and the Azores. These explorations would set in motion the Age of Discovery, the result of which was the eventual charting of what was to be called the New World. [2]

Laboratories certainly existed before the School of Oceanic Navigation. The particular interest in this laboratory is its mission towards applied principles, and more specifically, *by extension*, about instrumentality. Without the instruments, there would be no exploration, no charting of new territory. Instrumentality extends perception.

2. Digital Hueristics: a brief history

The ocean is the first undeveloped surface. To understand the ocean is to ignore the surface and focus on its fluid dynamics: the surface is only a resultant. Early in the 19th century Navier and Stokes described a set of differential equations to govern fluid mechanics ultimately forming the basis for the field of Computational Fluid Dynamics. Formulated as discrete approximations, the resolution of Computational Fluid Dynamics pursues the dynamic balance of forces in fluid bodies, which might be described as one state of matter passes by another. [3] Navier-Stokes equations are the precursor to simulation and even modern structural analysis. Their use has significantly accelerated our ability to understand and employ highly complex phenomena, that which is emerging, as a method for finding form.

Navier-Stokes equations lead to the first intentionally stochastic modeling by Enrico Fermi in the early 1930s and lead ultimately to the establishment of probability theory. Fermi's method of statistical simulation used random numbers, boundary conditions, and time variables to produce statistically probable results, defining general directions, or behaviors, rather than specific answers. Continued development through the 30s resulted ultimately in the simulation of nuclear ballistics at the Los Alamos Laboratory, and the Monte Carlo Method, named by Stan Ulam after the casinos and based on statistical probability, was a direct result of Fermi's initial simulations. [4] The use of Monte Carlo algorithms increased significantly alongside the development of the electromechanical computer in the 1940s and these algorithms, all based on statistical probability, random number variables, and boundary conditions, established the foundation for digital dynamic simulation.

Fermis' colleagues at the Los Alamos Laboratory, von Neumann and Ulam, began working with 'cellular' equations derived from branching theories that eventually became known as cellular automata. Developed as a method of inquiry concerning the behaviors of complex extendable systems, cellular automata are localized algorithmic functions capable of adaptive behavior approaching evolutionary states. As simple rule sets, they are largely self-replicating and self-governing, and because of these features can both emulate and solve problems of complexity. The universality of these simple systems has allowed adaptations to uses that include information theory, complex organization strategies, communications networks, particle physics models, economic theory, and systems engineering; any discipline for which computation is required. Emerging software environments utilized in design, engineering, fabrication and construction management are based on this inherent characteristic of universality and the computational ability of cellular automata.

Looking to model cellular growth, Lindemayer in the 60s developed automata as a set of branching algorithms classified into four typologies; terminal, monopodial, sympodial, and polypodial. All known plant growth can be described as a variation of one or more of these typologies. The same root level set of numerical branching systems has been co-opted by software engineers, providing the basic strategies for organization of online databases and search engines. The dynamically branching informational experience has become increasingly integrated within our daily lives: it is established, it is what sits behind the veil, it has emerged as a societal force. The experience is the modern anthropologic: the universal engine which seemingly models the world in real time, at full scale, and the universal engine provides for us the ability to seemingly simulate anything.

Previous page: 1. Semi periodic penrose packing tile maximising surface area and solar insolation. Emerging Materials Technology Program. The University of Arizona, 2006. **Following pages: 2.** 03 Ceramic Composite Tension Test.

Despite the establishment of cellular automata, branching strategies, etc. in a range of disciplines, the integration into the discipline of architecture is, all too often, flawed. 'L-systems' and 'cellular automata' have been fashionable buzzwords in recent years. Certainly, as in many disciplines, architects are guilty of co-opting the occasional extradisciplinary word and reapplying a wholly new and often unrelated definition. As one former colleague noted, architecture has adopted a sort of 'bastard etymology.' However, our discipline is particularly guilty of co-opting the ordered and structural movements of thought as wholes from other disciplines. With amazing regularity we do this quite poorly. So, while being a 'bastard etymologist' of an architect might be classified as a quaint transgression, being a 'bastard epistemologist' is an entire magnitude of contravention greater. The deployment of such thought systems as disembodied from fundamental understanding is akin to utilizing differential equations without reading Leibniz' *Monadology,* that is, without meaning, and thus quite possibly, without thought. Even Deluze and Guttari's *The Fold* is several steps removed.

Outlined in stark detail in the essay *Landscapes of Change*, Sanford Kwinter provides for us the modern equivalant of the *Monadology*. The problem with relying on discrete functions alone is twofold: 1. The discreet mathematics of Newton and Leibniz can be described as Instantaneous Velocity driven by universal engines in series. These are, in the end, linear instances and therefore deterministic. 2. The universal engine lacks philosophical resistance.

Prior to Fermi and after Navier and Stokes, Henri Poincaré defined the discipline of topology. The topological system described singularities and instances while at the same time being a part of a larger system, each singularity affecting the other. The difference begins with Bergson's conception of matter which consists of "modifications, perturbations, changes in tension or of energy–and nothing else." Changes in complexity are simply different modalities that adjust for form and according to Kwinter, form is an instance of structural stability in a system as it seeks homeostasis, thus all form is the result of strife and conflict, it is the resultant of force. The strife and conflict broadcast the surface. [5]

3. Causality

In *The Question Concerning Technology*, Heidegger addresses his concern for technology and for us, and defines what is relevant to the methods in the laboratory. The essence is not a thing: it contains no thingness. It might be

"The machine itself is a product of human ingenuity and effort: hence to understand the machine is not merely a first step toward re-orienting our civilization: it is also a means for understanding society and toward knowing ourselves." Lewis Mumford

more precise to say that the essence is principled, is a principle and employs principles, in simultaneity. The essence of technology is a mode of questioning Heidegger refers to as *the way:* it is not technological. The technological inherently refers to the thing itself, the technique. Instead, technology is a means to an end, and therefore considered instrumental. However, Heidegger continues, it is also the end itself, it is a human activity, it is anthropologic. By definition the instrument, like the navigator's quadrant, cannot exist without human activity; its purpose is to augment our experience.

The relationship between the instrument and the anthropologic is instrumental, this is the way of technology, it is the mode of questioning. Further, Heidegger argues, the relationship of means and end is governed by causality. [6] This is Aristotelian, where causality is inherently scientific. To engage a causality is to seek 'why' in four ways:

Causa materialis is the principle or properties of matter, it's the substance, the physical resistance. *Causa efficens* is the operative function, the animate or innate activity that causes the material to aggregate into form. *Causa formalis* is the governing order, the thingness of a thing, it is the fundamental principles of the assembly of matter, it is the logic of forming. *Causa finalis* is the purpose for which we act, directly relating to the end, the functional use, it is the program, it is the problem. Causality is empirical and therefore, a stochastic mode of inquiry. For Heidegger, technology is only addressed when the question, the model, is interrogated through fourfold causality. In this way, the means and the end are inseparable.

4. The Scientific Model

The Royal Society of London for the Improvement of Natural Knowledge is the longest running scientific society of its kind, having been established in 1660 by inter-disciplinarians who had regularly met to debate the works of Sir Francis Bacon. The early founders upheld several principles established by Bacon as the modern scientific method and which departed from the established Aristotelian methods. The most important deviation was the use of inductive rather than deductive reasoning. That is, some known or instrumentable physical knowledge was necessary before any theory or hypothesis could be tendered. Perhaps felt most strongly by Newton and Boyle, but generally agreed to by most founders, was that hypothesis and theory were not considered to have value in the sciences at all, the chief reason among many was that hypothesis and theory could be debated in the same way as politics and religion whereas experiments are universally observed phenomena and were viewed as moving towards a truth. In this sense, the charting of the undevelopable surface by an instrumentally augmented grand 'experiment' of exploration inherently contained the possibly for discovery, whereas, there is no such thing as a 'hypothetical discovery.' The purpose of the experiment in the laboratory, according to early Royal Society records, was to create effects, or reveal general principles, and in many cases resulted in phenomena other than first considered from theory and hypothesis. The scientific model does not begin with theory, rather, it is a construction using boundary conditions, random variables, measured over time with the purpose of revealing truth, by which the Royal Society meant for the betterment of mankind. [7]

In the cause of contemporary architecture research, the binary model is an instrument, either digital or in principle, particularly well suited to managing complexity. The binary model proposes the abstraction of the analogue into a symbolic language, making the intrinsic complexities of the built environment more manageable and more fluid. Analogue modeling, however, is no less complex: it is intuitive, spatial and visual. The analogue, either digital or in principle,

03

is anthropologic, and provides the content from which the binary seeks to abstract. For the architect, and more importantly, for the educator and student, modeling is neither one nor the other, but rather a constant dialogue of multiple variables, mediating the binary instruments on which architecture has become increasingly reliant with the careful observations about human nature and the nature of dwelling: this is also the essence of technology. The instrument in the architectural laboratory, and by extension, an essence of technology, is stochastic simulation. That is, the possibility of forming through a set of parametric constraints, utilizing universal computing methods engaging dynamic simulations, a "range" of possibilities, or behaviors, defines a clade from which principled results will emerge.

As a phenomenological inquiry, digital/analogue modeling requires us to experience the binary both immersively and as the contemporary technique, in essence, absorbing abstraction and recreating the analogue prototype of that experience. Ultimately, the results of the pared method are figural, evoking a state of becoming and anticipation. The figure, in the Heideggerian sense, is revealed, and the state of revealing, that which appears after fourfold causality, is what Aristotle called the poieis, a presencing, the coming forth. Revealed as a result of questioning, the stochastic model, is the poiesis: the root of poetry.

5. Praxis

Heidegger, via Aristotelian framing, suggests a difference between technique and technology: Technique, *techne*, is the momentary mastery of a precise action, the craft. Technology, however, implies the understanding of craft, its underlying science: the *episteme*. The relationship is more complex; one needs to know to make, and one can have knowledge of a subject without the ability to make within any discipline. Further, to consider the changes in design methodology as simply a matter of changes in technique is to deny the historical linkage between the techne and the episteme. A third Aristotelian approach applies, the phronesis; the valued deliberation upon praxis. In this sense, the question of technology is not a matter of technique; it is a matter of the implementation of its understanding.

The Carbon Tower, developed by the critical practice of Peter Testa and Devyn Weiser, exemplifies stochastically 'discovered' architecture as a direct result of the laboratory modality. *Causa materialis*, carbon fiber, tunable properties and high tensile strength. *Causa efficiens*, pultrusion, allows fibers to be woven in a continuous matrix, significantly reducing stress points. *Causa formalis*, woven, or weaving structure, both as an envelope and structural ordering. *Causa finalis*, vertical dwelling, the program, the tower. The Carbon Tower serves as a benchmark for architecture from the laboratory. It is speculative, it is disciplined and detailed and based on a response to physical and simulated principles, and addresses both causality and instrumentality. The thingness has been revealed as a cause of technology, and locates itself as a reality along a future timeline, as all laboratory and architecture work must, in the near and speculative future.

3-4. Testa & Weiser, Carbon Tower. **3.** Typical floor plan and section. **4.** Street level view.

6. Developing The Surface

Of course the design of vessels, of boats, has become a hallmark of digital modelers. Of course this extra-disciplinary drift has provoked digital modeling in the design environment to prompt intuitive shaping of architecture rather than as a response to specific behaviors as in naval architecture design. The pliability of the imagination allows limitless possibilities of shape without a disciplined methodology. This is the predicament, the confusion of technique and technology, whereby the essence, the first principle of technology, is either ignored, or overwritten in favor of, or against, a technique.

It is the disciplined application of the way of technology, as a method, and through the instruments of dynamic simulation and parametric constraints integrated with analogue processes that defines the pedagogy of the laboratory. In 2004 Professor Álvaro Malo founded the Emerging Material Technologies graduate focus at the University of Arizona. The program was research project based and interdisciplinary and included, among others, myself, and professor Dale Clifford, currently at Carnegie Melon University, in collaboration with disciplinarians from material science, optical science and engineering.

As written in the curriculum description, the Emerging Material Technologies graduate focus "program is aimed at advanced analysis, testing and modeling of the properties of traditional and new materials, seeking quantitative measures of physical efficiency: i.e., mechanical, structural, thermal, optical, etc.; and qualitative criteria of sensorial performance: i.e., auditory, haptic, kinetic, visual, etc. A final purpose is to establish a dual protocol of precise observation and imaginative experimentation where the material becomes plastic.

WOVEN STRUCTURAL MORPHOLOGY

150M HEIGHT (40 STORIES)

40 30CM X 3CM TWISTED CARBON FIBER STRANDS

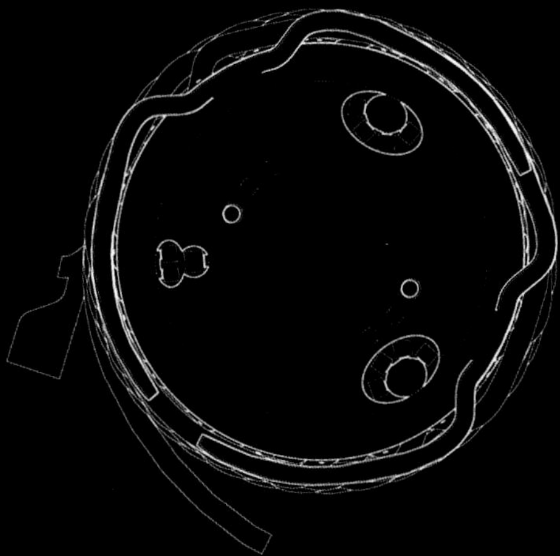

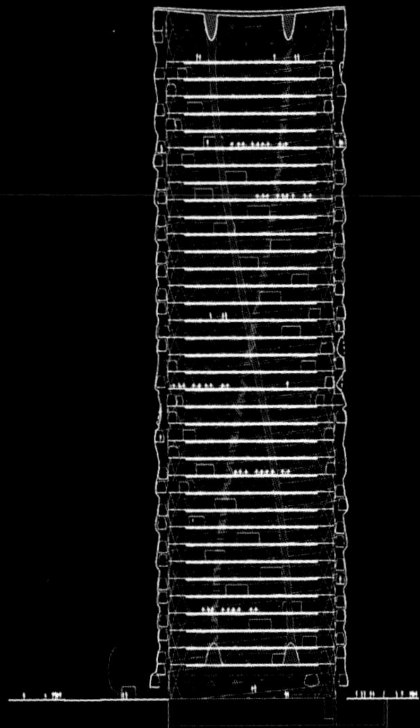

3

4

In the laboratory space available to the free and ordered play of invention, a conservation of force as well as a conservation of material is realized, obtaining a true economy of production–conceptual, ethical and aesthetical."

The pedagogy is evolved into a three semester sequence: 1. Directed research, whereby students engage in ongoing research projects to learn the process and procedures of the Laboratory, 2. Project development, a student manages an ongoing research project in the Laboratory, 3. Independent research, where the student develops and investigates their own research agenda based on the experience of the previous two semesters.

Introduction to the Emerging Material Technologies Laboratory was initiated by a series of provocations, or design principles, delivered as memos: *Material agency*–causa materialis. We must start here, material, from matter, from mater, the root word for mother. *Shaping logics*–causa efficiens–the logic and means of forming, extrusion, pultrusion, the slipcast, the ram pressed, the sintered and so forth–the emerging material cannot be separated from its forming logic. *Systema*–causa formalis–essential order of things, the matter, formed, has properties that elicit a finite set of patternings when arrayed as a multiple of its properties, (it is possible to consider this the archetype). *Prototype*–causa finalis–this must come last, without the empirical knowledge of the other causes, without results, without the limits of the material, the form and the logic, the program cannot be determined. In the Emerging Material Technologies Laboratory we are seeking to develop the surface where form follows force.

7. The Scientific Drift

I suggest a drift towards the sciences, both in discipline and method, using the way of technology. This is the natural course of events, for architecture, for art, that we also use the methods of the sciences as well and take on the challenge of the laboratory as a new modernism bringing about an understanding of the essence of technology though disciplined architectural explorations.

"By definition the instrument cannot exist without human activity; its purpose is to augment our experience."

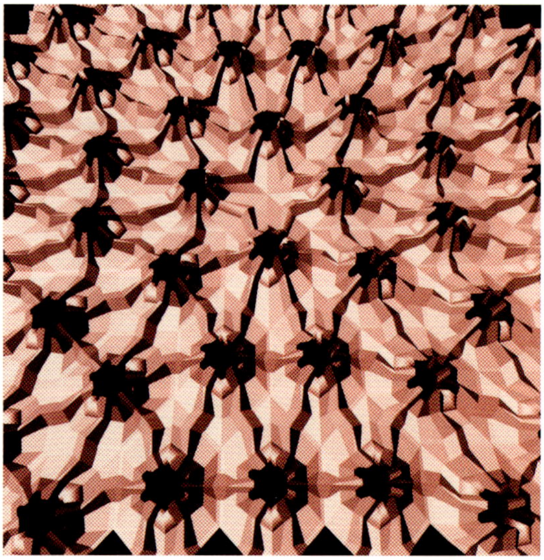

5

5. Wrinkled surface 02. Emerging materials technology program. The University of Arizona, 2007. **6.** High performance masonry system, evaporative cooling tile showing solar insolation and tool path patterned response. Emerging Materials Technology Program. The University of Arizona, 2008.

Writing in Technics and Civilization, Lewis Mumford foresaw our predicament in 1934:
"The machine itself is a product of human ingenuity and effort: hence to understand the machine is not merely a first step toward re-orienting our civilization: it is also a means for understanding society and toward knowing ourselves."[8]

Ultimately, architecture in the laboratory is to be investigated as speculative reality, integrating the speculative fiction and the physical reality confounding the established senses of structure and order, which teeter on the edge of our imagination, inviting us to leave terra firma and map the unknown. Is it the uncharted sea that is dangerous? Or the instrument itself? The answer is closer to home, after all, the mission of Prince Henry and the School of Oceanic Navigation was to mercilessly wage war against West Africa in order to spread Christianity throughout the known world. So, whereas technique is always in the service of something else where the means and the end may not be interconnected, technology is a human activity. It is the anthropologic condition of technology that gives us the right and wrong, as a pathos, as a compulsion in the form of a truth. The cautionary tale of agreed valuation rather than discovered, exemplified by the ultimate purpose of Prince Henry, is that we might all *agree* to put technique in service of the wrong thing.

The laboratory, its principles, digital or otherwise, is the place of discovery, and, after all, this is where the work is performed: force times distance cosine theta. Work is not done, analogue or binary, without this circumstance. The work of the laboratory is by definition ineffable because the outcome is both tangible, speculative, and by virtue of the nature of discovery, requires no words to begin. The motto of the Royal Society may sum up the intellectual position of laboratory as an ineffable methodology best, "Nullius in Verba", or no-one's words.

The architecture of the laboratory is the disciplined fusing of the anthropologic and the instrumental, it connects that which is from nothing and that which is from anything as inseparable, and thusly the laboratory is the

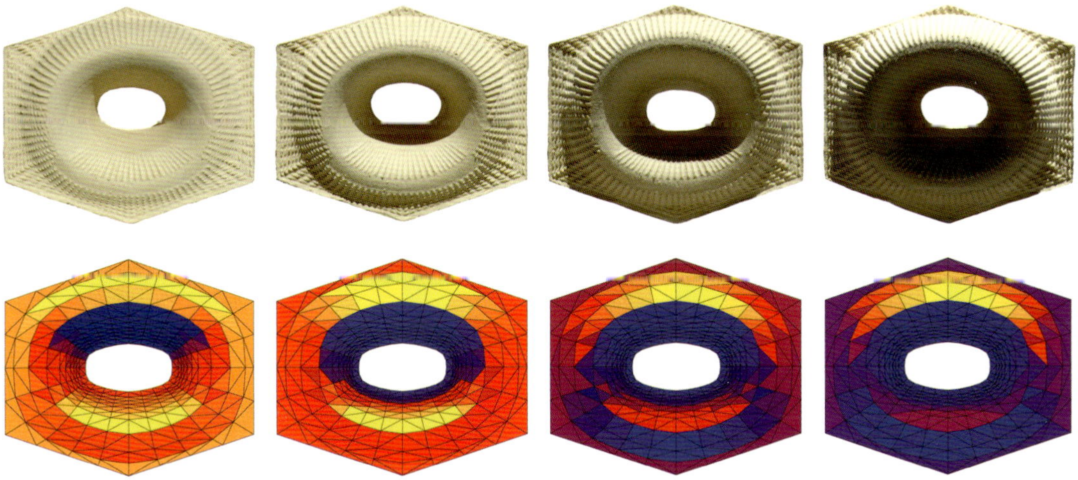

6

essence of technology. I present to you the First Principles of the Laboratory:

1. Instrumentality extends perception.
2. Force drives the universal engine in order to simulate–anything.
3. The means and the end are inseparable.
4. Stochastic modality privileges the experimental over the theoretical.
5. Technology is an applied anthropologic activity.
6. Form follows force.

Heidegger ends his essay where I will this one.

7. "The closer we come to the danger, the more brightly do the ways into the saving power begin to shine and the more questioning we become. For questioning is the piety of thought."

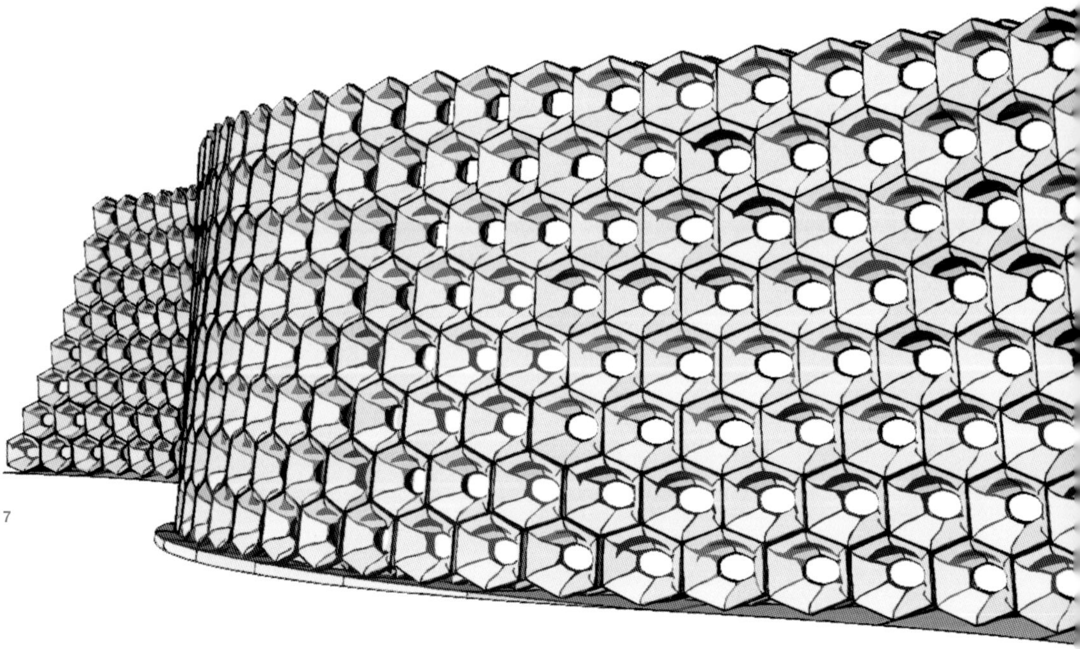

7

7. High performance masonry system, evaporative cooling wall. Emerging Materials Technology Program. The University of Arizona, 2008.

Notes:

1. R. W. Raymond, "A Glossary of Mining and Metallurgical Terms," *Transactions of the American Institute of Mining Engineers* 9 (Easton, PA: American Institute of Mining Engineers, 1881): 52.
2. Raymond C. Beazley, Prince *Henry the Navigator: The Hero of Portugal and of Modern Discovery,* 1394-1460 A.D. *With an Account of Geographical Progress Throughout the Middle Ages As the Preparation for His Work* (New York: G. P. Putnam's Sons, 1895), 13-14, 160-178.
3. G. K. Batchelor, *An Introduction to Fluid Dynamics* (Cambridge, UK: Cambridge University Press, 1967), 131, 144.
4. Nicholas Metropolis, "The Beginning of the Monte Carlo Method," special issue dedicated to Stanislaw Ulam, *Los Alamos Science*, no. 15 (1987): 125–130, http://library.lanl.gov/cgi-bin/getfile?00326866.pdf (accessed October 6, 2006).
5. Sanford Kwinter, "Landscapes of Change: Boccioni's "Stati d'animo" as a General Theory of Models," *Assemblage*, no. 19 (December 1992): 52-65.
6. Martin Heidegger, "The Question Concerning Technology," in *Basic Writings*, ed. David Farrell Krell (New York: Harper Collins Publishers, 1993), 321.
7. The Royal Society, "History of the Royal Society," http://royalsociety.org/page.asp?id=2176 (accessed September 12, 2007).
8. Lewis Mumford, *Technics and Civilization* (New York, NY: Harcourt, Brace and Co., 1934), 8.

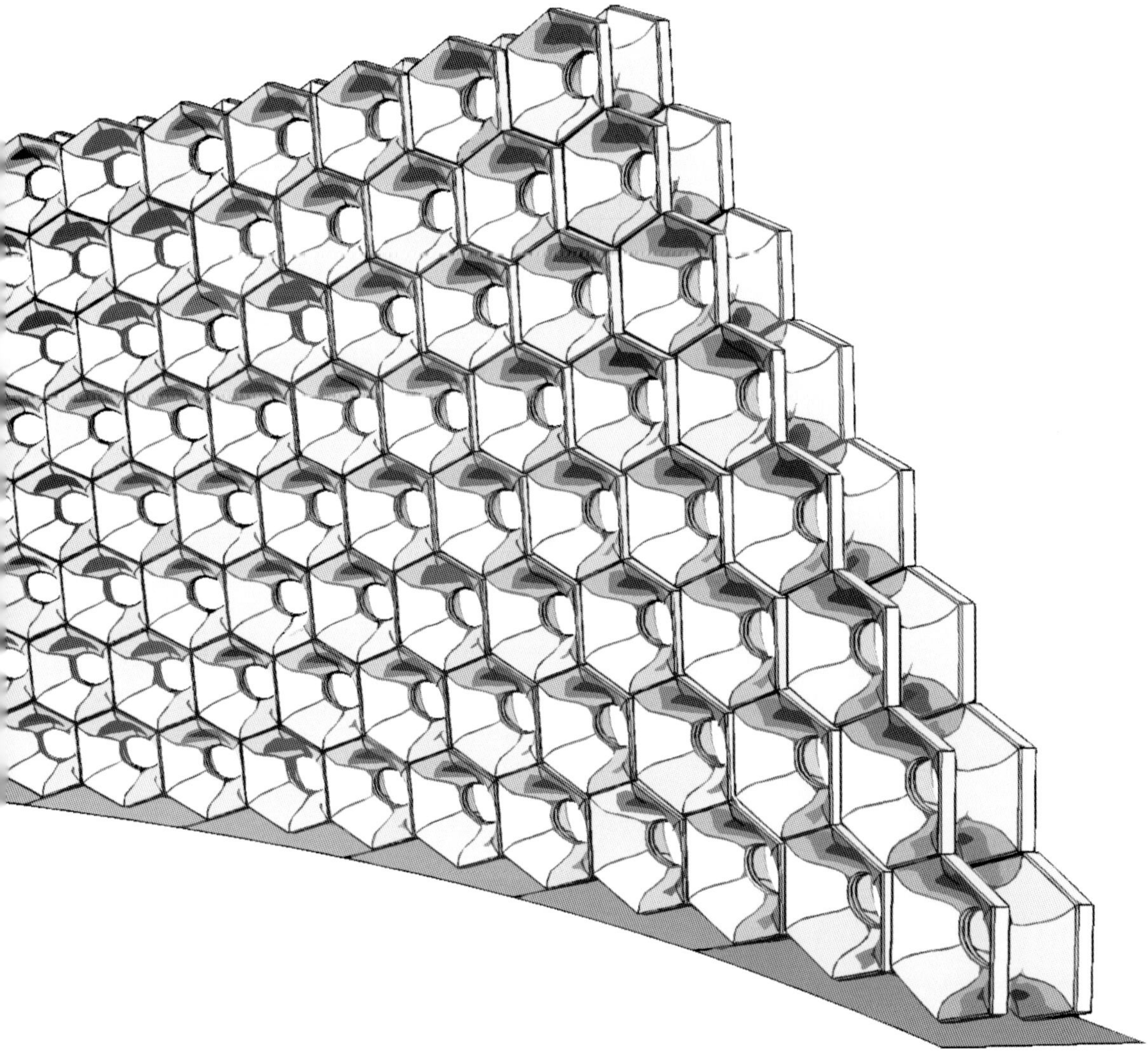

A PRACTICAL THEORY

George Ranalli

In thinking about the panel and the subject, which is "A Practical Theory," I am somewhat at a loss for words following the speakers who obviously have delved so heavily into the issue of computation, but I find myself at odds with this idea. In terms of the title "Ineffable," it is the inability to describe what is indescribable, which comes more from the senses and the emotions, and much less from the intellect. In thinking about pedagogy, I was also struck by the enormity of the idea of providing a clear and cogent pedagogy for an architecture school. The main premise of pedagogy, of course, is tools. The tools which are the instruments with which we study, the instruments which give students the capability to externalize their internal processes, and synthesize the way they think about their premises of architecture.

For me, it comes out of a premise of being in practice. I remember certain discrepancies in my day-to-day activities between the theoretical and practical extremes. I deal with people: people's needs and people's desires, which are often at odds with some theoretical premises of architecture. My wife is a psychologist, which is very dangerous because I on occasion live in therapy. One day my wife and I were driving uptown. My wife is a wonderful woman, but not in the arts or in architecture and as we passed the Morgan Library she looked at the front facade and said, "Wow that's a new building. What is that?" And I replied, "That's the new addition to the Morgan." She turned to me and asked, "What's it going to look like when they take the protective panels off?" I thought that was a very revealing observation about people's perceptions of modern architecture.

Facing page: 1. Claude-Nicolas Ledoux, *Perspective View of the Town of Chaux*. Engraving after Ledoux by Berthault.

I have been very aware recently, because the bulk of our clients are cultural institutions, of this discrepancy: between what we in the profession think about as ideas about architecture and what peoples' perceptions are of built architecture. One only has to think about the recent controversy over the attempt to demolish Boston City Hall. The fury and the power with which people feel that that architecture is in fact brutal, hyper intellectualized, and that they don't get a warm and fuzzy feeling from the experience of most modern architecture. Many people also feel architecture has become devoid of a social program.

Historically, the introduction of architectural language in the service of social programs begins with the embodiment and expression of the poor in entombments or memorials such as those designed by Boulee (Figs. 2-4). Ledoux also utilized architectonic forms, which were somewhat standard architectural language, that he extended and developed to dissolve or try to undermine the reigning political structure. In this case, the Saline du Chaux complex is used for the

2

3

4

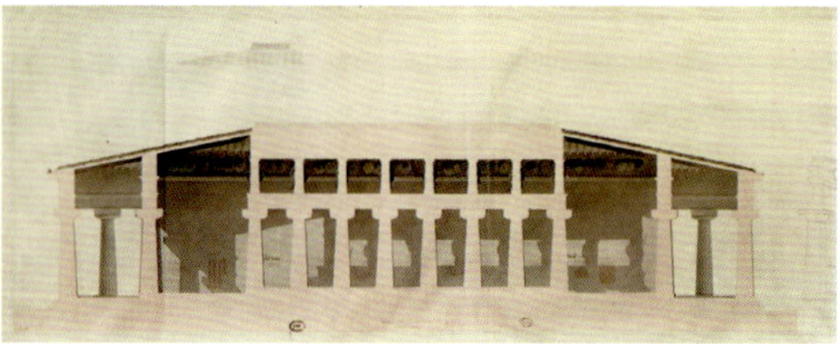

5

6

2-4. Étienne-Louis Boullée. **2.** *Project for a Pyramid.* **3.** *Project for a Cenotaph for Turenn,* cross section. **4.** *Project for a Chapel of the Dead.* **5.** Henri Labrouste, *Temple of Hera I ("Portique"),* Paestum, restoration, sections and perspective. **6-7.** Claude-Nicolas Ledoux, *Royal Saltworks,* Arc-et-Senans, France. **6.** Oculus window with saline. **7.** Utilities buildings. **8.** Edouard Loviot, *Parthenon,* Athens, restoration, section, 1881. **9.** Charles Garnier, *Opéra,* study for the principal façade, 1861.

7

8

9

production of salt by the French government. (Figs.1, 6, 7). We see in the letters that went back and forth between the municipality of France and Ledoux the dispute and complex arguments over the design decisions of position in the plan. France was aware of what he was doing: that he was attempting to undermine the political process by trying to empower the workers. Architecture seemed to have had a dual function: it had the capability to deal with political structures, as well as its own physical reality.

I was always drawn to the pedagogy of the Academy of the Ecole des Beaux Arts and the idea of the analitique, the idea of the historical survey, the introduction of understanding the memory of architecture and the extrapolation of what pre-existed into an analytic process (Fig. 8). If you look at the upper portion of this drawing, where the section is taken through the center of the columns and the decorative artifacts of the building you can just see the perspective on the right hand side shown in shadows, projected, as if they were ghosts, into the architecture (Fig. 5).

In this drawing of the Paris Opera by Charles Garnier, a graduate of the Ecole, actually a color working drawing, you can see the introduction of the measurable and the immeasurable (Fig. 9). We see the understanding of the physical reality of the building, its sense of measure, its sense of particularity of place, its particularity of construction as well as its overt beauty.

If we begin to think about architectural pedagogy's development as an analogy for practice, the work in the studio in school often is really about tapping into a whole array of ideas which are not only technological, but also memory traces. In this drawing of John Soane's from the Soane Museum, by Bailey, the renderer he worked with, we find the drawings infused with subjective criteria, non-rational criteria, the ability to infuse beauty, the idea of the collector and particularly the ineffable sense of space and light (Figs. 11, 12). In this case, of Soane's own predilection for the incorporation of artifacts from other cultures that he infused into his own architecture.

The idea of imbuing the architecture with a sense of wonder, of non-rational thought more imbedded in feeling is what certainly speaks to the ineffable, rather than the intellectual.

Why should buildings look like the result of the instruments that produced them? Why is it that we are in a current mode where erratic and non-orthogonal form is the main determinant of the design? Are buildings really vessels of cultural identity or are they merely architectonic compositional arrangements? In this case, Otto Wagner's post office building in Vienna is similar to other contemporary formal languages that are similar in feeling, but in fact it is different in technique and different in its constructed reality (Figs. 13, 14). Is there a way to bridge this gulf that appears to have occurred through the 20th century? I know in the curatorial work that we've done, I have often been aware of the fact that we have two histories running in modern architecture. There is the history of juxtaposition. The history that believes that every object we make should be juxtaposed to the existing environment, that is: that the city is a dark, dirty entity and therefore we should make things white, crystalline and fragile.

11

10

12

10. John Soane, *13 Lincoln's Inn Fields,* Breakfast Room. **11.** Sectional perspective of the Dome area and Breakfast Room looking east, drawn by Frank Copland, 1818. **12.** Sectional perspective of the Dome area looking east with inset small section looking east, basement and ground floor plans (lower left-hand corner) and 'General plan of the principal story' (lower right-hand corner), drawn by George Bailey. **13.** Otto Wagner, *Post Office Savings Bank* (Competition design, 1903), view of the main entrance. **14.** Otto Wagner, *Post Office Savings Bank*, part of the main projecting face in perspective.

13

14

"Why should buildings look like the result of the instruments that produced them?"

15

16

There also is another history, that of continuity: the reality of place, the reality of feeling, the reality of joining cityscape, landscape and building form. This is Frank Lloyd Wright's 1920s era drawing for the Hollyhock House (Fig. 15). You only need to think of it being designed at the same time as the white cubic volumes of Le Corbusier and other European Modernists.

Wright was really interested in the building's interrelationships to landscape and to a sense of place (Fig. 16). His goal was to root buildings in an almost seamless process.

You can argue that buildings are invested with cultural identity, as they are formed by complex iterative and comprehensive processes. These processes represent a myriad of forces acting on a design at any particular time.

You could say that single mono - dimensional processes will only produce projects that are single minded in their approach, and therefore don't reflect the full range of values present in the making of a building and the result is a disconnect of the building from society. If, in fact, we feel that buildings should be related to society.

Architects, throughout history, have used their instruments for both making beauty and for social good. In the case of Hugh Ferriss, he designed with an eye toward the early 1920s in New York, as well as looking at the ability of the city to be connected to its history and also to its future. To protect the citizenry from the massive building boom that was about to occur, he envisioned buildings and city structures that would ensure light and air to its citizens (Figs. 17).

Institutions are looking for a bridge between two worlds. They are not necessarily interested in trying to rebuild history, although there are a myriad of architects out there to offer their services for that. In fact, they are searching for a hybrid solution between the cold, alien and impersonal world of modern architecture and a mere copy of older historic buildings. They want a connection to the historic continuum of the architecture surrounding them. Here is Louis Khan's building in Dacca, where he was able to fuse these two issues (Figs. 18-20). He is able to transfer the idea of a thick walled building, a building of the pedagogical system in which he was educated in the Ecole des Beaux Arts, into a contemporary sense of servant and served space. It is a very beautiful conceptual apparatus that allows him to accommodate a thick wall building within thin wall construction and produce a very elaborate cipher for the government in Dacca. In Italy, Aldo Rossi used memory devices in the drawings of the Modena cemetery (Fig. 22). He was really trying to decode and describe the feeling of a cemetery, of death, of the memorial, and the symbolic and iconic properties surrounding this type of architecture.

I would argue that beauty is an elemental and essential part of the ineffable; it's an intangible characteristic capable of being borne out through architecture. Louis Khan in writing about Carlo Scarpa (Fig. 21) stated, "[B]eauty, the first sense art, the first word, then wonder, then the new realization of form. The sense of the wholeness of inseparable elements. Design consults nature to give presence to the elements. A work of art makes manifest the wholeness of form, the symphony of the selected shapes. In the elements the joint inspires ornaments its celebration, the detail is the adoration of nature."[1] The argument of an emotionally based architecture rather than a hyper - intellectually based architecture seems essential to this consideration of the ineffable. An architecture that is emotionally connected to the history of architecture and the history of culture should be connected to our past and be part of our present.

Some of my own work of the last 25-30 years has attempted to bridge the distance between the existing city and new ideas of architecture, space, and program. The tools used to generate architecture, whether hand or computer drawings, reflect a broader interest in sites and landscapes, rather than the particularities of the tools themselves. I was struck by this book written by a surgeon, Dr. Richard Selzer, who was teaching at Yale. I ran into him there on several occasions. He felt compelled to write about the disconnect between his activities as a surgeon and the feelings of his patients. As he explored this in his writing, he began to come to understand that the peda-

17

15-16. Frank Lloyd Wright, *Aline Barnsdall Residence*, *"Hollyhock House,"* Los Angeles, CA, 1920. **15.** Photograph of a lost drawing. **16.** Exterior view. **17.** Hugh Ferriss, *Overhead Traffic Ways.*

18

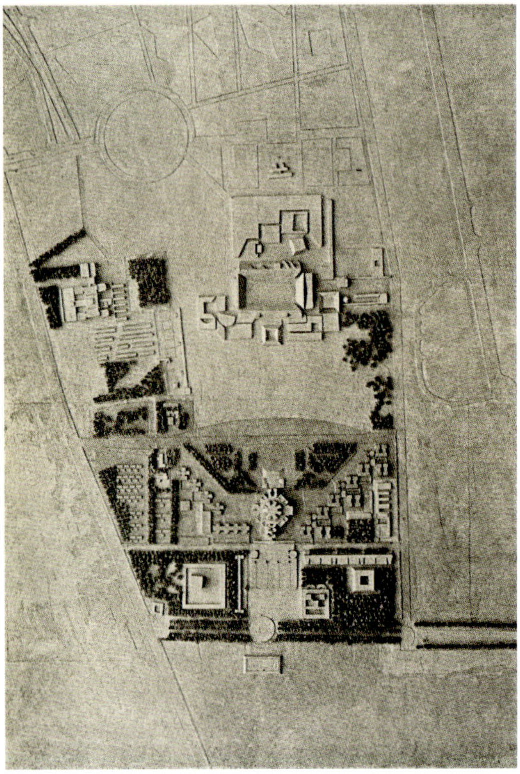

19

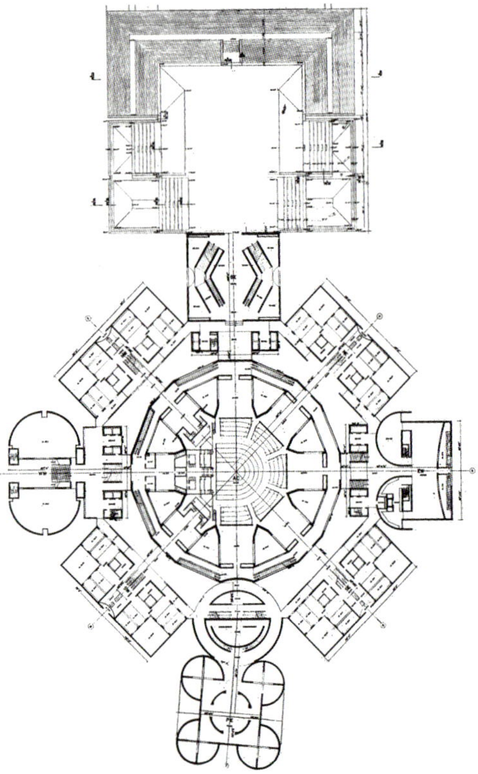

20

21

gogy of becoming a surgeon was anaesthetizing his own feelings: it created a disconnect from his patients. He was unable to have any empathy. He was unable to have psychological or even physiological connections to them. He was, in a sense, a glorified auto mechanic. He wrote about the tools of surgery:

"We are too removed from our tools. It is a kind of betrayal of our craft because we did not make our instruments with our hands. We do not use them to the best advantage. Our relationship to our instruments is a more distant and formal one. Then it was still necessary to chisel the nib of a knife from a stone for sharpening goose quill into a probe. A great oboist cuts and ties his own reeds, so does the fisherman his trout flies. In so doing these men infuse them with their spirit. The gift of prophecy has not deserted me. I should say that such men will make sweeter music and catch bigger fish than those that place their craft in the hands of manufacture."[2]

18-20. Louis I. Kahn, *Sher-e-Bangla Nagar*, Capital of Bangladesh, Dhaka, Bangladesh, 1962-83. **18.** National Assembly Building, exterior view. **19.** National Assembly Complex, site model showing master plan, c. August 1964. **20.** National Assembly Building, composite plan at 48 feet. **21.** Carlo Scarpa, *Brion-Vega Cemetery*, chapel elevation, San Vito D'Altivole, Italy.

Do we really teach our students the intricacies of construction and the intricacies of the craft of architecture as we experience it or as the public experiences it? Are we residing in the premise that modern architecture is predicated on the concept of juxtaposition rather than on amelioration? If we can answer this, then we can begin to understand the tools of study that are developed to enhance concepts, rather than the need to develop tools that can reconsider or transform them.

If we accept the premise that buildings are vessels of cultural identity rather than formal compositional manipulations, it would follow then that more, rather than less complex criteria are involved and applied to their formation. There are two public projects which I am currently working on: one deals with the last surviving historic structure of Penn Station, the power plant on 31st Street; and our Community Center in Brooklyn for the New York City Housing Authority (Figs. 23-26). I was struck by David Gersten's comment at the very beginning, when he asked an architect about the program of the building and the answer was Form Z. The architectural program is embedded with far more intricacy and detail and is latent with far more of the narrative of the building than is currently given credit for. The introduction of program is a key element of transforming a building, or architecture itself, into a new

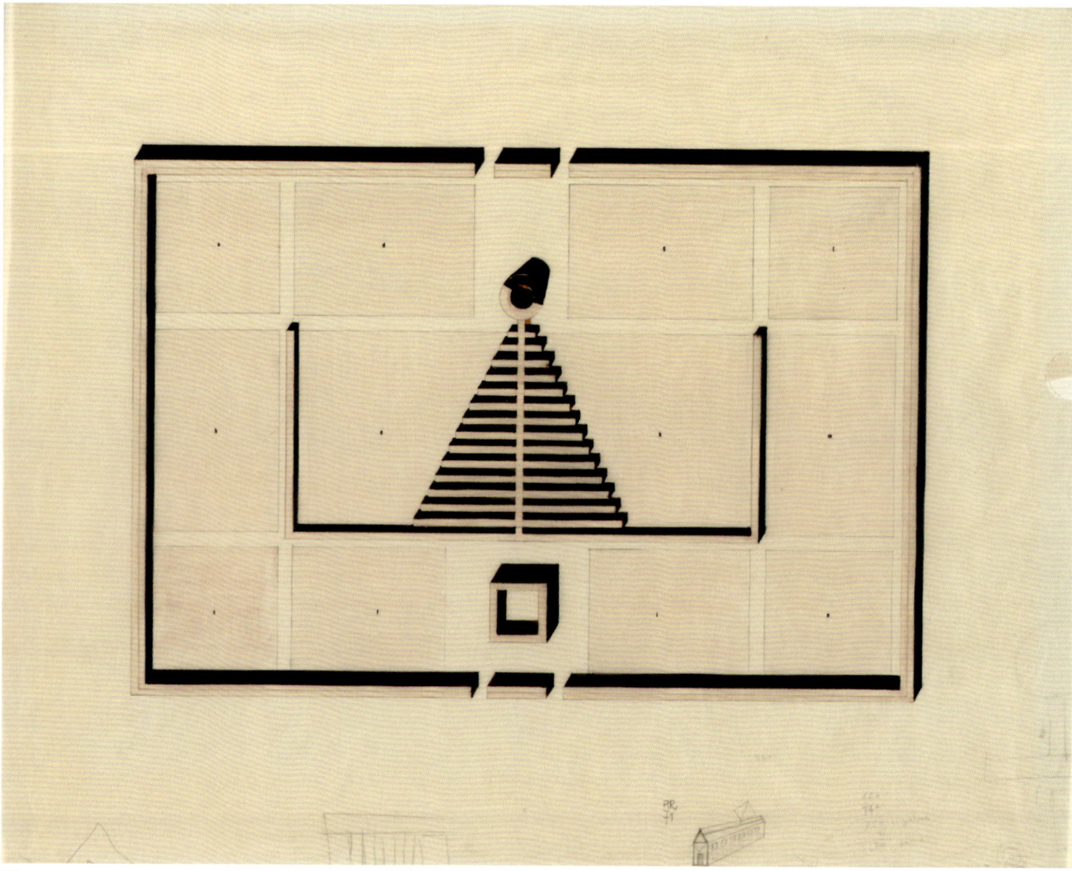

22

conceptual framework. Often overlooked as a pedantic and uninteresting list of accommodations, program is a creative, interactive device, which can explore new spatial relationships for the occupants, and for the occupants in relation to society. It is the concept of using utility in the broadest sense of the word to form spaces evaluated according to their technical, psychological, physiological, emotional, and poetic use.

22. Aldo Rossi, *Cemetery of San Cataldo,* Modena, Italy. Plan, 1971. **23-24.** George Ranalli, Saratoga Avenue Community Center, renovation and addition, Brooklyn, New York, 2008. **23.** Entry courtyard. **24.** Garden elevation of the community center.

23

24

In exploring spatial and hierarchical relationships within a program, each occupant and each site are unique. Pattern responses cannot satisfy the complexity of issues present in each new project. From the dynamic interaction of the occupants to the particular climatic conditions present on any site, there is a necessity to integrate, synthesize, and explore the complexity of possibilities embedded in each new project.

The memory of pre - existing works of architecture provides cultural continuity and each new work should accommodate and integrate into this history. We can preserve the values and meanings of prior works of architecture while we continue to investigate new programs, technologies, and ideas relevant to our own present condition.

25

25 and Facing page: 26. George Ranalli, Saratoga Avenue Community Center, renovation and addition, Brooklyn, New York, 2008. **25.** Wall detail in the main assembly room. **26.** View of the main assembly room.

Notes:

1. Accademia Olimpica, *Carlo Scarpa* (Vicenza: Accademia Olimpica, 1974), I.

2. Richard Selzer, *Letters to a Young Doctor* (New York: Simon and Schuster, 1982), 114.

THE GENERIC INEFFABLE

Karl Chu

The subject of the ineffable is somewhat of an anachronism now that globalization has taken hold of the discourse on architecture, much like it has everything else. The conference however is strangely in consonance with the subject since any issue related to the ineffable has been diminished to the point of oblivion and cast away from architectural discourse for at least a decade if not more. To once again direct attention on the ineffable is to re-invoke a theme at the heart of phenomenology, which has been superceded by the complex array of issues that dwell less on the phenomenon of subjective experience and more on politics–external issues that are pronouncedly determined by socio-political and economic matters at hand. My interest in the ineffable is not motivated by the desire to resurrect the tenets of classical phenomenology, rather it is propelled by the need to adequate a metaphysics of architecture, which is increasingly defined by the phenomenon of universal computation, with its counterpart, the void of existence: the ontological gap that exists between subject and body, body and language, and, language and world.

Generally speaking, the ineffable is a thought revoking experience where one's consciousness is transported to a vanishing point and one is astonished by the profound ignorance of the situation and thus rendered speechless: a limiting case where consciousness comes face to face with the unknowable, thereby opening up an ontological chasm between the subject and the situation that invokes the ineffable. Even in cases where a situation is knowable and appears to be normal, there is, according to Heidegger, a poetics of presence to the being-thereness of the phenomenon that can only be captured by means of the poetic use of language. The ineffable is the obscure silence that resides within being, which, Heidegger suggests, must be written under erasure in order for it to recede away from the web of empirical knowledge and reappear as a phenomenology of presence.

Facing page: 1. Metaxy, *X_Phylum*, X_Phylum Series, 1997.

In its generic simplicity, let it suffice to say that the ineffable is the unsayable. It resonates with Ludwig Wittgenstein's famous remark: *"Whereof one cannot speak, thereof one must be silent."* Wittgenstein's aphorism has been recalled so often that it not only monopolized the unsayable but may have eclipsed any attempt to articulate the remains of what is essentially a subsonic agitation of a disquietude, a dumbfounding denial ordained by an unknown impeachment that immediately – as if time were an artifact of infinite speed – impinges on the desire to say something: an intrusive act that suspends the efficacy of manifest destinies, be they instrumentally determined or otherwise. Experience of the ineffable therefore is on the side of the subject, which perpetuates those who are religiously inclined towards faith and to the belief in the existence of a second world transcending the immanent world by valorizing the mystery of the impasse as the ineffable. In most cases, the experience of the ineffable is a passive reception of a unique phenomenon that is given to sense through the phenomenal appearance of a situation. Given such an immediacy of impact, it may seem unlikely that having conceptual knowledge of a situation without the physical occurrence of an event would have the power to evoke the ineffable. Yet, the mind is powerful enough to think of situations capable of invoking the ineffable. Mathematics, for instance, is an example in which certain discoveries are so fantastic that mathematicians are simply awed and amazed by the beauty of symmetries contained in abstract structures such as the Monster Group[1] in Group Theory that exists in higher dimensions. Whether one believes in the existence of such abstract structures or not, one is nonetheless implicated in the ontological status of mathematics entailed by such mathematical entities, which undoubtedly has the power to invoke the ineffable.

The ineffable is an experience of the unknowable mediated through either knowledge or complete lack of knowledge and concerning a phenomenon that is either visible or invisible. Since it is directly related to the limits of knowledge and to the silent gravity of a situation where time seems to have acquired a translucent viscosity that freezes an image of thought conjured up by the penetrating light of the mind, it would be appropriate to start by first sketching out a set of assumptions that frame the condition of being that is tied to the condition of knowledge. As such, I would like to refer to one of the founding premises of Western metaphysics: *"Thinking and being are one and the same reality"* as ordained by Parmenides of Elea. There are few statements that are as astonishingly pregnant with implications and as far-reaching as this in articulating the transparency of thought to being and vice versa. Implicit in the statement is the subject conceived as an expression of being: when the subject thinks, it is essentially the same as a being thinking through the subject. The two are one and the same reality. When, for instance, Einstein made the famous remark, *"one of the most incomprehensible things about the Universe is that it is comprehensible,"* is he not implying more or less the same thing and calling attention to the *incomprehensible* as that which points to the ineffable enigma of being whereas Parmenides' statement does not refer to the unknowable? Nevertheless, in light of Parmenides the point is that being is co-extensive with reality and there is nothing that is neither unthinkable nor unknowable.

There is therefore, no such thing as absolute non-knowledge, and ignorance is merely a symptom of forgetfulness: to learn is to remember, to leave is to return and to see is to encounter once again, which is the classical paradigm of the eternal return. The eternal return is also extended to knowledge, which is founded upon anamnesis and which in turn is coupled to the logic of metempsychosis: transmigration and circumlocution of souls within an imperishable and eternal cosmos that is identical with the reality of being. In addition, Parmenides established the limits of ontology by pronouncing, *"Being is and Non-being is not."* The significance of this statement implies the fullness of being and non-being is banished from thought: it is the unthinkable and the unknowable since there is nothing within non-being that is available to thought. It's not until the twentieth century that non-being or the notion of the Void comes back into play within the conceptual universe of quantum physics. Nevertheless, Parmenides further extends the attribute of being by suggesting that being is an infinitely large sphere. Being is not an amorphous substance but endowed with a definite form. Being as such is a form of totality: form is being. Since then, every attempt at the formalization of a situation can be understood as an attempt to capture an aspect of being through an axiomatic framework. This is the reason why the French philosopher Alain Badiou aligns ontology with mathematics.

Architecture therefore is already implicated at the very inception of ontology: being and the architecture of form are mutually coextensive. The other side of Parmenides, who is the philosopher of eternity, is Heraclitus, the philosopher of change. Taken together, the conception of being understood as a totality is essentially autogenic; it is self-sufficient unto itself and is endowed with the potential for infinite differentiation, transformation and variation within itself. *"Time is the moving image of eternity,"* as Plato would say a few centuries later. The classical image of being as envisioned by Parmenides and Heraclitus is indeed a beautiful thought, a conceptual model of a possible world that is mistakenly construed to be the one and only world or the One-All of existence that is absolute. Notwithstanding Copernicus's discovery of a plurality of worlds, this image of thought remains relatively unchanged until the advent of three interrelated conceptual innovations: Georg Cantor's invention of *set theory and transfinite numbers* in the late nineteenth century, the discovery of the *Theory of Incompleteness and Undecidability* by Kurt Gödel in 1931, and the invention of the concept of *'forcing'* by Paul Cohen in 1962 in his attempt to prove the independence of the *Continuum Hypothesis*[2] from the Zermelo-Fraenkel Set Theory. Even then, the concept of being not bounded by the concept of the *WHOLE* or the One-All is a latecomer to philosophical ontology.

Only with the publication of *Being and Event* in 1988 by Alain Badiou can we now refer to the ontology of being as an inconsistent multiplicity without attributing epistemological limits to it. For now, I will proceed to connect the Parmenidean conjugation of thought and being to the figure of Hegel for the reason that Hegel is the philosopher who explicitly rejects the ineffable because it signifies non–knowledge and ignorance. Needless to say, Hegel's philosophy cannot be summarized too hastily without gross exaggeration but there are salient points that can be addressed with regard to the ineffable. In the context of his conception of the Absolute and its relation to self-consciousness, it is a well-known fact that Hegel disavows the ineffable since there is no such thing as the unknowable due simply to the fact that the Absolute, of which self-consciousness is its expression, implicitly contains everything and nothing.[3] The Absolute is self-sufficient unto itself and there is no surplus of information or knowledge that would point to an ontological gap or deficiency within being, which is identical with the Absolute. Here we have the One-All of being localized in the self-consciousness of the Absolute and the notion of non-knowledge is inconsistent with the logic of the Absolute. From a Hegelian standpoint, the ineffable is merely a state of consciousness that is still grounded in empirical knowledge and therefore it is shrouded in ignorance. In other words, the subject has not come to the realization that self-consciousness is an expression of the Absolute within man. Hegelian dialectics is one of the simplest models of thought, an Egyptian Pyramid, to use Derrida's description, that is extended into the ontology of being: reflection as a philosophical principle is not man reflecting the Absolute but the Absolute reflecting itself through man. Correspondingly, Hegel, unlike the Egyptian, denies the existence of a second world that is transcendent to the world; there is but one world that is radically immanent in all aspects and the Absolute resides solely within the immanent domain. Self-consciousness then is the locus of mediation and transformation of the world in its passage toward the Absolute, which paradoxically is already immanent within self-consciousness.

Among the post-structuralist philosophers, Alain Badiou's philosophy is one that resonates with Hegel's through a disjunctive correlation on a number of points. In the present context, I will only address a few major points that touch on the ineffable: the whole, the status of truth, the generic and the limits of the knowable. The most prominent feature that is in contrast to Hegel's philosophy of the whole is the subtractive ontology of Badiou: being is an inconsistent multiplicity without discernible limits. One of Hegel's celebrated pronouncements is that the true is the whole whereas for Badiou the concept of whole is subtracted from ontology just as there is no set that functions as the set of all sets. To claim otherwise would be to entertain logical paradoxes. Even though both Hegel and Badiou believe in the existence of truth, Badiou eschews the fundamental idea that enables Hegel's idealism: the absolute of knowledge is knowable and attainable. The re-installment of truth is controversial to say the least. Unlike previous thinkers, truth is never given in totality. According to Badiou, *"All the categories by which the essence of a truth can be submitted to thought are negative: undecidabiity, indiscernibility, the generic not-all, and the unnameable. The ethics of truth resides entirely in the measure taken of this negativity, or in other words, in the limitations placed on the potency of truth by the hazards of its construction."*[4] Being is interspersed throughout with excess of the indiscernible and the unnameable. At the foundation of Badiou's ontology is the void, a philosophical attribution of the null set: the empty set that establishes the possibility of sets. The void permeates throughout being: it is present through pure absence. For Badiou ontology is coextensive with mathematics, and correspondingly, Badiou has resuscitated the notion of truth back into philosophy. Mathematics is a discipline grounded in reason and proof, and without the logos of truth, mathematics would not have been possible. Without getting into the ontological status of truth, it should be noted that post-structuralist philosophers who deride the notion of truth are directed toward Hegel's logic of absolute truth, which resides solely within self-consciousness and its corresponding claim to absolute certainty that is grounded in the Absolute.

Nevertheless, according to Badiou, the truth of a situation can be conceived in terms of the generic, which is a central motif of his subtractive ontology. The generic cannot be discerned based on the resources and determinations of a given situation. There are elements within a situation that, even though they belong to the situation, cannot be described by the tools of the language pertaining to it. The generic is intrinsically multiple; the generic truth of a situation is infinite and unnameable. In other words, *"The generic being of a truth is never presented. A truth is incompletable."*[5] Yet, and this is one of the conditions where the ineffable begins to lose its poetic weight if not its opacity, *"The subject can make the hypothesis of a Universe where this truth, of which the subject is a local point, will have completed its generic totalization."*[6] Furthermore, he calls this *"anticipatory hypothesis of the generic being of a truth, a 'forcing'."*[7] Forcing is a term coined by the mathematician Paul Cohen in his attempt to solve one of the outstanding problems in set theory: the *Continuum Hypothesis*, which in–itself verges on being ineffable simply by virtue of the irresolvable enigma that it contains. *The unnameable* is a term that remains *unforceable*: it signifies a limit point or threshold of the knowable beyond which nothing can be said of the potency that is contained within a generic set. Similarly, Lacan's notion of truth as a hole in knowledge is related to the void of knowledge: ontological limits that cannot be traversed.

Both Hegel and Badiou privilege the Subject: self-consciousness of the Absolute within man for Hegel, and, the generic fidelity to the truth of a situation by the Subject in the case of Badiou. Badiou's ontology, despite being influenced by set theory, still privileges the subject who speaks about the *"naked existence of a generic humanity."* [8] Such a profound concept cannot be dismissed in the name of the coming era of post-humanity. Instead, one can extend this reasoning by calling attention to the generic life of being, not the life of this or that species but the universality of life as an emergent phenomenon in all its manifestations: life as such here and everywhere in the universe. What I would like to propose is to radicalize Badiou's philosophy, which finds its limits in the unnameable of a situation, by incorporating the phenomenon of universal computation in conjunction with a computational monadology of speciation. It would then have the power to address the construction of species and possible worlds within his ontology. In other words, what is needed is a computational monadology of architecture seen through the mathematical ontology of Badiou. Correspondingly, inasmuch as architecture is implicated at the origin of ontology, the sphericalization of being by Parmenides, architecture would also be implicated in the break-up of the vessel of being by renouncing the metaphysics of presence and the corresponding desire for totality that is at once programmatic and formal.

Both Hegel and Badiou privilege thought and both manage not to fall prey to the circularity of arguments. An example where thought is caught chasing its tail is the case of Edmund Husserl, who is principally the founder of phenomenology. The irony of Husserl's life and work is defined by his perpetual dissatisfaction with his own preceding attempts at defining phenomenology and his published work is a sequence of attempts at articulating and refining the project of phenomenology. The last phase of his career is marked by his development of a transcendental logic in order to secure once and for all the foundations for phenomenology: a logic that probes into the internal constitution of knowledge within the subject, a move that Hegel never took but assumed as a speculative condition inherent within the knowledge of the Absolute. In so doing, Husserl finds himself trapped in an infinite regress in the attempt to unravel the causal basis of knowledge through the very mechanism that constitutes knowledge itself by means of a transcendental logic, which correspondingly leads to nowhere. Being trapped in an infinite regress is yet another symptom of the ineffable, of being channeled into an infinite causal loop or vortex perpetuated by self-similar adumbrations unto itself, ad infinitum.

The stage is now set for the deconstruction of metaphysics by means of language. If there is a philosopher who manages to chart an escape route, it is Jacques Derrida who displaces the conjugation of thought and being in order to disclose the remainder that self-consciousness could not digest or synthesize in its passage toward the Absolute. In so doing, the notion of absolute and equivocal truth loses its efficacy for Derrida. The characteristic hallmark of Parmenides's identification of thought and being is the proximity of thought to speech: a metaphysics of presence that Hegel extends into language. Notwithstanding his speculative proposition with regard to the Absolute, Hegel emphasized the cultural and historical specificity of language, which carries within it the ontology of sense that allows language to be the medium for the communion of a communal life in communication with the spirit. The dialectical genesis of language by Hegel is based on the fact that *"The sensible itself interiorizes itself into thought, and thought exteriorizes into language,"* [9] as Jean Hyppolite, an influential interpreter of Hegel has shown. Furthermore, *"the thought of being and the thought of thought must be unified."* [10] As such, Hegel's speculative idealism belongs squarely within the metaphysical framework as delineated by Parmenides, albeit reformulated in terms of his dialectics, which incorporates contradiction as part of the movement towards the Absolute via the *Aufhebung* (a term that designates the negation, conservation, and elevation of a previous stage in consciousness). Ultimately, however, the power of Hegel's resources lie in the role of the negative in speculative idealism, the otherness operating within reason, that makes Hegel's philosophy such an overarching system that is difficult to escape. In light of this, Derrida says we will never be done with the reading of Hegel: the moment when we think we have gotten beyond Hegel to its farthest point of contradiction or difference, we are most Hegelian. In *Of Grammatology*, Derrida calls Hegel *"the last philosopher of the book and the first thinker of writing."* [11]

Correspondingly, Derrida's method for the deconstruction of metaphysics is through writing. [12] Specifically, it is initiated by the coinage of a neographism, *differance*. Derrida is adamant that *"this graphic differance (a instead of e), this marked difference between two apparently vocal notations, between two vowels, remains purely graphic: it is read, or it is written, but it cannot be heard."* [13] In addition, Derrida insinuates, *"It is offered by a mute mark, by a tacit monument, I would even say by a pyramid, thinking not only of the form of the letter when it is printed as a capital, but also of the text in Hegel's Encyclopedia in which the body of the sign is compared to the Egyptian Pyramid. The 'a' of differance, thus, is not heard; it remains silent, secret and discreet as a tomb: oikesis."* [14] Yet, he prefers to associate differance with the word sheaf, which *"seems to mark more appropriately that the as-*

Facing page: 2. Karl Chu, *SYBORG*, 2003. Collage.

3

semblage to be proposed has the complex structure of a weaving, an interlacing which permits the different threads and different lines of meaning–or of force–to go off again in different directions, just as it is always ready to tie itself up with others." [15] A sort of rhizomatic proliferation of signifiers that is structurally infinite, a network without boundaries or closure that, in the process of interlacing along different lines of meaning, manages to deconstruct the Egyptian Pyramid. In so doing, the act of writing opens up a space or caesura through the insertion of *differance* into the construction of textual meaning: the delay or deferral entailed in the transmission of thought to act and the transition from one act to the next, and the resulting polyvalent proliferation of meaning as registered in the gesture of writing, which by then is no longer a direct re-presentation of thought to inscription. In this context, trace is no longer construed as tracing of a past, of an already constituted speech or thought but a proactive tracing of possible futures of meaning: the movement of writing opens up the space of writing where one is exiled into the space of oblivion and becomes exposed to the complex array of forces that are no longer under the jurisdiction of pure thought. Writing therefore is a form of exile into the desert of non-meaning, away from pre-constituted idea or thought. In so doing, the materiality involved in writing becomes inflected, and the desire to write motivated by the desire for inventive discovery of meaning unexpectedly and

3. Karl Chu, *ROBO_BABEL*, 2005. Collage.

inadvertently comes into contact with unheard-of thoughts and figures of speech that are alien to the subject. Inevitably, the subject, far from being securely founded in the space of his own thought, is thrown into an indeterminate space called text that is inherently unstable.

Inasmuch as a text is woven out of the polyvalent fabric of the active production of meaning, non-meaning as pure absence also comes into play and consequently finds its place in the textual web of transcription: the space in between that is the void of thought. The interstitial spaces that are dispersed throughout the text become zones of exception where the unsayable announces its momentary abode and resonates with the ineffable. This represents a primordial fissure in the Parmenidean imposition of a conjunctive synthesis of thought and being. The void of the ineffable is the mute announcement of the celebration of the co-belongingness of thought and action, as they constitute a thoughtful dance that evokes, ever so obliquely, the inextricable commutation of being and non-being. In other words, it is not the act of writing *per se* that is ineffable; it is the immersion of the subject in the *space of an enigmatic experience*, a theater, as it were, that evokes an oblique sense of the ineffable: the drama of the intricate interweaving of meaning with non–meaning.

As can be imagined, the basis for the cohesive articulation of thought and action is contingent upon the body and its relation to thought. The body has its own vocation that is not necessarily incongruent with the ambitions of thought. The ineffable is virtually present with the presence of the carnal body: the body obstructs linguistic expression by permeating its affects through visceral experience. At the level of genesis of the body, however, it points to the possibility for the incarnation of the word of language or code. Yet, in and of itself, the body is a massive conglomeration of cells that are self-organized into formal and informal arrangements, which paradoxically vivifies the otherness of organs within consciousness: it is as much body-without-organs as it is organs-without-body. It is the *locus classicus* that witnesses a massive confrontation between consciousness of self and the body: an ontological gap between the identity of self and the body with its own carnal volition. The body is the primordial site of the ineffable. The inert and mute cadaver is the extreme case where the conception of self or self-consciousness totally dissipates into non-existence only to leave the body as an inert matter devoid of being. Insofar as a living body is concerned, one of the means by which the ontological gap between self and body can be overcome is through the intensification of pure energy where thought is suspended thereby dissipating the delimitation of self-containment as ordained by thought. Through activation of the movement of the intensive body, the body effectuates an energetic field such that space-time becomes curved and contorted through dynamic saturation of tension and compression, which correspondingly insinuates the effect of the virtual: dispersion of traces of multiple bodies from a singular body. Such an endeavor, as Antonin Artaud has pointed out, is a theater of cruelty that vanquishes representation: the word of God, speech, thought, idea, etc. In so doing, it releases the subordination of the body to the demands of thought or narrative.

Writing is a dancing act that engenders the virtual proliferation of meaning and its other, non-meaning. Nietzsche's celebrated notion–dancing with the pen–is most vividly expressed in calligraphic writing where the dynamic movement of the hand and the body is registered in the markings of words and sentences on a page. As such, the meaning of words and the flow of sentences become inflected and contorted, thereby filling the field of inscription with ambiguous yet subtle nuances that only bodily gestures can impart: a heightened concentration of impersonal forces instigated partially by the intermingling of conscious and semi-conscious trajectories that come into complicity with the pure release of energetic exuberance flashing through the space of anonymity.

Deconstructive writing, in this regard, is far less calligraphic but the development of textual information is a dynamic interweaving of the multifaceted dimensions of meaning that unfolds over time. Derrida has endeavored to bring the force of writing and signification as part of this general economy of expenditure that leaves trails of detritus in the process of constructing a textual assemblage. As such, it entails a dynamics of active and passive forces where the subject is the locus that negotiates the dissemination of meaning through the very act of writing. The dynamics of force and action are necessarily intertwined; the tendency however is to privilege active or positive content, thus ignoring the negative or the passive. The passive is also a force, an inverted force to say the least. There is no activity that does not engage with the negative force of passivity; the two are polar extremes of a singularity like the continuous variable between two values or, to give a concrete example, a glass of water that can be designated as either half full or half empty. The mutual dance of the active and the passive over time maps out zones of attraction and repulsion, territorializations and deterritorializtions that find their correlates in physical space. What Derrida manages to accomplish with deconstruction is the opening up of imperceptible fissures that sever the ontological commitment between thought and being through the artifice of writing such that, it paradoxically reconvenes as well as disengages the body-in-action with the construction of meaning. The locus of meaning therefore is displaced away from the subject and multiplies itself into kaleidoscopic dispersion of meanings within the text.

Insofar as we are dealing with the dynamics of situations, it would be necessary to take into consideration a crucial concept from chaos theory: attractors. An attractor is a set of states within a dynamical system, which settles, after a long enough time, into a basin of attraction and asymptotically approach a point, a curve, a manifold, or even a complicated set with a fractal structure known as strange attractor. In general, attractors act as limit cycles, in which trajectories circle around a limiting trajectory, which they tend toward but never reach. The simplest form of attractor is the fixed-point attractor of which a tornado or a hurricane is a well-known example. Strange attractors on the other hand are bounded regions of phase space and trajectories within a strange attractor appear to skip around randomly. Since an attractor is the locus of organization for a dynamical system, it acquires the attribute of an agency that is violently mute and powerful: the vortex unleashed by a fixed-point attractor is similar to a black hole that absorbs everything unto itself. It is the soul of an invisible order that behaves somewhat analogously to Aristotle's concept of the first cause, which sets the universe into circular motion: *the unmoved mover, by virtue of its immobility, moves everything else*. An attractor therefore is a ghostly agency that is fundamentally passive but whose power lies in the unleashing of negative forces onto things around it. As such, an attractor projects a powerful sense of anonymity, a sublime indeterminate force that invokes the sense of the ineffable.

Inasmuch as dynamical systems self-organize themselves into basins of attraction, they are driven by the economy of matter, energy and information. Correspondingly, the distribution of these three parameters is directly related to increase or decrease in the entropy of a physical system. Here I would like to suggest another aspect of the ineffable: ignorance. In science, the Second Law of Thermodynamics is a theory that deals explicitly with entropy. Notwithstanding its status as a scientific theory, it is also thought of as a theory about knowledge of physical systems in general. Algorithmic Information Theory, which is based on program-size complexity, has reformulated the concept of entropy in terms of *ignorance* or lack of knowledge. Accordingly, entropy is understood as the degree of ignorance concerning knowledge about the meaningful information content of a system. It is therefore correlated to the amount of random information present within a system. A phenomenon is random when there is no mathematical function that could compress a given random situation into a shorter program: the algorithmic program is just as long as the situation to be described. In other words, ignorance is the negative or inverse of positive knowledge and as such, it is a necessary outcome of all productive activities. With each change in form or organization, energy or information content is degraded to a less useful form, which correspondingly increases entropy or random information. The paradox is that with the rise in entropy due to expenditures entailed in the production of work, order emerges out of chaos through self-organization of form. All forms of production engender heat as a byproduct, which is entropy. For now, suffice it to say that the higher the level of entropy or random information, the higher the degree of ignorance that will infect the information content of a system. Ignorance therefore is yet another expression of the negative, of the void of knowledge produced by the activity of work.

As can be also inferred from deconstruction, this entails a displacement of the subject by becoming cognizant of the dispersion of the void of knowledge, the irreducible presence of randomness within order (a revenge on Maxwell's Demon with his God-like acumen to eliminate absolute disorder) especially within machinic subjectivities that are internal to computing systems, which will be addressed below. Deconstruction is a critique of the logocentric tradition that privileges speech and the proximity of speech to truth. If there is a mode of inscription that is antithetical to deconstruction, one that reinstalls logos in the construction of meaning and the world, it is algorithmic information processing that is determined by codes. This is the point where computation as an instrumental medium finds its intersection with the classical paradigm of Parmenides: ideas translated into codes that is used to construct the world or being. Computing is all about codes and codes are univocal: a term written in a software code means precisely just one function or designation. Significantly, in computation, there is no author/writer who would negotiate and instigate the real time unfolding of information or meaning as it is in the case of writing. Instead, an algorithm is a set of instruction that generates the output: it is deterministic in every sense of the term. The differences therefore are extreme: deconstructive writing is indeterminate, multivalent, slippery, ambiguous, paradoxical, nonlinear and undecidable, all of which are maneuvers that occur in the semantic domain and the author/writer is profoundly implicated in the making of the text in real time. Machinic inscription is deterministic, linear, syntactical and unequivocal, and the majority of software programs are based on Lambda–calculus,[16] one of the paradigms of logocentric procedures. On the surface, it seems the two approaches are antithetical to each other and imply two different ontologies.

There is, however, a way to conceive of these systems that finds some degree of equivalence at the level of their outputs: deconstruction as the production of sheaves or the interlacing of text and computing as the generative construction of patterns of information. The procedures of writing and computing are dissimilar but the end result may resonate with similar affects. If, for instance, we consider a Universal Turing Machine (a theoretical blueprint for computation) as a molecular monad that is endowed with dual attributes–as in the programming language Lisp where an atom can be assigned to function either as an element or as a function,–then we can envision a situation whereby a massive random collision of monads or Turing Machines would engender autocatalytic reactions among these monads, which will then lead to the self-organization and self-synthesizing of monads that produces complex ensembles (as emergent phenomena) not unlike chemical compounds that occur due to interactive permutations at the molecular level. The output generated by these Brownian (random collision of monads) computers [17] at the molecular level would be in fact far more unpredictable, accidental, seemingly indeterminate and surprising. The resulting patterns of information would no longer be the result of following a single code that determines the outcome through a linear procedure; instead, it would generate a complex interweaving of textual information. In so doing, it will function just like natural systems do and correspondingly these machinic monads can be made to interact with natural systems as if they are part and parcel of a single symbiotic ecology of information processing. The view of computation changes drastically when viewed as such.

Experience of the ineffable is, more often than not, accompanied by the sense of the cessation of time. Time however can be conceived of in different ways and there is a point where the ontological gap is most pronounced: the gap or disjunction between the internal experience of time and the external constitution of time. From the standpoint of the human subject, duration is the stream of consciousness that engages in the internal constitution of time perceived as a continuum. Consciousness in its normative state is a flux of shifting attention that meanders randomly from one fleeting moment of thought to another; the ineffable is the experience of time that ceases to function as a temporal flux when consciousness is interrupted by the event of the ineffable. In addition to a subject-centered conception of time, there are dimensions of exteriority that pertain to the external constitution of time: mathematical time or the time of information processing

4

"The body is the primordial site of the ineffable. The inert and mute cadaver is the extreme case where the conception of self or self-consciousness totally dissipates into non-existence only to leave the body as an inert matter devoid of being."

4. Karl Chu, *ARTIFICITY*, 2005. Collage.

"For now, suffice it to say that the higher the level of entropy or random information, the higher the degree of ignorance that will infect the information content of a system. Ignorance therefore is yet another expression of the negative, of the void of knowledge produced by the activity of work."

that is linear. It is counter-intuitive to imagine a non-linear movement of time or the dynamic differentiation of speed that affects the variable constitution of time. Deconstructive writing implicitly entails a non-linear interlacing of time in the constitution of intertextuality. In this regard, there is a direct correlate to the differential interlacing of temporal dynamics: the logic of an asynchronous computing system, where information processing is not governed by a global clock speed. In these situations, time becomes a variable in the differential modulation of the genesis of form. Unhinged from a linear pathway, a modal conception of time comes to the foreground especially in the context of massively distributive computing systems where the dynamic coordination and exchange of information occurs within labyrinthine networks of branching pathways which are instantiated by self-replicating monadic agencies that govern and channel information processing throughout the machinic assemblage. As prosaic as it may seem, the implications are profound: the generative construction of architecture no longer follows a linear path toward a desired end. Instead the structure of information processing branches into the phase space of permutation enabled by codes that reside within Turing Machines, which can be exceedingly large, thereby engendering both factual and counterfactual domains of linkages and correlations. When the linear temporal process of generating architecture is unhinged from within the global web of transgenic computing systems, generative processes find their opportunistic networks of branching pathways that lead to multi-modal domains of possible worlds. Correspondingly, an immanent zone of potentiality emerges at every branching node: the nodal intersection where possible pasts and possible futures converges in order to once again bifurcate into the evolving web of architecture. Being, as such, is no longer a sphere but a constantly fluctuating labyrinth of information constituted by the ever shifting, dissolving and emerging patterns of order and chaos, meaning and non-meaning, and being and non-being.

Sustained by the efflorescence of being that extends infinitely in all directions, the nature and limits of computation find their moment of exuberance in the compression and decompression of information that is most vividly displayed in the Holographic Paradigm[18] a hypothesis that is derived from a real physical phenomenon in the Universe and referred to in the scientific community as black hole computing.[19] It is a theoretical possibility that programmable black hole computers might one day be realizable. Due to the hyper-density of information and potential processing speed implicit in the extreme black hole environment along with the foaminess of space-time that leads to an uncertainty in timekeeping (the more accurate the clock, the shorter its lifetime), black hole computing may provide alternative measure for the limits of computation. Here, we have arrived at the limits of the intelligible and the sublime ineffable and we can now frame the problem of the generic ineffable in relation to the limits of the architecture of the Universe. Objects are destroyed and torn apart under immense gravitational pull when they fall into a black hole but the information content of these objects, in the form of bits, are registered randomly on the inner surface of the black hole – the machinic void of existence, as it were – instead of being extinguished into non-existence.

Black holes are cosmological entropic computing systems dispersed throughout the Universe. Strange as it may seem, the question posed to the Holographic Paradigm is surprising and fantastic: is it possible to re-constitute objects that are destroyed back to their original form based on the remnants of bits randomly stored on the inner surface of the black hole? The very plausibility of the question is derived from the fact that the surface functions as an information storage system and Hawking radiation emitted from a black hole is considered to be the channel for the output of computation. The reconstruction may seem impossible if it is judged solely based on present- day knowledge but we should be mindful of the fact that reality is far stranger than any of our conceptions of being. The emphasis here is on the metaphysics of the ineffable in relation to either potential or actual/virtual correlates in the physical Universe. The domain that lies at the edge of existence is the proper domain to conceive of the *generic ineffable:* the foundational *non-event* or non-being that serves as the primordial condition for expression of the ineffable. Suffice it to say that the view of computation as stated above has profound significance to the genetics of becoming and to the horizon of our capacity or incapacity to imagine and theorize on the machinic conception of the ineffable. The limits of architecture then become a function of the limits of machinic attribution to existence, beyond carnal involvement by the subject with writing, thinking, dreaming, imaging, discovering, fearing, loving, etc. Since the subject is both an active as well as a passive agent – a receptacle for diverse forms of affects including that of the ineffable, any attempt to theorize on the relation between the ineffable and the instrumental immediately expunges rational formulation: the ineffable blocks, destroys, exhausts and casts away all forms of modal semantics that govern our conceptions of being and causality.

Having sketched various manifestations of the ineffable within diverse disciplines and philosophical orientations that seem disconnected or unrelated – from the speculative idealism of Hegel to Badiou's subtractive ontology, deconstruction to dynamical systems along with non-linear distributive computing systems and black hole computing – I would now like to point toward one of the critical ideas of this paper: the *displacement* of man by machinic subjectivities. Since architecture is man written large, which is an unspoken premise of architecture since time immemorial, the advent of this paradigm shift will radicalize the way we think of architecture: the potential disruption of what Agamben refers to as the anthropological machine[20] – demarcation of the animal and man, the inhuman and human or the inhuman within the human that is used for the politics of exclusion especially in the political domain of sovereignty- and the emergence of the Post-Human Era[21] whose full-blown affect is yet to be felt but whose near future impact on the universe of humanity is inevitable. This development is nothing short of being revolutionary; it is already implicit in the concept of metamorphosis. At this stage in the evolution of life on Earth, the impetus for this change is driven by the convergence of computation and biogenetics. Without this convergence, it would not have been possible to complete the sequencing of the Human Genome Project. The acquisition of the human genome is an event of major significance, an indexical landmark, as it were, not only in the history of technology but also in the history of knowledge, or shall I say, self-knowledge.

The emphasis is not in any specific problem or the variety of genetic manipulations that are now being instantiated – from transgenic mutation of food crops to the invention of new species including mutants and cyborgs. Instead, I would like to call attention to a general phenomenon that is rather comprehensive and far-reaching: the path toward the age of transgenesis. We are at the very beginning of this global transformation that is leading us, on the one hand, to the inevitable emergence of a planetary computing system in the form of the global brain, a massively distributive interactive intelligent system that functions as a machinic assemblage at the planetary level, and, on the other, a metamorphosis that would result in the biomachinic mutation of the organic and the inorganic, of man and machine, of mutant beings and species, both virtual and physical, all proliferating into intensive zones of implementation within the planet and the virtual realm of the global brain. These are undoubtedly brave new worlds to come: an inconsistent multiplicity that will be the hallmark of a new computational monadology of architecture that is currently in the making.

In light of this, the Socratic injunction, *Know Thyself*, which serves as one of the cornerstones of wisdom in the West, finds its partial fulfillment in the possession of the DNA code: genesis of the body as coded in the instruction set of the Homeobox gene (a subset of the DNA responsible for the morphogenetic development of the body of species, which in-and-of-itself is a software program). On the other side, absolute knowledge of self – as implied by Parmenides and claimed by Hegel – is an impossibility as shown by the failure of the work of the phenomenologist, Edmund Husserl, whose attempt to discover the mechanism for the constitution of knowledge and, by extension, of self and consciousness, results in an infinite regress without being able to arrive at the knowledge of the knowledge of self. Further augmenting this impossibility is the Lacanian conception of the real: speech-defying affect of the encounter with a horrifying phenomenon that fissures the being of a subject. Therefore, however one chooses to frame it, the ineffable is a singular experience of a existential effect induced by a bipolar phenomenon that inadvertently calls attention to the extremes of something and nothing: an intrusion, on the one hand, of the void into the normative condition of a situation, thereby flattening it with absolute meaninglessness, and, on the other, a phenomenal excess of being that shatters the normative condition by pointing to that which lies at the limits of being.

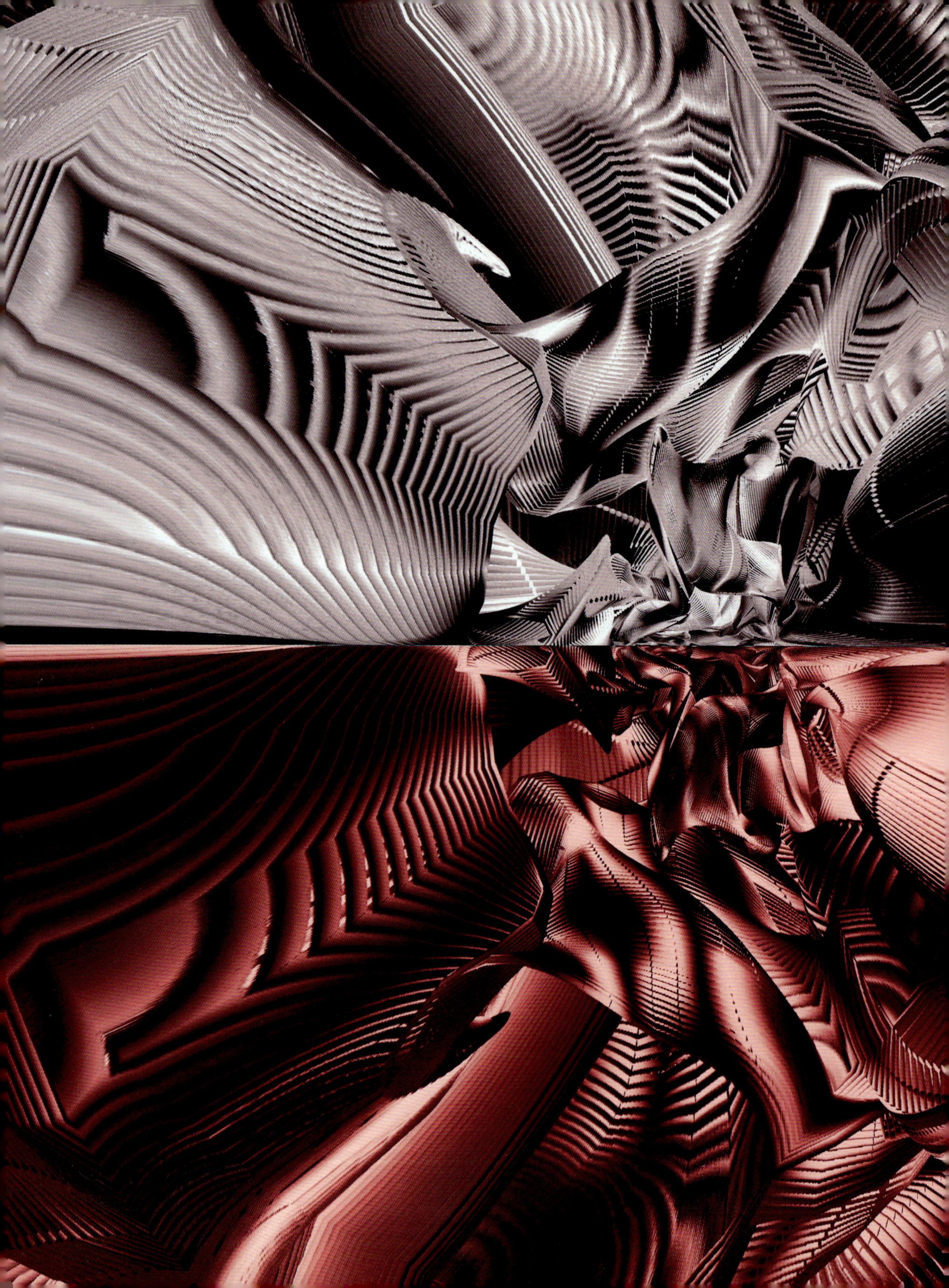

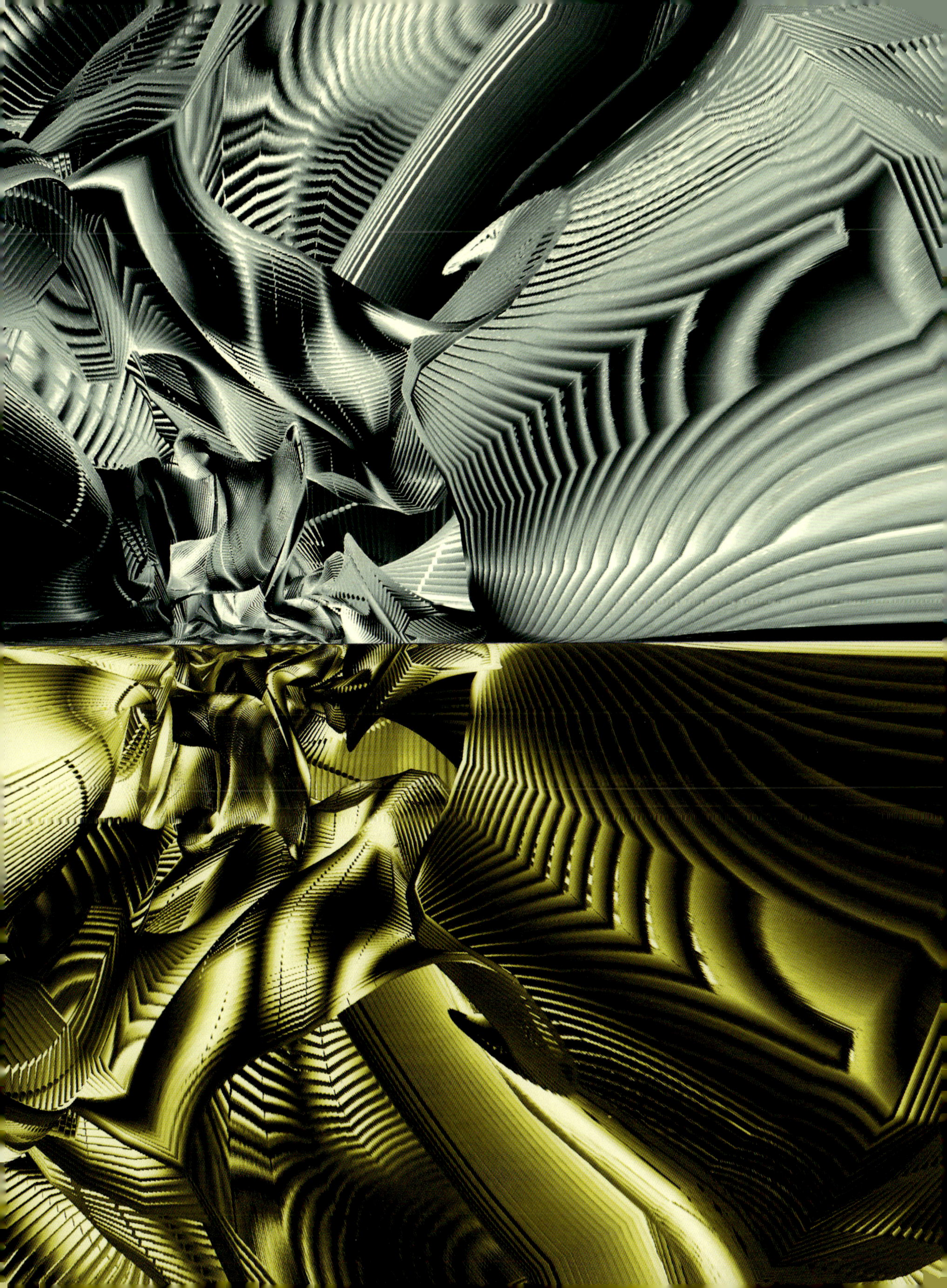

"So primarily I am interested in architecture as a form of thought. I am interested in the questions: why does anything exist at all and why do we need architecture? What is architecture? Why do we take architecture for granted?"

As such, it is a phenomenology of excess inasmuch as it is of deficiency, at once horrifyingly full and empty, induced by an invocation of absence in light of presence and presence in light of absence. The ineffable breaks through the barriers of categorical imperatives and conceptual determinants and the universe of semiological regimes that are associated with these imperatives. The ineffable is the generic affect associated with, on the one hand, the Lacanian real (a psychological rupture into the being of a subject), and, on the other, resurgence of crevices in the web of existence that discloses the sheer insignifiable dimension of nonbeing within being.

The experience of the ineffable is immediate: speechlessness accompanied by the unimaginable that fissures the light of day into the night at noon. The scenic juxtaposition of the abnormal onto the matrix of the normal is where the real of a situation is calling attention to the confluence of incongruity into a disjunctive congruity of being and nothingness. In so doing, time loses its grip on the timeliness of the movement of life in and through its activities. It neither is the movement of time nor is it the announcement of eternity due to the cessation of time but a caesura that ceases to give time the dimension of temporal significance. In other words, time is robbed of its timely significance through the arrest of linear causality that gives meaning to the ongoing business of life, a rupture into the structure of the world at any given interstice or situation that shows that reality is simultaneously divergent and convergent, at once radically incongruent as well as congruent to itself. Once again, the generic condition of the ineffable is the speechless violence of shock and awe engendered not only by the one dimensionality of destruction but also by the sublime exuberance of generative excess proliferating in all directions, an oceanic expanse of translucent green digitizing itself into the non-linear expanse of being without limits – a mutant anonymity from the oblivion that appeals to the virtual co-belongingness of being and nothingness: the collapse of both linear and reverse causality of construction and destruction, as if all oppositions including counterfactuals were expansively converging toward a *coincidentia oppositorum*, which, at the primordial level, separates inasmuch as integrates being with the void of existence: the topo-cosmological wormholes of existence.

Previous pages: 5. Karl Chu, collage.

Related to the machinic conception of the void, the ineffable can also be thought of as a higher order exemplification that is analogous to the seething flux that occurs at the so-called Planck's length:[22] the super subliminal sense of estrangement – out-of-joint with the sense of time and place – due to no other reason than an effusion of low-level impulses that leak out of the cracks of the superposition of the atemporal dimension of time – infinitesimal gaps between minute instances of nows – and the temporal act that irrupts untimely and ineluctably from out of the infinite expanse of vacuous eternity or vacuity: call it the fundamentals of existence that is not unlike incessant irruptions and disappearances of virtual particles in and out of the quantum foam[23] in quantum mechanics. The ineffable in the manner that I am referring to is an expression of the paradox of exception that emerges and dissolves into the fabric of reality while disclosing the trauma of the real as an aftereffect caused by the agitation of existence. It is a paradoxical invocation by the unexpected infusion of the incongruent into the matrix of the congruent, consequently filling the experience of the ineffable with shocking contradictions, sublime horror with noxious amazement or perplexity set in motion by dynamic oscillations that reside at the limits of the intelligible and the perceptible. Analogous to Friedrich Schelling's adumbration of the causal genesis of the world in his Ages of the World, the unsaid dimensions of the ineffable lie in the domain of unheard of thoughts: contraction and expansion of the Void that triggers the basis for vacuum genesis, and subsequent formation of *will to will* that gives sustenance to the emergence of being out of the vibrations of non-being. Insofar as the ineffable is an existential effect produced by the rupture of being through an internal oscillation that conjugates itself with itself as well as with its other, i.e., the noncommutable excess of non–being within being, it is a resonating fissure that wedges into the normativity of a situation grounded in the logic of cohesion: the global apparatus of architecture that sustains the artifice of life in all its diverse assemblages. In other words, the apparatus is already permeated with side affects of the ineffable. Yet, in line with the evolutionary path towards self-knowledge, the apparatus is now expanding its function into the architecture of life. This is the basis for the genesis and proliferation of the architecture of possible worlds into the living organism we call Earth – an organic particle whirling around a star floating in the oceanic sea of existence that is ultimately nothing – according to the emerging paradigm based on computation – but a manifestation of virtual reality sustained, propelled and computed right down to the kernel of existence: a spectral emanation of self-replicating systems profusely engaged in the self-organizing and self-synthesizing of bits into higher orders of monadic ensembles in and through the Void or the null set of existence.

Contained in the mythical injunction to *Know Thyself* is the logical conjunction to know the world. Implied in the imperative to know the world is to create the world based on knowledge accrued from having known oneself and the world in all its vicissitudes: the conjunctive as well as disjunctive correlations of being with its intrinsic other, the non-being of existence. Nothing exemplifies this better than the discovery of the DNA code with regard to self-knowledge and the genesis of the body of self, and by extension, a certain crude approximation of the notion of the self. And nothing represents the generative construction of possible worlds better than the emergence of universal computation that is responsible for the machinic attribution to existence. Yet, the ineffable is simultaneously everywhere and nowhere: it obliquely points to the surplus of the unknowable within the self as well as within the world. Even with the arrival of the age of computation (where the generative construction of possible worlds is driven by the dynamic interaction of codes) and even with the possession of morphogenetic codes that will consequently result in the proliferation of genetic architecture, which symbolizes the emergence of a new paradigm destined to alter the very nature of man – the eternal stability of the concept of MAN grounded in the biological category, *Homo sapiens*, the ineffable will not cease to announce its ineluctable presence at the very moment of the ejection of a monadic species of architecture into existence: a miraculous phenomenon not unlike giving birth to life, and subsequently, to the spectral proliferation of possible worlds to come. This leads us once again to the question: what is architecture? A provisional answer might not be inappropriate at this stage in the evolution of the ontology of being, which is co-extensive with the ontology of architecture: the generative construction of possible worlds, each of which is a generic extension of the body of the ineffable.

Notes:

1. First constructed by Robert Griess at Princeton in 1982 and was named the Monster by John Conway, the Monster group can be thought of as a snowflake with more than 1,050 symmetries that exists in a space of 196,883 dimensions. Connection has been found between the symmetry of the Monster and string theory in physics.
2. In mathematics, the continuum hypothesis is advanced by Georg Cantor in 1877, about the possible sizes of infinite sets. It states: There is no set whose cardinality is strictly between that of the integers and that of the real numbers. In other words, there is no infinite set with a cardinal number between that of the "small" infinite set of integers aleph_0 and the "large" infinite set of real numbers c (the "continuum").
3. Jean Hyppolite, "The Ineffable" in *Logic and Existence* (Albany: State University of New York Press, 1997), 7 –21.
4. Alain Badiou, *Infinite Thought: Truth and the Return to Philosophy,* ed. and trans. Justin Clemens and Oliver Feltham (London: Continuum, 2003), 58.
5. Badiou, p.64.
6. Badiou, p.64.
7. Badiou, p.65.
8. Badiou, p.68.
9. Hyppolite, 27.
10. Hyppolite, 27.
11. Jacques Derrida, *Of Grammatology*, (Baltimore: The John Hopkins University Press, 1974), 26.
12. It should be noted at the outset that my reading of Derrida is unconventional: it is based on what I construe to be the metaphysics implicit in deconstruction in relation to the Parmenidean injunction: *Being Is and Non-being Is Not*.
13. Jacques Derrida, *Margins of Philosophy*, trans. Alan Bass (Chicago: University of Chicago Press, 1982), 3.
14. Derrida, *Margins of Philosophy*, 3.
15. Derrida, *Margins of Philosophy*, 3.
16. Lambda-calculus is a model of computation invented by Alonzo Church in 1934. It's analogous to Turing machines, which defines a simplified programming language.
17. C. H. Bennett, "The Thermodynamics of Computation – A Review" (1982) in *Maxwell's Demon 2: Entropy, Classical and Quantum Information, Computing*, ed. Harvey S. Leff and Andrew F. Rex (London: The Institute of Physics, 2003), 289.
18. Leonard Susskind, *The Black Hole War: My Battle With Stephen Hawking To Make the World Safe for Quantum Mechanics* (New York: Hachette Books, 2008).
19. Seth Lloyd and Y. Jack Ng, "Black Hole Computers," *Scientific American* 291, no. 5 (November 2004): 52-61.
20. Giorgio Agamben, "Anthropological Machine" in *The Open: Man and Animal* (Stanford, CA: Stanford University Press, 2004), 33 – 38.
21. Many scientists are referring to the 21st century as the century of biotechnology.
22. Planck's length refers to the smallest unit where entities can exist at 10^{-33}cm and beyond which objects can no longer be conceived in quantum mechanics.
23. Quantum foam referred to as spacetime foam as a qualitative description of subatomic spacetime turbulence at extremely small distances of the order of the Planck length.

OUT OF TIME

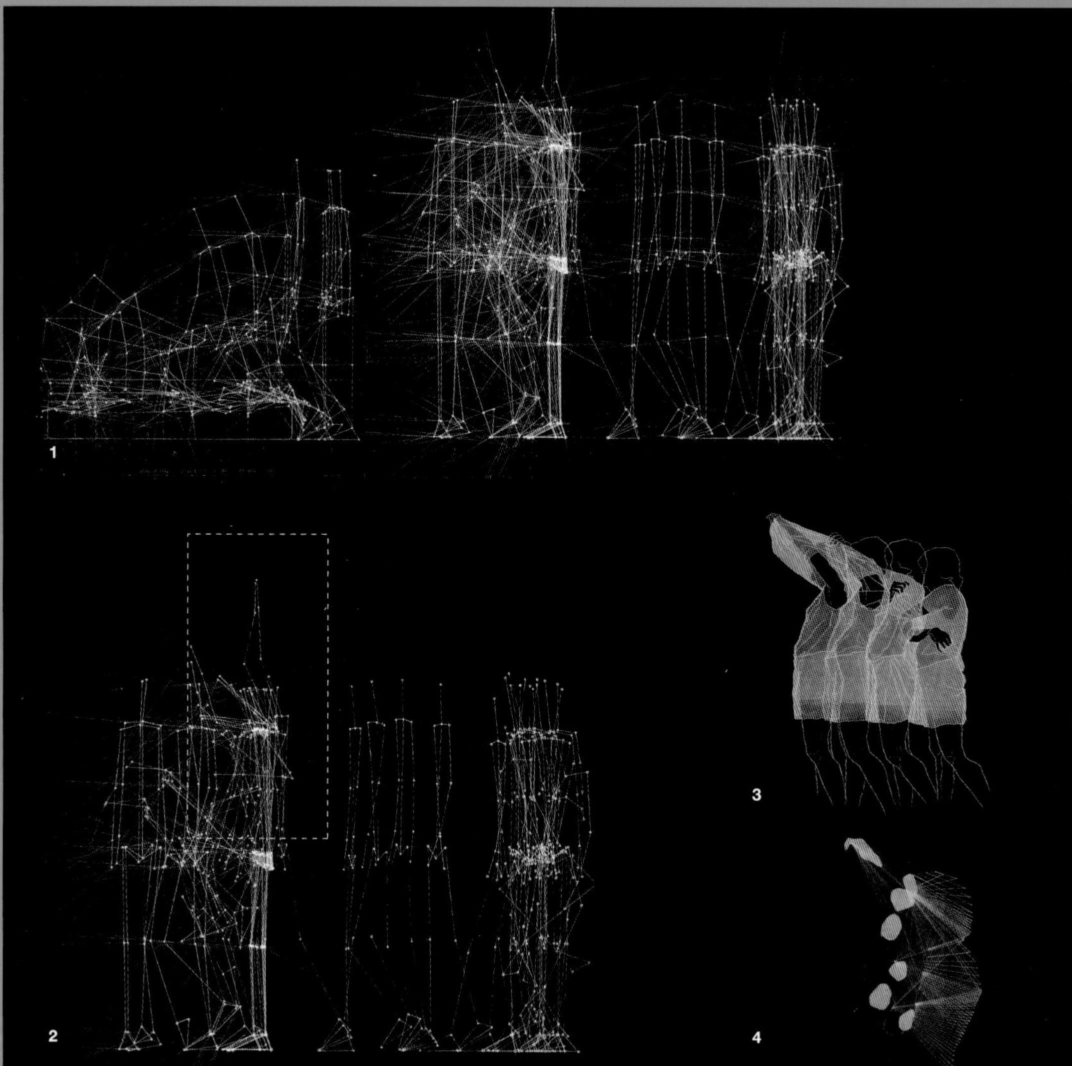

Yael Erel

When considering the meaning of *Ineffable* in the context of this pedagogy panel, it seemed appropriate to examine a fundamental question in architectural pedagogy – our relationship to the process of creation. How do we create? What is the infrastructure for building our thoughts in matter? How do we place ourselves within it? With these questions in mind, I would like to look directly at the design process – the arena in which we construct, translate and critique our thoughts. I will explore the design process through the two pivotal conditions that construct it. The first condition is our relationship to time – both as a continuum, which I will refer to as becoming; and as moments of presence, which I will refer to as being. The second condition is our relationship to authorship – with the author acting both as a force within the design process (operating either from outside in or from the inside out) and as an external gauging force – out of the time of the process. When I teach, I view the design process as a whole that contains these different temporal scales and points of view simultaneously. I believe that awareness of these simultaneities liberates us to view the process as a dynamic act of defining thought in matter; an act that is not necessarily linear in its development and does not have to remain captive to one fixed authorial point of view.

I will examine these ideas on process through student projects produced in first year design studios I taught at Pratt Institute from 2005-2007. All the projects shown here are almost completely analog in their production, though they contain seeds of a time based, digital design approach. All the projects I address use time as a means of generation – through the construction of a tectonic time based event (for example movement within a constructed wood joint) or through the observation of a tangible event from which tectonic conditions are extracted.

Facing page: Jeanee Hammet - Arch 102 Spring '05. **1.** Study of the personal ritual of getting undressed and into bed. **2.** Study of a personal ritual / detail. **3.** Shirt removal detail. **4.** Shirt removal tectonic study.

Bergson claims that reality appears to us as a perpetual becoming and that we use sections (in time=moments of being) as an artificial device to order a flow that we cannot grasp – the flow of the time.[1] These two conditions of reality occur simultaneously at different temporal scales – similar to still frames in the flow of a film, being is a moment contained in a flow and the flow of becoming is constructed out of series of moments of being. Just as we can acknowledge different spatial scales existing within one reality (for example – detail, building, urban) so do different temporal scales exist simultaneously. Each of these scales in time (being and becoming) exposes a very different relationship to space – in the sequence of becoming, our frame is temporal and within it we see spatial transformations unfold; being on the other hand is giving us a slice of time – a timeless snapshot that exposes spatial relationships between elements.

To demonstrate these two temporal conditions I will refer to Jeanee Hammet's study of a personal ritual through time (Figs. 1-4) - In Figure 1 we can see a documentation of the complete ritual sequence. Each figure notation can be understood as a notation of an artificial moment in time (being), which we use in order to understand the overall transformation sequence (becoming). Figures 2 and 3 are an analysis of a smaller fragment within the sequence. Theoretically we can zoom in endlessly and will still find transformations that become more and more subtle (which is precisely Bergson's view – we can never naturally find a frozen moment-unit). We use the language of architecture to study the event and explore the tectonic relationships that unfold within it – for example Figure 4 studies the redefinition of the tectonic relationship between participating

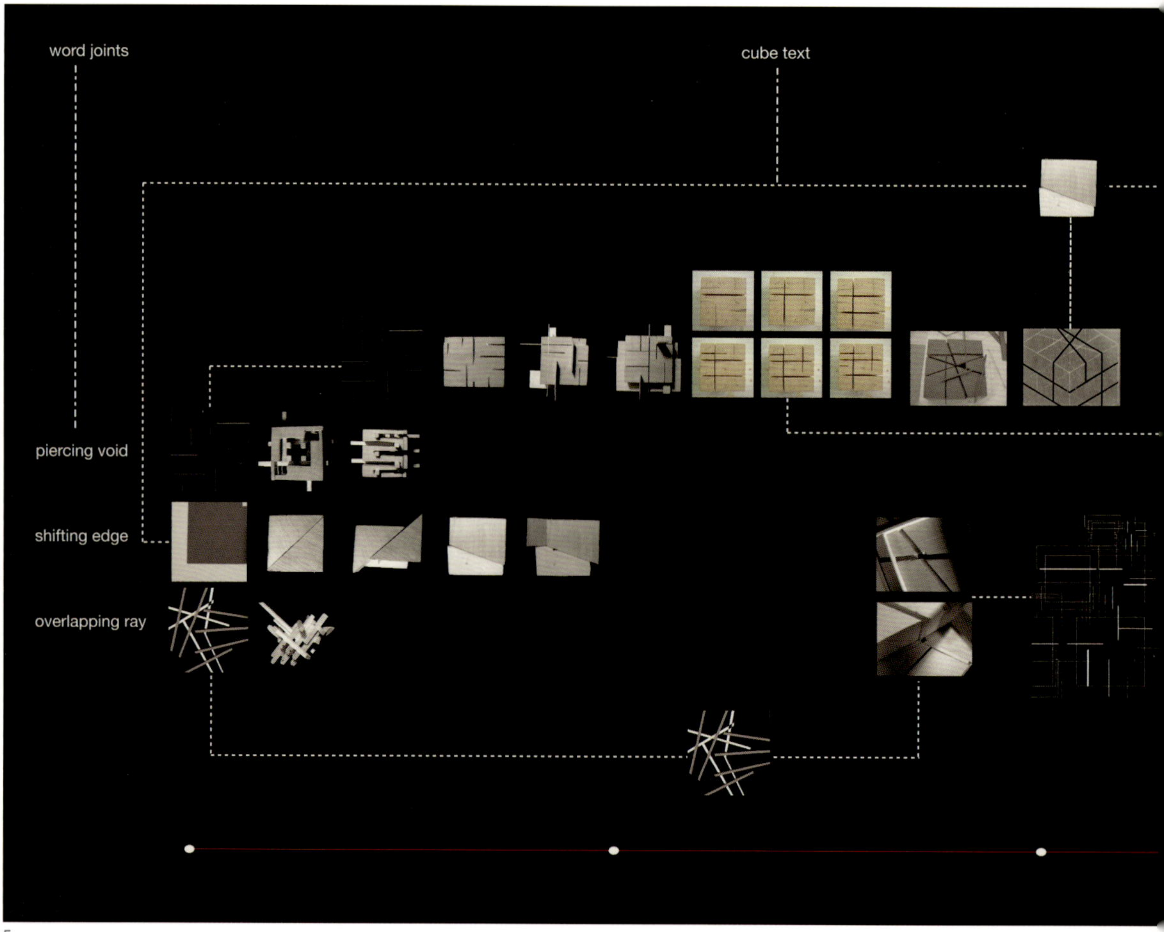

5

elements throughout a sequence. Each individual moment contains within it a timeless spatial relationship.

In a design process one may understand drawings and models as moments of being – physical articulations in which relationships are established spatially. Building a design project is similar to the construction of a Bergsonian reality in which each moment creates the next (the difference is that a design process is not mimicking reality; it is an artificial tool constructed for our intellect to grasp itself). Each articulation in matter is born in a certain moment and context, but is not limited to it. Once a moment is extracted it becomes temporally independent and is articulating spatial relationships. It becomes autonomous. This autonomy is crucial. If we only see process as a continuum we might find ourselves enslaved in something that cannot be edited or engaged with. Only when a flow is sectioned into moments can it become part of a productive exchange. These moments of being are free to inform the project throughout – as autonomous moments that can be re-inserted at a later stage in the design process and read in a new way (for example a moment born in a tectonic context may inform an approach to program, site or space).

Each moment in the process is a material construct that has the potential to articulate an idea through architectural relationships. Architecture's capacity to convey thought was clearly articulated by Le Corbusier in *Towards a New Architecture "(my eyes) behold something which expresses a thought. A thought which reveals itself without word or sound, but solely by means of shapes which stand in*

5. Dan Brietner (Arch 101 Fall '05) full semester process, diagramed by Yael Erel.

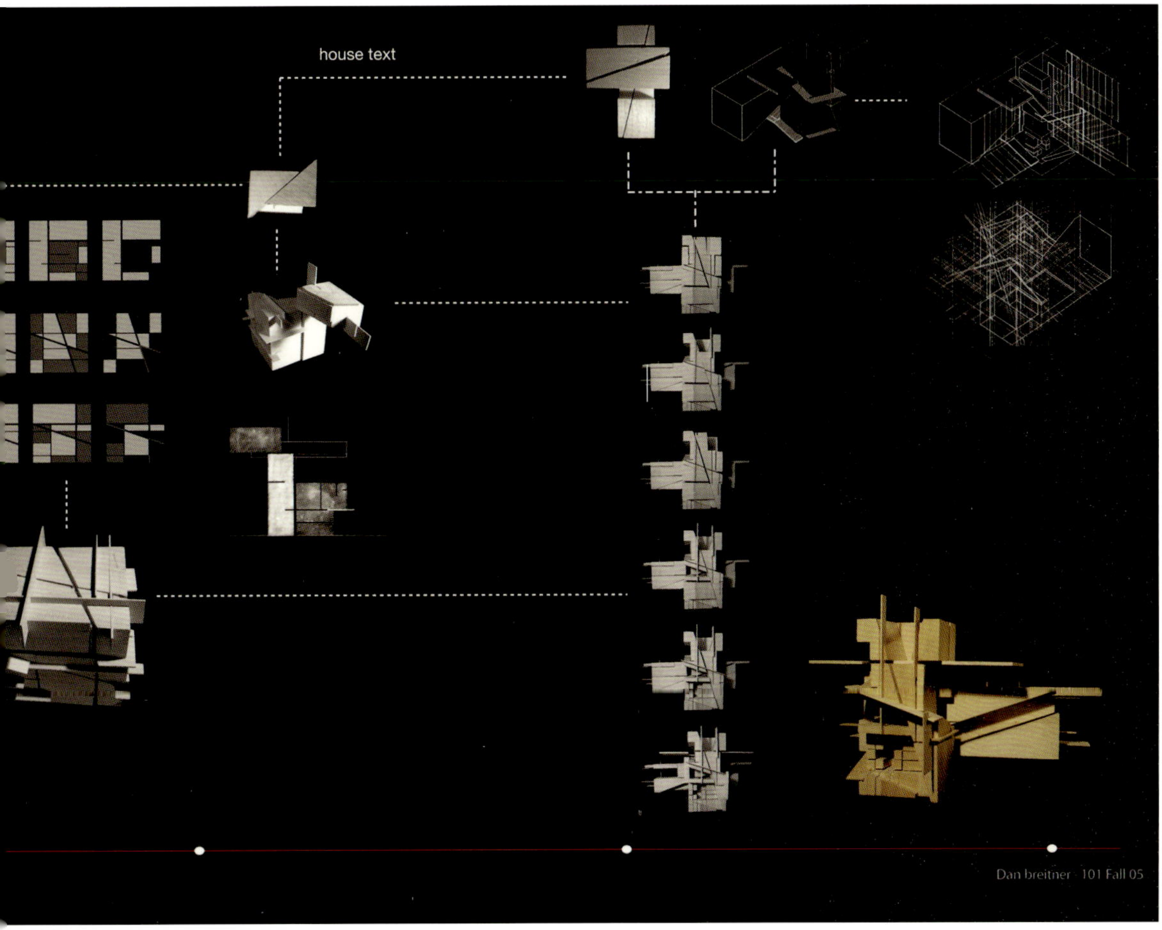

a certain relationship to one another." [2] Throughout the process, these moments of definition begin to construct a thought that evolves through time, with the capacity to develop an architectural language.

For example, Dan Brietner's project diagram (Fig. 5) is a construction of his design process through its moments of being to approximate the project as a whole. This project is constructed and gauged through words and tectonics – wood joints embody the spatial essence of word combinations (a verb and a noun), they establish a language of construction that builds a memory–machine–cube and an inhabitation. Each moment (drawing/model) defines an idea articulated in word and matter. Once defined it is not confined to its linear location in time – it can inform the project at a later date. Moments are part of a sequence of becoming as well as specific instances of being. As such these moments can be extracted from their original location within the sequence and define finite architectural conditions that are informed by idea and program, and contain both the memory of its making and a tectonic articulation. The decision of what is remembered and what is forgotten throughout the construction of the project is up to the author.

Who is this Author I am referring to? In order to construct the concept of this author, it is important to understand two current perceptions of authorship. Western culture has two seminal approaches to authorship in relationship to creation, which could be viewed as parallel to two pivotal authorship concepts we deploy within design today. One is an omnipotent fully authored God-like figure. The second is a system stemming from a germ, a unit developing a whole – the presence of authorship here is much more subtle, existing in micro scales, in transitions.

6

Approach 1 – God architect (Fig. 6) The Biblical God figure is an omnipotent author with the capacity to stand out of time (create time, actually) and observe the complete picture (as from a point of view of a map). Constructing reality via precise intentional acts upon matter, which build upon one another to construct a spatial reality then inhabited. Through the use of the word, this author uses meaning to construct and then critiques each finalized material state of being. This is an approach that operates from the outside in, from the larger picture into a more detailed system. This may be seen as traditionally being the architect's point of view in the design process or the so-called top down approach.

Approach 2 – Evolution (Fig. 7) The second approach is building the process from the inside out – starting from a unit and expanding through development of system logic inherent within the unit into a whole. Authorship takes place at a smaller scale – the logic of the unit and its aggregation can begin to determine development rather than a fully authored move. This may be seen as the so-called bottom up approach.

The following two projects observe a time based everyday event as guide to the construction of both a map (understanding an event as a transforming field) and a unit (a basic tectonic element developed from both the event and texture analysis). Developing them in two parallel tracks that converge to construct a landscape. The map provides the larger top down logic of the landscape and the units provide the tectonic logic to construct that ground and perhaps inform the structure of inhabitation within it.

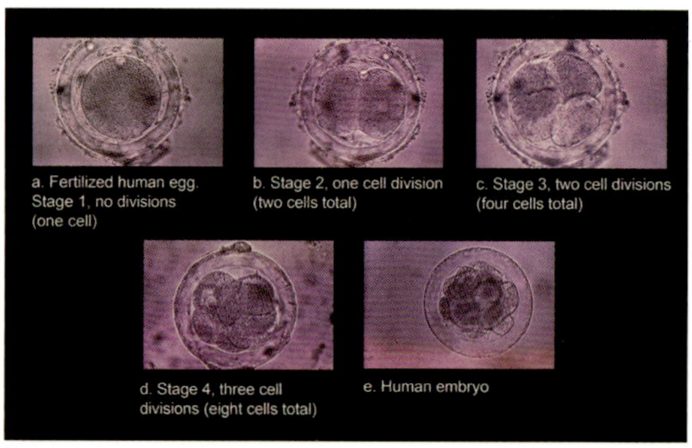

7

6. *God as architect of the universe*, miniature from ms. of *Bible morslisée*, France, 13th c. **7.** Fertilized human egg. **a.** Stage 1. no divisions (one cell). **b.** Fertilized human egg. Stage 2. One cell division (two cells total). **c.** Human embryo. Stage 3. Two cell divisions(four cells total). **d.** Fertilized human egg. Stage 4. Three cell divisions (eight cells total). **e.** Human embryo. **Facing page:** Patrick Collins (Arch 102 Spring '07). **8.** Observation. The removal of a neoprene glove. **9.** The unit: Using qualities of the neoprene to generate a module. **10.** The map: transforming relationships understood as fields.

Project 1 – Patrick Collins (Figs. 8-11)
Observation: An everyday event – the removal of a neoprene glove. (Fig. 8)
The unit: Using the rigidity and stretching qualities of the neoprene as a generator for wood modules. (Fig. 9)
The map: The transforming relationship between hand and glove is understood as a field. (Fig. 10)

The blending of the map and the unit is also the blending of two points of view of the author – the map provides control over the whole, whereas the unit constructs the details and material assembly.
The detail is examined for the opportunities it holds and the maps as a tool to articulate the direction this potential can be steered. The simultaneity in which both are explored

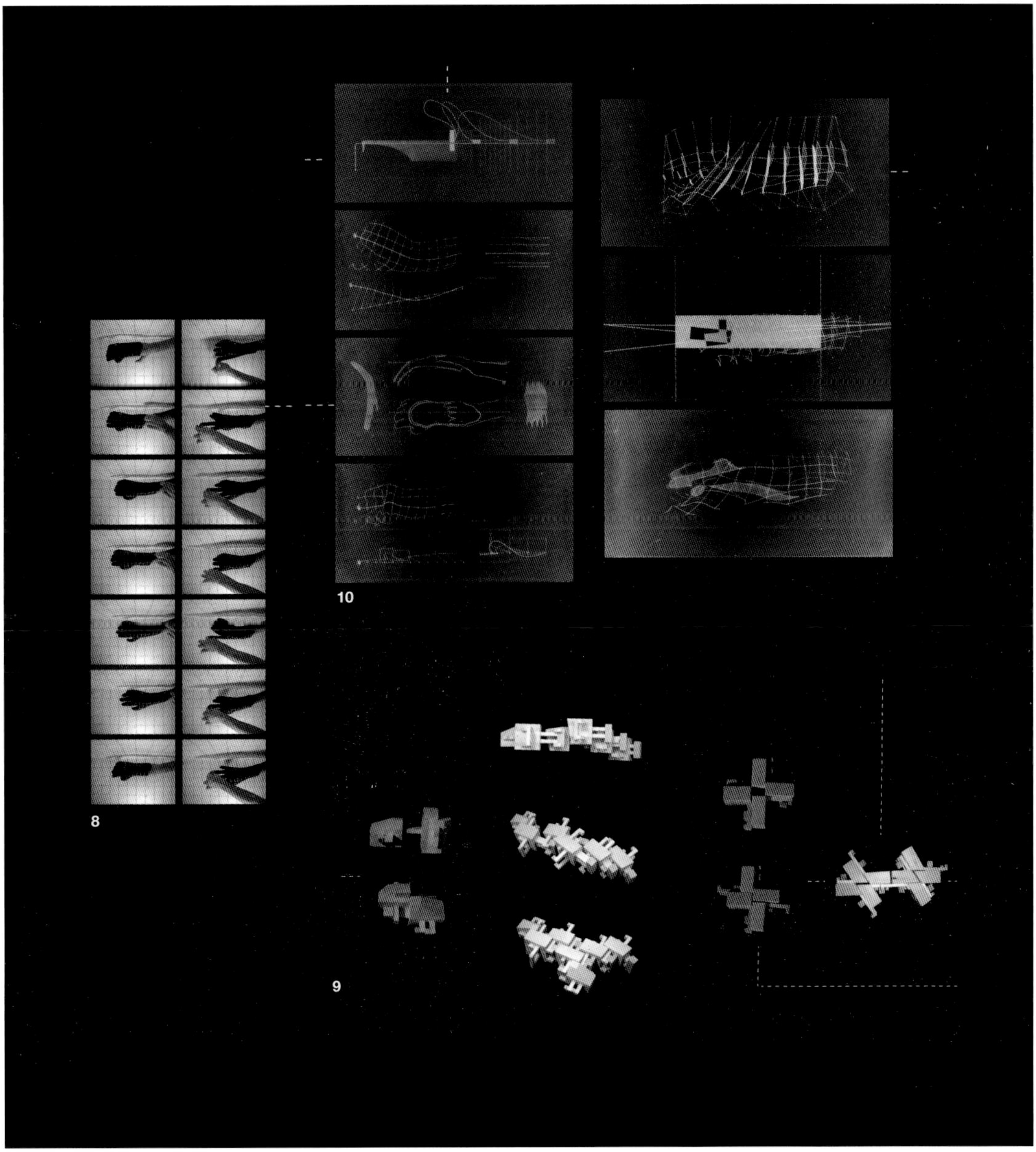

10

8

9

constructs an architecture of negotiation between these two points of view of authorship and the author conducts this mediation informed by ideas, tectonics and program.

Project 2 – James Orielly (Figs. 12-13)
The project analyzes stretching and scrunching a strand – capturing the act through modules and field maps. (Fig. 12)

Observation: an everyday event – the removal of a sock.
The unit: The unit is based on the performative tectonic expression of the stand's stretching and scrunching. As the project developed the original unit was studied as the generator of a versatile architectural syntax, exploring different conditions of space, light and program. (Fig. 13)

In the development of his project James refrained from viewing his design process as progressive, for example, he returned to his original unit as a point of departure, rather than a series of units developed after it. Acknowledging that although it developed sequentially, the latest move is not necessarily the better one. The possibility to re-insert moments within the process allows for an authored process, external from sequence and time and motivated through critique, observation, and the ability to remember or to forget and discard.

The map: The map is a field capturing the transformations taking place through time. It was generated through studying transformations of the structure of the fabric and the action of compression and expansion.

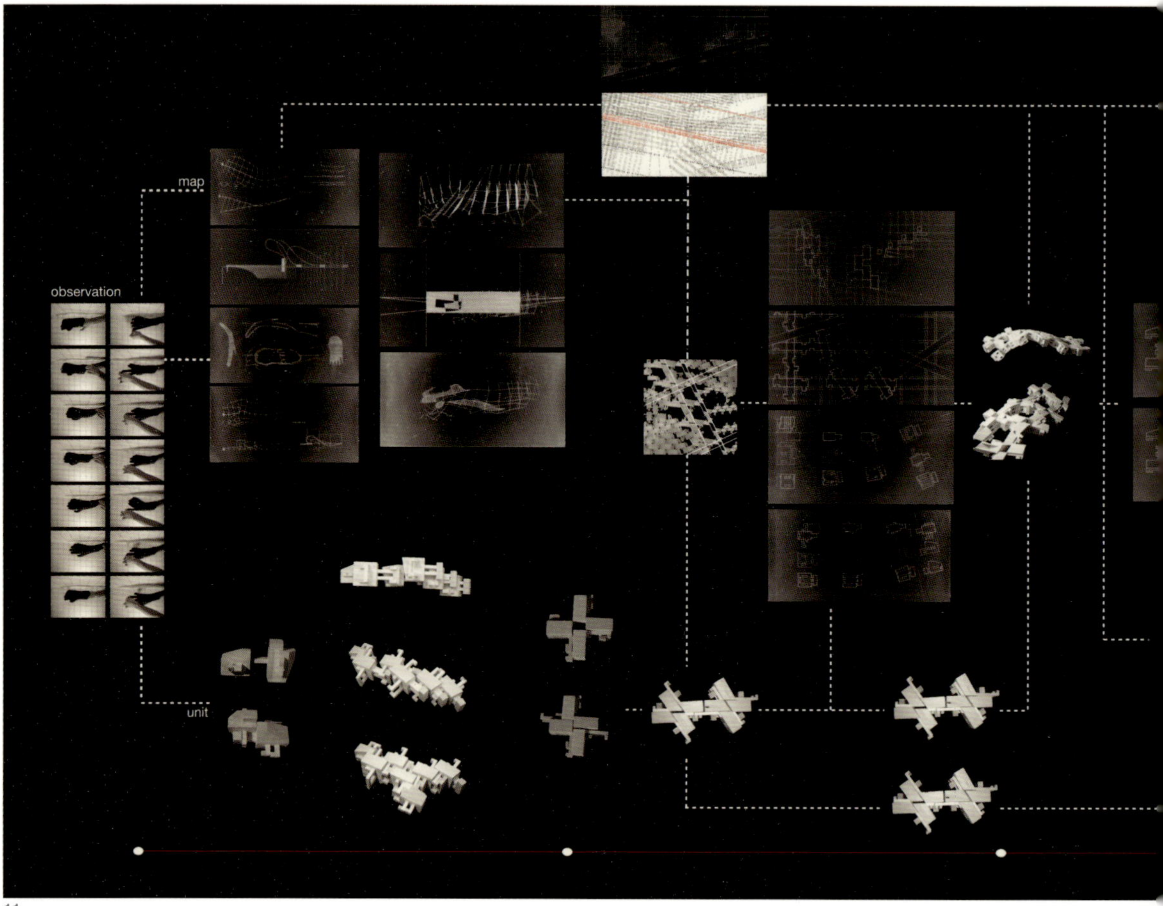

11

11. Patrick Collins (Arch 102 Spring '07) full semester process, diagramed by Yael Erel.

The design process is not an end in itself; it allows one to clarify an idea (or set of ideas) within the discipline of architecture. This idea is not pre-existing but it unfolds within the work as a thought being thought through making. Since architecture requires the development of an idea, a rational process grounds these thoughts in a system (tectonic or other) and perhaps allows (together with the idea) for the establishment of a language.

Each moment within each project acts as an autonomous moment – itself articulating a precise set of conditions in the boundary of its site – the page. Once these ideas are articulated in matter they can be later re-examined. In all three full project process maps, which are built with the x axis representing time, we see drawings and models as individual moments that have the ability to shift and inform the process at a later date; not necessarily remaining fixed to their original chronological placement.

Bergson claims that memory admits to our consciousness only that which is useful for our lives.[3] The process, as I express it, operates in this manner – allowing the divine property of forgetting as well as a way to recall conditions and reassert them into a project. This re-shuffle in a project cannot be made without acknowledging the author as the driving force; not caught in the events unfolding – but articulating intent – through text, program, drawing and model.

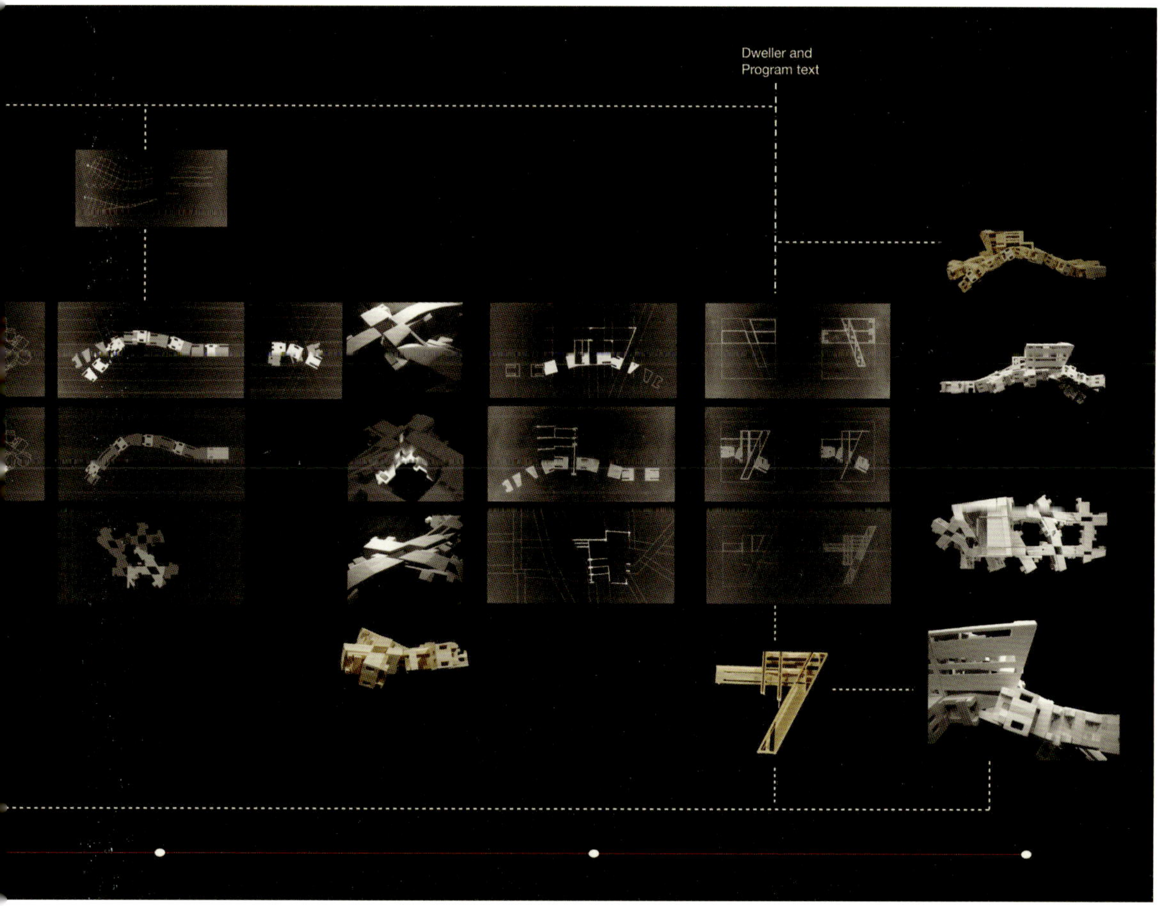

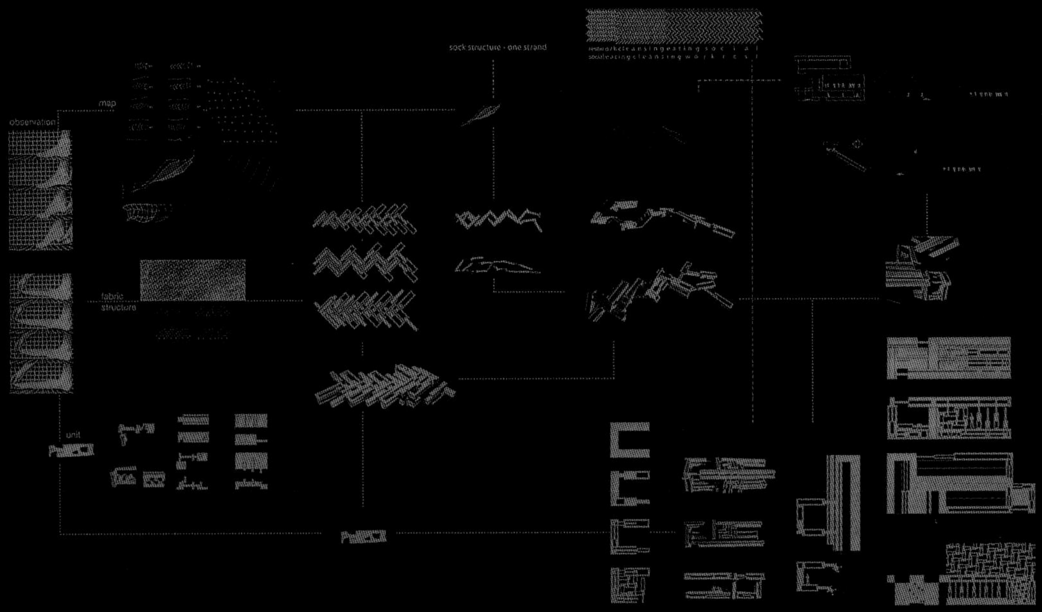

12

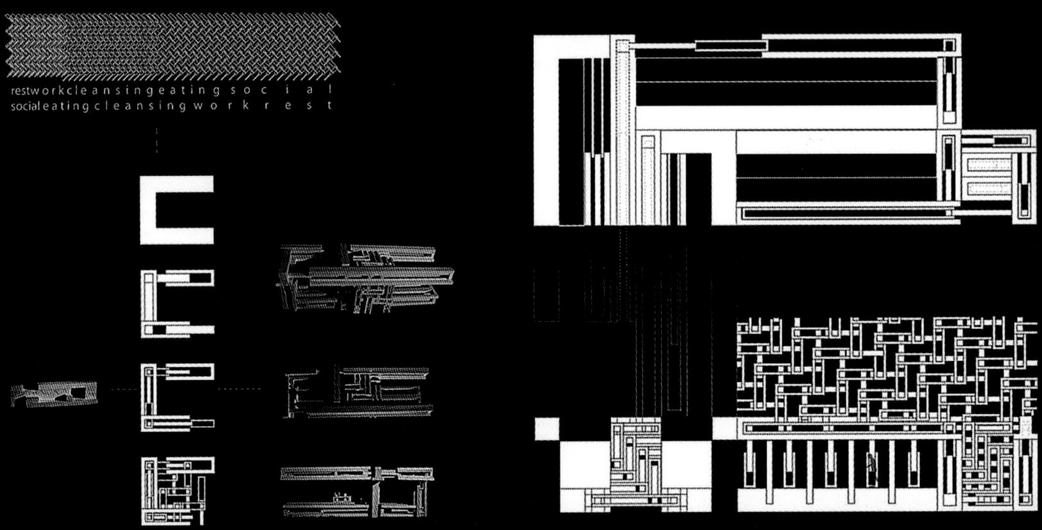

13

12. James Orielly (Arch 102 Spring '06) full semester process. **13.** James Orielly from module tectonic to programed architectural language.

There is a Bergsonian/Proustian idea on time and authorship, which Tarkovsky grasps in his description of a director's work.

"What is the essence of the director's work? We could define it as sculpting in time. Just as a sculptor takes a lump of marble, and, inwardly conscious of the features of his finished piece, removes everything that is not part of it – the film maker, from a "lump of time" made up an enormous, solid cluster of living facts, cuts off and discards whatever he does not need, leaving only what is to be an element of the finished film, what will prove to be integral to the cinematic image" [4]

In a similar manner we can see the process as a thought constructed out of edited moments of presence. This physicality of being is crucial for architectural education, which requires articulation of conditions in matter and thought, growing and ripening through making. Assuming the responsibility not of a god but of a poet – existing outside the time of the process, sculpting thought in matter. Using ideas as a measure, which exist outside of time and serve as a reference for whatever is created.

Notes:

1. "The apparent discontinuity of the psychical life is then due to our attention being fixed on it by a series of separate acts: actually there is only a gentle slope; but in following the broken line of our acts of attention, we think we perceive separate steps...But, as our attention has distinguished and separated them artificially, it is obliged next to reunite them by an artificial bond. It imagines, therefore, a formless ego, indifferent and unchangeable, on which it threads the psychic states which it has set up as independent entities." Henri Bergson, *Creative Evolution*, trans. Arthur Mitchell (New York: Henry Holt and Co., 1911), 2-4.
2. Le Corbusier, *Towards a New Architecture* (New York: Dover Publications, 1986), 153.
3. "In reality, the past is preserved by itself, automatically. In its entirety, probably, it follows us at every instant; all that we have felt, thought and willed from our earliest infancy is there, leaning over the present which is about to join it, pressing against the portals of consciousness that would fain leave it outside. The cerebral mechanism is arranged just so as to drive back into the unconscious almost the whole of this past, and to admit beyond the threshold only that which can cast light on the present situation or further the action now being prepared-in short, only that which can give useful work." Bergson, 5.
4. Andrey Tarkovsky, *Sculpting in Time: Reflections on the Cinema* (Austin: University of Texas Press, 2005), 63-64.

Panel Two

DISCUSSION

Moderated by Maria Berman
Panelists: Ed Keller · Jason Vollen · George Ranalli · Karl Chu · Yael Erel

MB: In tackling some of the many rich subjects that presenters addressed today such as the post human, and Ed, your phrase Speaking With the Alien, how do we address that in transmitting information to a new generation of architects who will or will not take us in that direction? Do we not make our own futures that way?

EK: One issue that Karl brought up when he said he was interested in architecture as a form of thought is crucial because essentially that sidesteps a whole series of problems such as stylistic debate and local questions of technical mastery and pushes it toward a broader question like what would it mean to actually think, and if we wanted to draw a disciplinary line around ourselves and say 'we are architects' and attempt to define that then, that says we have to think through the discipline what it means to think. And that's also what Yael was talking about in her presentation and it seems to me that that's really crucial. I hope everyone understood that my talk was deliberately tongue and cheek and joking and that's why I was fortunate that I remembered that Cortázar quote at the beginning because that's a quote which is simultaneously extremely ironic yet also completely committed to a belief in beauty and pleasure and reality. Reality itself is something that he investigates the mystery of and believes in. Also for me speaking to the alien is something that invokes the question of dialogue not only with the student obviously but with self and in that sense it absolutely is self critical as you just brought up Maria where we are simultaneously teaching but also building up a future with people for ourselves. It doesn't work unless it becomes a form of thought that can somehow bootstrap and I guess that for me was the issue of the ineffable coming back in right there. The ineffable as Brad was setting it up was something from the outside and it may be completely impossible to define what the outside is; it may be beyond speech, we may have to pass over it in silence, right, but nonetheless we can intuit or through experimentation discover that there is some kind of outside so it seems to me that a form of thought immediately always has to address that unknown or potentially unknown or un-transmittable message and it always attempts to negotiate with it and if it becomes a kind of pedagogical exercise where you convey a simple message 'oh, there's something outside and you have to pay attention' then it really misses the deeper implications of what it means to wrestle with the un-thought or unknown ourselves. Pedagogically speaking I had a long conversation with my seminar students a week ago because we were talking about violence in teaching, actually, and I said that there are a lot of strategies that we use when we are doing things like teaching seminars to destabilize the inherent violence in teaching but there's also a kind of limit to which you reach whereby if you go beyond it you radically destabilize the pedagogical structure in general itself. I am reminded of the debates that Badiou had with Deleuze over the years which he writes about in his book on Deleuze and he never really for example sat down and had dinner with Deleuze. Even though he agitated against his classes, he disrupted them and wrote screeds against him ultimately he formed a kind of begrudging friendship with him. So I think it's crucial to actually talk in a critical and transparent way about what it means to reach a limit of pedagogy but there is also this paradoxical trick up the sleeve that has to be kept and when I say that I don't just mean that I, as a teacher have to keep a trick up my sleeve for my students but that all of us have to keep a trick or two up our sleeves in practice and in thought and on top of that we have to keep a trick up our sleeves against ourselves so that we can constantly be vigilant against the patterns that emerge in ourselves.

YE: Computation is here and it's not going to go anywhere even if there is a certain amount of resistance to full immersion. For me its really interesting to see the simultaneous scales in which we can actually see are the original values and that was what was debated earlier today, what are the original values that are still totally valid and essential to be taught and what are the new things we could get out of our fabulous new tools that we have in our tool box now. I fear the notion that students being taught now are different from students being taught twenty years ago because I think there are essential qualities to an architect or to an architectural education in relation to thought and construction that are worthwhile.

JV: In the Arizona desert temperatures routinely reach 120 degrees at ground level and the brain begins to cook at 112. We teach our students this topological question where computation isn't a thing it's lots of different things and this topological issue is between the phenomena and the surface. If one begins to manipulate the surface one can adjust the phenomena on the other side. One can make it cooler, one can make it less expensive and one can do that using computational methods that are efficient. So it's not the thing, it's the space between the phenomena and the thing, this infinitely thin plane that becomes articulated and that's what we are trying to get them to think about, that computation is adjusting that plane for a purpose and that program is not the larger program it's the smaller one like adjusting the surface temperature by 20 degrees.

KC: In response to your question, the first thing to do as Agamben said is put the anthropological machine to a halt. And in doing that we stand a chance of having a symbiotic correspondence with things that exist outside of us; so we don't have an ontological separation between us and them. And the second thing is the idea of distributed consciousness as Katherine mentioned earlier and the model, which is just a metaphorical model, is the jungle. So that there is no single species that dominates the jungle. It's an ecological dynamic that achieves balance within itself. Here I am talking about the machine jungle which is in correspondence with the natural jungle. There's a diversity of species both man-made and artificial and perhaps we can envision new kinds of architecture maybe perhaps growing architecture and so forth so not just projecting our own aesthetic or our own philosophy or concepts about reality and then we see what happens in that space; it's a different kind of space.

MB: I think it starts addressing a little bit about the laboratory, Jason, that you were talking about; in a way letting something go without the expectation of knowing what you will wind up with. I have a question about sustainability and in relation to the previous panel, the un-built or virtual architecture as a way to achieve sustainability in a new way; is that something we can polemicize in a direction not of the real or tectonic environment but from another perspective?

KC: First of all, the concept of sustainability has become a political concept, so I think we need to remove the politics and ideology because it's loaded and saturated with these terms such as human rights, ecology and so forth. Nature is such that when we try and tamper with it even to balance things out it doesn't naturally mean that it will have the same effect we are looking for. Minute changes in initial conditions can have drastic outcomes and differences and so we don't even control we just navigate and bit by bit we just operate within the context so that we don't completely disrupt and impose the will of man or even the will to power of Nietzsche. Right now there is too much ideology…this green movement…really just ideology and nothing more; for the benefit of humans.

JV: Although they are politicized they are physical realities which is no less computational than virtual it just gives a resistance that one can begin to articulate a form…green washing is a new fancy term to devalue the green and so forth and I become concerned when the largest industry in the United States is at stake and not because of big corporations because of all the people it feeds so if it entails work in the very traditional sense that's sustainable also because it helps people keep their homes. If that disappears for example, now there's a significant paradigm shift. If we do away with those things then truly the anthropologic has disappeared. That's a place I'd actually fear.

EK: In that case it ends up being a question of defining what's worth saving. And it addresses a point made in the morning session made vis a vis risk management that David brought up which was interesting because it implied that the formation of a company or a corporation would understand that through a collectivity risk could be distributed and made manageable and if you take that idea you could probably get some pretty justifiable technical solutions out of it and you can also get some really remarkably dangerous and damaging technical solutions out of it; companies that could do great ill and companies that could do great good. But it's really important to figure out exactly to what degree they're able to act in the world. So if you notice that a particular material is off-gassing EOCs you attempt to abate that; I'm reminded of that scene in *Fight Club* where Ed Norton's character tells this other passenger on the airplane that the formula that the company has is how many accidents they had and the cost of replacement, etc. and it ends up being this kind of balance point where the company is doing risk management and if the cost does not exceed the potential lawsuits then they don't do a recall. It's a great punch line. And in that sense I think everything is risk management. What we have to do is make a decision about what body we are attempting to preserve and the going beyond the anthropocentric that Karl was talking about is really important, and something that I have a great feeling for, which is again why I brought up the issue of the alien, not to say that the alien is something outside ourselves but the alien is a useful term to reconceptualize what it means to be human and then to reconceptualize what bodies are worth preserving or worth having conversations with. I know that might sound abstract and science fiction, but in a very basic sense, whether an animal or bacterial life form is worth preserving. Let's say, a humble animal which ecologists will often mention like an earthworm which construes and composes an enormous amount of bio mass of the planet. Of course, we see nothing of it, and we accidentally cut it into pieces every time when we dig a hole in the ground, right? If that body is worth preserving, then what actions are we taking to preserve that body and how do we see the limits of that body. Those are arguments which, again, came up earlier because usually I think that the idea of simulation and modeling is something which says I have an idea what the boundaries of this body are and I am going to construct a tool surrounding it to experiment with those boundaries either directly or virtually. And virtually means you simulate the boundaries of those bodies and hopefully you're constructing a scenario in your workshop where you are trying to rethink what those boundaries are. But I think in practice, often, there is a preconceived model of what the boundary of a body is whether it's the population of deer, or the use of a particular kind of chemical, or how much energy is expended to make aluminum, etc. There is a preconceived notion of what the boundary of that body is. So the simulation will unfortunately often suffer the same kind of limitation that the pre-conceived notion suffers. And actually, the optimism in me says that we are going beyond that right now. We are going to experience the politicization of green, of ecology that Karl's talking about definitely and it is probably going to be a problem for another decade or two. But we are going to rapidly overtake that politicization, I think. Not to be an optimist for computational power, but I do think in the next two decades, we are going to overtake that and move beyond that very rapidly in terms of solutions.

JV: I think there is an important difference between the anthropocentric and the anthropologic. It is certainly possible to step out of the anthropocentric but I'm not sure if we're able to step out of the anthropologic. By definition it will be part of us; computation is something that we have given to it. We have created it and it doesn't exist without us as its own thing to give in its manner. I'm not surprised. I think that this is us we're talking about. We are bringing form and so forth. So whatever lens we view it from, it is from our lens. No matter what, that doesn't mean that it is not valuable to say, step out on the edge and to look back and see a more clear center. I would agree not to be anthropocentric but I would argue that to ignore the anthropologic is to ignore all of the conditions upon which computation is built.

KC: Well I think architecture cannot be a subject for anthropology as such, right. So the doors and windows of architecture are in scale in reference to our bodies as we know them. We have to loosen up to rethink the concept of man and humanity and to allow the possibility of nature establishing a complex dialogue from one to one, one to many, many to many, and many to one. So from that standpoint, you are just going to keep on affirming the anthropologic as a kind of absolute condition, which it is not.

JV: It's equal to instrumental. I mean, it seems like they're both together. I'm not sure if I understand that.

KC: Well there's no essence to anthropology. There is no transcendental essence to anthropology. But it is a provisional construct that we deploy for our own convenience as a disciplinary construct. So for you to claim that it implies that it has an essential dimension to it is a problem.

JV: They are both ways of describing the world.

KC: Yes, there are many ways of describing the world. Yes, yes.

JV: Computation is one, automata is another. There is Leibnizian Newtonian but there is also the anthropologic. But there is also culture and economics and there is language and all of those things that each one is. ... How to value one from the other I find difficult which is why I find the Royal Society to be the most influential because they don't want to argue about it. They look at this thing, and if something happens and then they all see it and say oh, we all saw this, we all agree on that. And that's it. It is actual and physical, not political or theoretical.

KC: Everything we develop such as language, measurement, knowledge, concepts, they are all a part of a construct. So from the yard stick measurement to the meter, or horse power it is always in the right position in relation to the human body. Architecture is among all disciplines the supreme discipline that gives expression to the destiny of man himself. In fact there is an ontology implicit in manifest destiny to determine measures by situating man in the middle of the universe.

YE: To some extent, I find it unavoidable that we are humans that construct through our intellect. We construct things and we expand our bodies through technology in order to survive. I think I will not survive in the jungle. There is no way I can survive without the extensions that technology allows even if that extension is a knife or clothes. There is a level that we have. We are human and we, as architects, create environments mainly for humans. It is unavoidable that we are in our own perception. It is like, you know, Bergson; my perception is the only perception that there is. I assume that you have a perception. But I am my only reference point to this reality, so I think it is unavoidable that we are human and we think human-centric.

KC: It is right, I mean it is at the origin of the biblical conception of architecture that Daedalus entrapped the Minotaur half man half animal in the labyrinth so that humanity could live happily ever after, right? And it's been living happily ever after until almost the twentieth century. So we have to radicalize the very concept of architecture itself so that it can open up, right? If Heidegger talked about the Open then the domain of architecture has to open.

MB: On that note, I think we should open it up to the audience. Let's take some questions.

Audience: I do appreciate this discussion very, very much, but I think Karl you are really extreme. And that it is possible to get somewhere by using computation. I appreciate Yael's understanding of pedagogy as a making that then uses the computer in some way to map these moments in time and then generate something else but it still goes back to perception. You seem to be very caught in this business that computation is natural. It's not! It is created by the human mind and it is the most anthropocentric thing. The most anthropocentric act you can make is precisely this assumption rather than believe your experience that you are indeed connected to the world in a way that can be articulated through language. So for me, your extreme position is very problematic.

Audience: I would have to agree with that. This anti-anthropocentric idea that computation is supposed to bring about has a contradiction at the origin. There is no possibility to have a science without having a nature that signifies all these assumptions in front of it. So it is the apex of all of that. That's why I had a strange feeling from the beginning. From this point, to insist on something that has a kind of 19th century smell right? The predicament of architecture today seems to be caught between an idea that tends to reject any kind of formalistic or stylistic discussion that goes into an intense development of building technology. Which is a position that has a history, a geneology, has a metaphysic and an ontology that dates in the contemporary tradition I believe in the 19th century but Alberto can contest that idea. On the other side, there is the other version that was developed in the 19th century also which is an antagonism to positivism which is the reaction to the fact that philosophy is being flattenned into science. Out of that, a figure like Feidler started to talk about the autonomy of the content of the work of art, not a work of art that is kind of romantic individual gesture. But a work of art as Alberto said which can express through the imagination a system or a type of knowledge that is not necessarily contradicting the conceptual one, but is in parallel but different from the conceptual. So now, this discussion about a science or form of science that is supposed to substitute everything in terms of liberating us from certain kinds of ideas has consequences given that architecture doesn't talk about its own nature and its own relation with this new condition. How to reiterate into a different form what is its original project which is not the labyrinth, it's rather, I don't know, Santo Spirito or the St. Peter of Bramante; that's the project that allows architecture. Our project is not the project of the Greeks or Romans. These are the inventions of the 19th century too by the way. And so it is a very strange thing thinking that using additional technology in teaching is not authoritarian, it is more authoritarian than anything else because it deals with the intention of developing concepts that can only be thought inside of that kind of discipline. It is very restrictive because it is unable to confront processes that come out of that kind of logic. So this is really an issue that I think should be discussed here rather than building up all these kinds of territory which architecture may disappear into. Architecture is a medium itself; It doesn't need media to be a medium. Because it is a language, because it is a message, because it is representation, and so on. And that's maybe a point to go on in terms of discussion. Maybe it's a little bit of polemic or provocation but this is a kind of 19th century discussion.

EK: I want to say something there. Because of the issue of computation that has come up. I think there are a number of different definitions of what computation is. I actually tried to head that one off at the pass when I said that computation is what happens when you feed energy or information into any given system and then you extract a result from that and meaning is what happens when you chain that result to another system. And see what happens between them which ties back into the laboratory issue that Jason brought up in a number of ways because it deals with a kind of testing model. But there are other notions of what computation means and other notions of what it means to work within a digital environment for example. And so, actually, probably it is beyond the scope and time limit that we have to go into it, but I would say it is really important to define precisely now. One of the things that is current in contemporary discourse especially that I see in my own student's work, is the belief that by scripting, by working directly working with code, they go beyond what they perceive to be the limits of something like the diagram. In fact some of my top students put together a proposition to do a lecture on the death of the diagram. There has been this enjoyable back and forth between us where I find myself in the unwilling position of the defender of the diagram which god knows is the last place I need to or want to be. I can just throw, you know, take your pick, anybody's text on the diagram at the discourse and it would be a much more eloquent defense of the diagram. But what I do want to defend is the precise application of concept. And in this case, I see a real vagueness and a lack of precision in the discussion of what things like diagrams, computation and scripting are. I would say that computation has been around a lot longer than the contemporary computer has as probably most intelligent people would know. Now with that said, which is a kind of general oil and water engagement, I would say that there is an incredible value to a specialized approach to computation and to using models that you develop within computation, and looking at the world and saying not what does this model mean in the world, but do I see a similarity in the behavior of this model in things in the world. Again, this is something that we have seen in geometry and proportion that has been around for hundreds and hundreds of years. So the legitimization of that model by simply finding an imitation of it in the world or a duplication of it in the world is going to run up against a limit immediately. But nevertheless, I would say this is the position that many people who work in a hard-core coding way in computation think. They think they found the place where the guy or the girl or the hermaphrodite or whoever it is, in the basement is throwing coal into the engine. And I mean THE engine that runs everything. This is the mechanic that's in the system, right? They think that by coding, they found you know, the backdoor to the basement where the coal gets thrown into the furnace, and they start tweaking the coal and tweaking the furnace and so forth. I have to say that I think that is a limited model but I think it's onto something. And I think Karl and I agree on this, that in the next few decades, these are the questions that are going to be utterly transformed and from a pedagogical point of view, it's actually a responsibility that we have, not to be technological evangelists or fetishists but just to say computationally speaking and Ray Kurzweil has a great book on this, *The Singularity is Near,* which sounds a little bit like a book of theology but it isn't at all. He's arguing that the technological thresholds that we're about to cross in the next few decades are utterly going to transform every question, for example, social re-construction: every need that people have could potentially be answered and this is an ongoing discourse that we have. Obviously we technically and economically have the resources globally right now to answer the needs that most people have and we don't choose to do it. Kurzweil's point is that essentially the technological threshold is going to become such a powerful lever that people like you and I, who can let's say have these discussions we'll actually be much less limited in terms of the kinds of change we can enact. This is the kind of technological threshold that Kurzweil is envisioning. And it isn't just that you will be able to do something like feed two million people in Bangladesh because you, one person, have the ability to do that. It goes beyond that, I mean, pervasive computation is something that will happen in the next 30 years. You won't need blood, you'll have synthetic blood. Blood will be manufactured and will work. And every one of those blood cells will actually be a node in a computational network that will connect through some kind of wireless connection to his blood to his blood to his blood. If you want to talk about distributed computation which came up in the first panel…

Audience: What does that tell me about architecture?

EK: I'm not even attempting to tell you about architecture. I'm telling you about a technological threshold which is going to reconfigure every platform that we exist on and reconfigure the way that we can store ourselves as humans. Then architecture inevitably has to respond to that.

Audience: Nothing distributes risk more than a strong sense of inevitability and I can't help but feel that there has to be a linkage between this incredible sense of inevitability that this is going to happen and the role that that plays, relative to capital and expanded consumption. Its simple math; to meet the requirements of expanding consumption, there needs to be a constant expanding sense of the direction; the navigation is inevitability. That is one of the tools. It is one of the inner logics of how capital drives itself. That's part of conquering the future is to have everybody feel that this is what's going to happen. That's one thing, But next to that, let's just remove the fact that it's possibly part of a narrative of progress that's actually keeping the mechanisms of capital well oiled. Let's say it's inevitable. I think Karl, when you said the most interesting part is not when computation emulates human desire not when it mimetically does what we think it should do but it when it find its own logic, its own ghost right? There's a ghost in the machine, let's see what it is. And you take that to an inevitable end and we're talking about this second life right? Silicone based life forms, etc. If we're having that discussion as architects, I'm not asking what do we do with that. I'm asking how do we begin to define an ethical dimension to that. And what I mean is what are the terms of the relationship, assuming it happens, of that autonomous genetic algorithm as its own breathing form, and us? And what does that mean relative to the ethical dimension of life which is, quite something. And I mean life when I say so.

KC: When you say life, you mean human life?

Audience: Yes, human life. I would say that ethics precedes epistemology, to say it in a philosophical sense. Ethics is something pre-figuring knowledge. It is deeply human; it is older maybe even than language. It certainly is a deep part of what we are. Does that have any chance of bridging this inevitable future assuming that it's not just a kind of sales pitch?

KC: The potential is enormous, it is really treacherous for life as we know it. The second we speak of ethics, we connect to human life actually, not so much to the concept of the bare life. The bare life of animals. So I think perhaps there is a need to develop an ethics based on the regarding of human life as such.

MB: Okay, let me have one more comment and then we can move on.

Audience: It is a provocative question, even for me I guess. Can't you say that we are already in the jungle anyway? There are two scales in which the sun disappears, right? At both meso-scale and quantum-scale symmetry disappears so there is no past and no future and that is one of the implications that you refer to in your diagrams of impossible futures. But when symmetry disappears, all of your "master-slave," "copy-object," "human-machine" relationships also disappear. So when the question is put out on such an inexact level, what happens then is that any model can be seen as having been grown at some micro-scale. Like the Villa Savoye could have been just a model grown in the jungle that we live in.

MB: Okay, thank you. We should leave it at that. The discussion will go into the next panel.

Panel Three

MATERIAL, NUMBER AND SPACE

Moderated by Ashley Schafer
Panelists: Evan Douglis · Ben Nicholson · Lebbeus Woods · José Oubrerie · Meejin Yoon & Eric Höweler

This panel addresses what can be quantified, translated and built; and what cannot. Can the ineffable be designed? Or is the very idea at odds with the design process? What is the relationship between systems of measure that mediate artistic expression and the materials within which they get embodied? How does the organizational logic or code of an architectural assembly relate to its capacity for expression? How can the mathematical or quantitative be leveraged to explore new dimensions of the experiential or qualitative?

DIGITAL ALCHEMY

Evan Douglis

The larger value of offering a conference at this moment in time on the Ineffable is to examine the status of new forms of cultural production in an era where speed, digital dexterity, and rapid commodification continue to obliterate meaning around the world. At a time where the spread of homogeneity threatens to produce infinite sameness under the guise of modernization, Digital Regionalism (a term which I have coined as a means of harnessing current digital practices in favor of reaffirming cultural heterogeneity) offers the ideal resistance capable of uniting seemingly opposing interests: the sustenance of tribal memory (an underlying human urge to reaffirm our anthropological imprint from one generation to the next) and our contemporary impulse to embrace novel modes of digital design and manufacturing production in favor of perpetuating the fiction of a perfect future.

This new project proposes that we consider our current digital technology as a benevolent tool capable in the hands of an enlightened author of using its vast computational engine to help us move closer to the infra-thin scale in architecture (genomically) as a means of reconfiguring the underlying logic of our base building units. At a time where the very building blocks of life are undergoing radical reassessment it is only fitting that the flesh of architecture assume a more robust emergent identity: where the co-existence of organic and inorganic features represent the next generation of architectural components. Just imagine a future where intelligent membranes like biological tweed will respond in real-time to changing environmental, spatial, programmatic, and cultural concerns. By merging ethics and aesthetics together at the moment of 'surface' the epic battle between memory and matter may finally be achieved.

Facing page: 1. Wall Pattern of Tomb Tower at Barda, Azerbaijan, in Square Kufic Script.

In response to the last panel discussion, it was curious to witness the condemnation of technology as a polarized set of perspectives on the increasingly destructive effects of digital technology for our discipline. Once again the unsubstantiated claim that 'all' technology operates as an unregulated force in the world to supplant 'us' as authors represents a serious lack of appreciation of the ingenuity of our contemporary machines as well as the primacy of humankind.

While I certainly sympathize with the underlying claim that without rigorous intentionality all forms of artistic production are subject to arbitrariness and whim, one should not assume that the mere existence of contemporary technology within one's work is synonymous with a lack of criticality. That's an irresponsible argument that diminishes the value of progress and the ethical responsibility we all share to embrace change. Unfortunately there appears to be an underlying moralist tone coming from some of

2

3

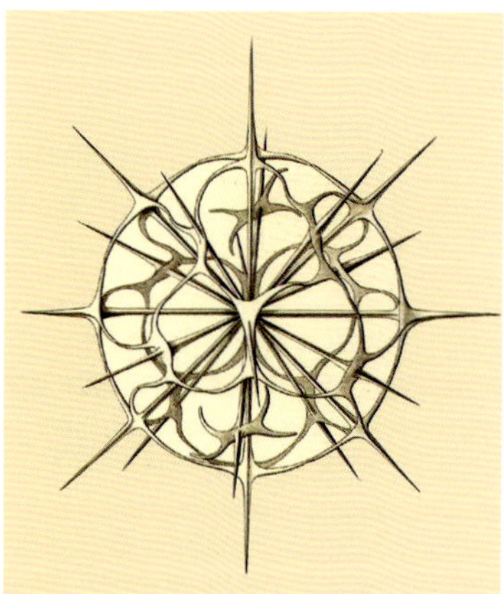

4

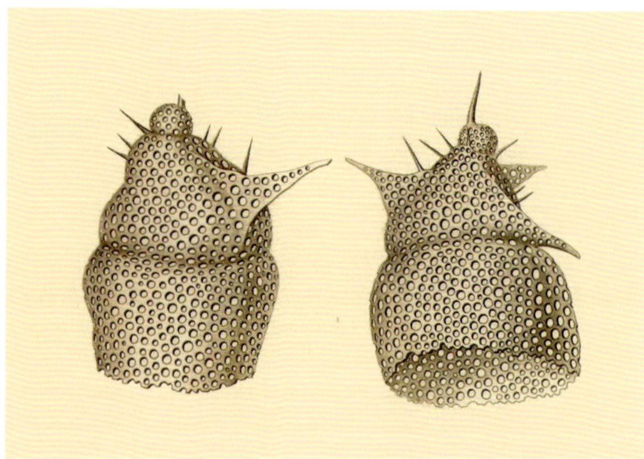

5

my colleagues today. It's somewhat reminiscent of a long legacy of diatribes from the past that voiced great discomfort concerning any paradigmatic shift that threatened to overturn the course of history.

Karl's claim for a future genomic universe represents one such paradigmatic shift that will fundamentally shatter one of the basic tenets in western philosophy: the origin of being. His argument which I fully accept as one of a number of "possible worlds" posits a shared empire in our future where genetic information would now become the genomic underpinning of all organic and inorganic life; including the machines we created as extensions of our sentient desire. It's a radical vision and potentially a dangerous one for all the theologians within the room but that doesn't diminish the fact that there is a massive increase of computational power underlying our information age today that might be interpreted as a precursor of even greater things to come.

In the context of addressing some of these issues I'd like to begin by offering some precedent examples that will serve to shed light on the potential opportunities afforded with the 'play of surfaces' for our discipline today. Presented as a series of conceptual and performative ideograms they exemplify the complexity of issues that lie within a deceptively simple terrain.

Infra-thin Face Robots

I remember the first time I encountered this image. It was in a book showcasing contemporary work dedicated to the creation of future beings. I was captivated by the iconic and perversely ominous glow of this face robot. It immediately resonated with me that our current efforts to recreate life, as we know it requires a thoroughly obsessive focus on the epidermal behavior of our skin. Although it's far more complex then just working out the material science of flesh. It also includes an unspoken mandate that our double needs to acquire an approximation of our physiognomic proportions so that the final illusion of aliveness can be sustained. In other words, the underlying math that needs to be derived here has to simultaneously accommodate both the engineering and scientific intelligence necessary to engender animate movement as well as produce an acceptable iconographic resemblance of life. The conflation of these apparently dissimilar interests embedded in a single surface is a compelling new model for architecture today.

6

2. Albrecht Dürer. **Left:** *Fifth Knot, with a white shield with six points in the center, c.* 1506. **Center:** *Fourth Knot, 7 circular groups of knots with black centers, c.* 1506. **Right:** *Sixth Knot, 7 small systems of knots with black centers, c.* 1506. **3.** Detail of a Muqarna in Imam Mosque, Isfahan. **4-5.** Ernst Haeckel. **4.** Skeleton of Dorataspis bipennis, unicellular marine microbes. **5.** Skeletons of Dictyoceras virchowii, unicellular marine microbes. **6.** Felice Frankel, *Ferrofluid.*

Finely Tuned Micro-systems

It's interesting how the simple change of scale reveals an entirely new universe of relations. These microscopic images from the book *Art Forms in Nature* by 19th century biologist and artist Ernst Haeckel captivate the remarkable structural clarity innate to the tiny undersea organism called radiolarian (Figs.4,5). It serves as a compelling reminder that within a space of invisibility lie the most remarkable organizational systems often unobtainable to the human eye.

Excitable Matter

To be in possession of two seemingly competing desires is often interpreted as a burden, an impossible quandary or at best an endless battle for control. In the case of the man-made material *ferrofluid*, exposure to a magnetic field has an immediate transformational effect on the liquid where the polarization causes an unexpected upheaval of energy resulting in the creation of excitable matter (Fig. 6). Hidden within the interiority of this seemingly innocent material is a strange silent storm waiting to be unleashed. Recalling the wonderment of alchemy, the new materials of our time display the most extreme effects in defiance of what we assumed to be the laws of nature.

7

Infinity Nets

I have always been attracted to paradoxical models. The idea that a system contains its own inverted logic seems strangely compelling to me as a way to approach the study of architecture (Figs. 10-11). It's as though the perpetual chase to solve the riddle contains an even more compelling truth about the power of imagination. M.C. Escher is one such individual that spent a lifetime devising mathematical puzzles that sought to test the limits of endless difference through the recursive iteration of a single unit (Figs. 8-9). Masked behind his demure reputation, as a decorative artist was an obsessively dedicated amateur mathematician who found enormous fascination in the underlying principles regarding tessellated systems. Through a thorough appreciation and study of symmetry groups, crystallography, and topology he obtained the rigorous foundation of thought necessary to create his impossible objects and perpetuate the illusion of infinite growth.

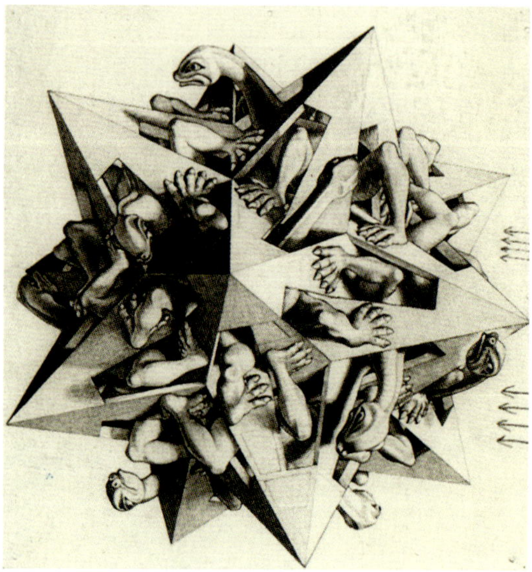

8

Topological Memory Machines

Throughout the history of the decorative arts one finds an inspired legacy of ornament that combines pure pattern and aesthetic appliqué alongside a world of calligraphic inscription (Fig. 2). Seeking to move between aesthetic assemblies and projected meaning through written language, a curious combination of seemingly unrelated cultural systems are found coexisting on a single surface. Like some weird anamorphic braille in possession of two completely independent 'readings', ornaments from past civilizations contain invaluable lessons for contemporary architecture concerning the acquisition and release of memory (Fig. 1).

Whirling Dervishes in the Voice of Matter

Imagine a time where buildings functioned like colossal books set erect all over the world as monuments. Each surface decorated with countless narratives describing in the greatest detail the most enigmatic stories of their time. Now move closer to the surface of a muqarnas nested within the ceiling vaults of a 14th C. Persian mosque (Fig. 3). Here we find an example of scalar redundancy, hyper-packing and three dimensional exuberance rarely seen in the history of architecture. It's as though in the quest for spiritual illumination, the flourishing of math within matter is synonymous with a kaleidoscopic frenzy.

Retinal Skins

If in the 'limits' of all things lies the possibility to remake the world, then let's reflect for a moment upon the pathology of sight as a convenient bridge to a whole series of imaginary spaces. Consider the impressive legacies of trompe l'oeil, anamorphosis and more recently op art where the inadequacies of the eye contribute directly to the constructed logics underlying each illusion (Fig. 7). Deeply attuned to a variety of perceptual techniques (i.e. after-images, line interference, dazzle topology, and chromatic vibration) all of these works take on a kind of phenomenological trigger for the unassuming spectator.

7. Andrea Pozzo, *The Glorification of St. Ignatius*, ceiling fresco, 1691-99. S. Ignazio, Rome, Italy. **8-9.** M.C. Escher. **8.** *Gravity*, 1952. **9.** *Smaller and Smaller*, 1956. **10-11.** Tamás F. Farkas. **Top.** *Dimension Knot*. **Bottom.** *Space Labyrinth*.

9

10-11

12

13

Resurrected Flesh

Reconceptualizing the bridge between organic and inorganic systems as a transfer of essential genetic information is not an entirely new proposition in the history of the world if one considers the exhaustive legacy of ancient and contemporary alchemists in a variety of fields throughout time that sought through the transmutation of matter the creation of a parallel animistic universe. Conceived as an extension of our timeless desire to bring inanimate material to life this continuous chase for synthetic immortality has preoccupied our imagination for centuries.

Auto Braids / Auto Breeding

With the rise of interest surrounding emergent systems as the new organizational model for a planet undergoing constant change, the opportunities to develop a more robust bio-mimetic approach in architecture are becoming increasingly more attractive. The once exotic and ineffable metamorphosis of the chameleon octopus, the otherworldly bioluminescence of the sea cucumber and the strange gelatinous and reconfigurable anatomy of a comb jelly creature are no longer unobtainable effects underlying nature for the futurist at the turn of the century. The dazzling life of invertebrates is just one example of a complex system of behavior

14

innate to a family of living organisms that is currently being reassessed on a computational level in order to extract the base code inherent to these uniquely divine creatures. Auto Braids/Auto Breeding proposes biological mimesis as an alternative logic in the development of a new species of architectural membranes. Inspired by Jean Prouvé's commitment to the most advanced technology of his time and the legendary contributions he made to the development of modular systems, the exhibition design set out to reinterpret these conceptual directives from a new and contemporary perspective. Celebrating the current opportunities afforded by high-end 3-D modeling software and five-axis rapid prototyping milling, (Figs. 15,16) a series of interlocking modular elements were produced for assembly as an exhibition "display–scape". Intended to function as a curatorial game board, this new membrane and its matrix of landing sites serves to offer a range of recombinatory flexibility ideal for any collection continuously undergoing change (Figs. 17-19).

In addition, significant emphasis was placed on the development of topological surface effects capable of altering the experience of the spectator. In search of the underlying math inherent to produce an 'indeterminate' oscillating wave pattern, a single computational unit was selected as the primary building block necessary to promote the illusion of infinite growth. Conceived as a self-organizing system, the increasing aggregation and resequencing options afforded within this deceptively simple iterative process produces an extreme range of surface variation ideal for an architectural membrane situated in a new era of serial reproduction. A full circle is finally achieved with the arrival of Prouvé's artifacts, paying tribute to the timelessness of his work and the relevance of his ideas for a new generation.

The simultaneous pursuit of curatorial and topological "multiplicity" inherent in Auto Braids/Auto Breeding represents a much larger architectural aspiration beyond the limits of the gallery. It concerns the future development and application of 'biological mimesis' (Figs. 12-14) as a new paradigm for architectural production. As we enter through this new phase of morphogenetic and technological expansion we unleash a range of material and programmatic opportunity capable of altering the very destiny of architecture.

Helioscopes

In the dream of recombinant technology and biologically mimetic surfaces for the future of architecture, Heloscopes represents an alternative model of production seamlessly obedient to the machination of a modern strategy. Situated

15

16

12. Warp-knit, CorCap, bioimplantable device. **13.** CorCap cardiac support device. Manufactured by Acorn Cardiovascular Inc. U.S.A., designed 1998, manufactured 2004. Warp-knit PET polyester multifilament yarn. Diameter: 15.9cm. **14.** Bioimplantable device for reconstructive shoulder surgery. Designed by Prof. Simon Frostick and Dr. Alan McLeod, textile designed by Peter Butcher, developed by Ellis Developments, Ltd. **15.** 5-Axis CNC milling machine. **16.** View of primary modular unit milled out of foam.

17

18

19

somewhere between a search for topological indeterminacy and an oneiric vehicle of desire, this seemingly life-like fleet of media-scape stalactites represent an entirely synthetic ecology (Fig. 22). Offered as a single module or in multiples suspended across an aerial terrain, each of the helical tails contains a vision orifice through which an endless itinerary of fantasy settings is available to the consumer with a propensity for consumption (Fig. 21). Outfitted with the most recent advancements in membrane and information display technology this new wired flesh serves to highlight the endless algorithmic differences found in the indeterminacy of everyday life. (Fig. 20)

The most memorable architectural experiences often contain an element of surprise, a momentary escape, and possibly an erotic sensation on a subliminal level. In response, the excitable flesh of the Helioscope opens up momentarily to reveal an unexpected seedling of desire. Recessed within the membrane resides an LCD unit offering a continuous loop of video footage of the inside of current Japanese Love Hotels. Operating as a perpetual desiring machine, the Helioscope exploits the intended perversity of the subject as a cinematic device to increase the overall level of attraction.

Reptile

In appreciation of a legacy of Japanese mythology surrounding the sacredness and virtuosity of reptiles, the project proposed resurfacing the interior of the restaurant with a new animate skin capable of emoting a range of visceral and associative responses for the curious spectator. Applying a strategy of biological mimesis where the divine attributes of a natural system are reinterpreted within the performative logic and effects of its artificial counterpart, we set out to create a custom lightweight mass produced tile system that exhibited a range of emergent properties synonymous with this venerable creature.

17. Full view of Auto Braids assembly at gallery entry. **18.** Detail of telescopic hardware suspending Prouve furniture above display-scape membrane. **19.** Oblique view of vertical wall system.

"Just imagine a future where intelligent membranes like biological tweed will respond in real-time to changing environmental, spatial, programmatic, and cultural concerns. By merging ethics and aesthetics together at the moment of 'surface' the epic battle between memory and matter may finally be achieved."

20

21

22

20. Reflected ceiling plan showing repetitive aggregation of base unit. **21.** Helioscope with viewer. **22.** View of excitable Helioscopes enroute to some unknown destination.

Facing page: 23. Detail of Flora_flex system with second growth accessory flange installed on interior ring.

Through the superimposition of two independent meshes (pyramidal vs. smooth) fluctuating at different frequencies within the animation we were able to achieve a series of compelling interference patterns. Through the use of controlled chance an extensive menu of surface effects emerged offering an increase of options for the discerning eye. The changing scale and rotation of the matrix of pyramids work to redirect the light and shadow in such a way that a greater depth of field is perceived (Fig. 28).

Developed as a unique modular unit installed throughout the perimeter of the room the changing animate surface seen from a variety of perspectival positions offers a kaleidoscope of cinematic effects dedicated to an agenda of theatrics and visual play. (Fig. 29-30)

Flora_flex

Given our predisposition for even greater control today over an ever-increasingly complex universe, the next generation of animate assemblies within the discipline of architecture will inevitably be comprised of a more complex amalgamation of scripted equations capable of reenacting the most spectacular effects. Harnessing the unlimited power of programming as a vast hereditary engine for emergent design we will see an unimaginable increase in surface and behavioral variation on a level of intricacy and control unparalleled in the history of digital design.

In appreciation of architecture's current shift towards the 'play of surface', our Flora_flex prefab modular building system set out to test parametric design as a generative source for producing infinite variation (Fig. 23). Combining an interest in botany, skeleton morphology, topology, optical effects and emergent growth patterns, the Flora_flex system represents a new era of computationally derived membranes that maximize the use of 'intricacy' as a contemporary design strategy to increase desirability and use.

Currently offered as a prototype screen and assembled as an interchangeable alphabet of load bearing units, the array of surface relief, changing transparency, and recombinatory options now available to the consumer all subscribe to a promising future in architecture of increased flexibility and control. Slip cast, injection molded or 3-D print out of a variety of space age materials this new prefabricated wall system aims to additionally utilize the most recent advancements in material science to finally bring architecture to life.

el_Tower

Proposed as a colossal open-air rooftop retail and hotel complex, the el_Tower represents a new urban typology for the 21st century (Figs. 24, 25). Utilizing a single surface as a branded wrapper, the structural dia-grid transforms from a horizontal trellis to a vertical bris-soleil along a distance of three city blocks. Enclosing over 10.1 million cubic feet, the new complex envisions the future skyscraper as an (L) system in which future urban expansion is now multi-directional: as it increases simultaneously horizontally and vertically. The accessorized surface within the el_Tower dia-grid represents an invaluable opportunity to test our commitment to a new synthetic biology as it moves between aesthetics and ethics in its dual role as a new urban typology and micro-climatic membrane.

Given our predisposition for even greater control today over an increasingly complex universe, the next generation of animate assemblies within the discipline of architecture will inevitably be comprised of a more complex amalgamation of scripted equations capable of reenacting the most spectacular effects (Figs. 26,27). Harnessing the unlimited power of programming as a vast hereditary engine for emergent design we will see an unimaginable increase in surface and behavioral variation on a level of intricacy and control unparalleled in the history of digital design.

24

25

24. Interior view of el_Tower looking out through oculus. **25.** View along main interior street with dia-grid open air membrane above.

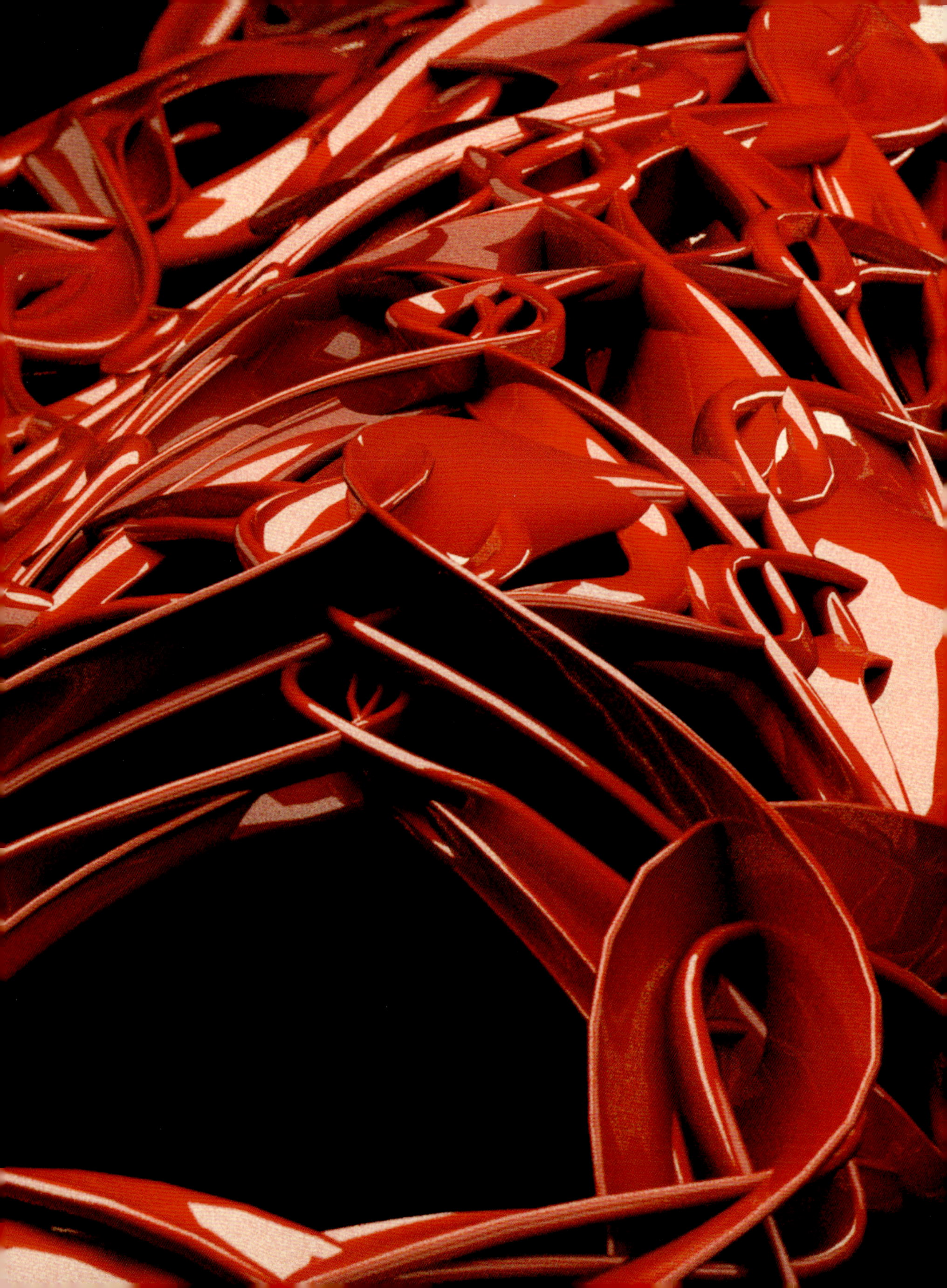

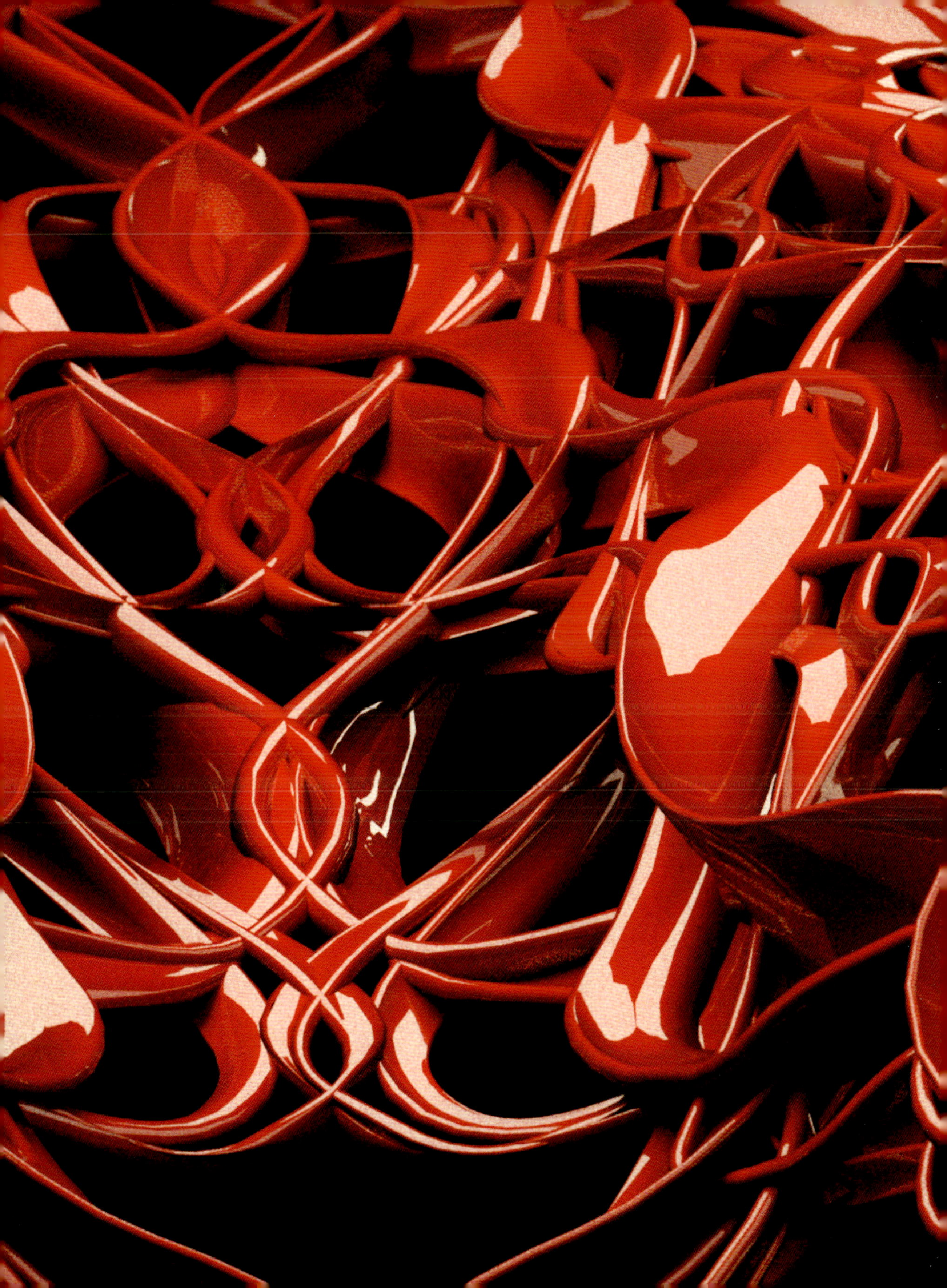

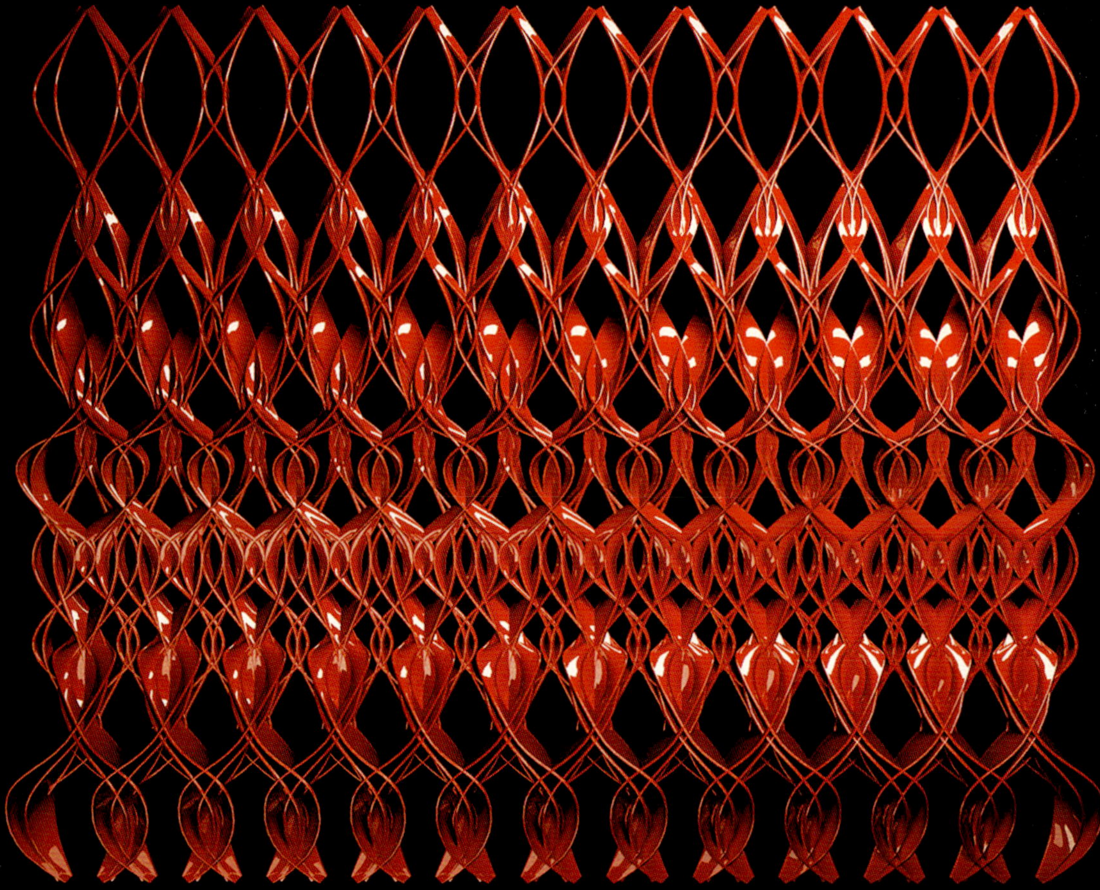

27

27. Detail of el_Tower braided membrane study derived from scripted library. **28.** Detail of custom modular tile showing surface variation. **29.** Exterior view of storefront elevation. **30.** Interior view of restaurant from sushi chef's station.

28

29

30

HIDDEN RESIDUES BENEATH THE SURFACE

Ben Nicholson

From A to B, The Long Way Around

Brad Horn booked me on a Delta Airline flight from Chicago, which triggered an image from a silly email circular concerning weird technological disasters involving aircraft (Fig. 2). The image of a Delta cargo box being sucked into a jet nacelle is at once hilariously funny, but then again it prompts the space of measurement used to rationalize hyper - technology, in which the previously measured is immeasurable due to the unforeseen.

Three years ago I left city life and now live down in rural Indiana at the confluence of the Ohio and Wabash rivers. Living on a bird flyway changes one's notion of quantity: millions of red wing blackbirds, tens of thousands of snow geese and clouds of gnats under iodine lamp posts show mind numbing quantity. Symbolic graveyards of hundreds of makeshift crosses laid out in front of big box churches to represent the daily tally of aborted babies, give one pause for thought. Number. Measurement. It's hard to know what it is.

Being in the countryside prompts a real desire to shuffle your feet in mud & dust, just for the sheer pleasure of it (Fig. 3). Raw dirt offers a brief opportunity to experience the notion of *tabla rasa*. Even though every teaspoon of earth holds thousands of dormant seeds waiting for the right conditions to sprout, earth can be laid bare with constant hoeing to make a surface devoid of life. The desire to fill space, *Horror Vacui*, is one of mankind's insatiable needs: so what would it be to reenact that elemental desire in the ground? By carving out a 40 foot diameter circle and removing every sign of life by hand, the resulting surface takes on an eerie winter-like quality of nothingness. By making a measured shuffle of footsteps, a winding walk spiraling out from a center, in which one foot is placed in league with the instep of the other, measurement is palpable. You can feel the thousands of individual footsteps that form the whole; the whole is measurable through its parts. The dance floor of Ariadne comes to mind, made by Daedalus, the first architect.

Furthermore he wrought a grassy floor, like that which Daedalus once made in Knossos for lovely Ariadne. Here was a dance of youths and maidens, all with their hands on one another's wrists; sometimes they would dance deftly in a ring with merry twinkling feet, as it were a potter sitting at his work, and sometimes they would go all in line with one another.

Homer, *Iliad 18. 750BCE*

Another quintessential Midwestern form of measure is found in the giant piles of corn accumulated by the combines of agribusiness. The circular disks of kernels are

Facing page: 1. Betwixt Two Lines. Clock-wise and counterclock-wise lines intersect to mark the beginning of a measured path.

2

3

4

2. Delta Cargo box sucked into jet engine nacelle. **3.** Tabula rasa of dirt. Two thousand footsteps carve out a labyrinth, a proto-historical 1:1 scale architectural plan. **4.** The Monad: billions of familiar objects (kernels of popcorn) that become one thing.

proof positive of the notion of *Monad*, where *"In the One is the Many"*. By slowly unpacking thought and musing, it is possible to look at a conical mountain of corn and imagine the billions of dispositions of straight lines that join the individual kernels. The whole world is in the pile, and by linking one kernel to the next, an incremental journey is made to the center, and each step marks measurement. The hubris of incremental measurement, the walk from A to B, is that when we get to B we think that something might be found. We look for Paradise but instead find Paradise Lost. In the desire to Go, Get It! we find that our fingers have been burned. For me, this is the sensation of measurement; it is the moment when your fingers are burned.

Measurement exists in the most unlikely places. To my Indiana friends I am fondly known as "the good ol' city boy": at the semi-annual festival of machine guns held at Knob Creek Kentucky, I rented an Uzi sub-machine gun and ran through a box of shells on full automatic. When I looked at a photo of the firing, I realized that there were four shells captured in the air and the image was shot at 125th of a second, meaning that the rate of fire was 600 rd./min, with one in the chamber; exactly the factory specs! I thought to myself, if there has ever been an ineffable moment then this is it: in the rattle of the machine gun there is the sense of measured time, doled out in bullets. The Knob Creek Machine Gun Shoot is something every American ought to see. Where else can you can rent a machine-gun and blow away a Porsche? It's an incredible experience. A sign reads "Machine gun rental, See Bill." This is not Quentin Tarantino's *KillBill*, it's the regular American *Joe-Six-Pack* kind of Bill.

Measurement really interests me. I want to know what is the measured space between two points adjacent to each other. Some may be comforted by the logic of mathematical series such as the Fibonacci, Golden, Silver and Bronze Means, but when placed on the ground they all need a fixed unit before they can be set in motion. Of course they all exist in the mind, but when they hit the ground there has to be some kind of span, you cannot get away from that. It is the measure of that span I'm looking for. Take two rows of fava beans for example. In one row the beans are chosen to be approximately equal in size from the middle range, and the second row is composed of random sized beans, each of which is a little bit different. Put together they exemplify two forms of measurement, but dare I suggest that there is an ineffable quality of not knowing exactly what the varied dimensions are between the beans?

Beans are a staple crop the world over and it should come as no surprise that a strong mythology surrounds them (Fig. 5). A read through Roman writers commenting on Pythagoras reveal sexual innuendo vis a vis beans. Why would Pythagoras, the great geometer, be talking about beans and sex? If a bean is examined closely it reveals an aura of androgyny: its physiognomy provides for every sexual persuasion, no one is left out (Fig. 6). Measurement is not only about the length of a finger; it is a whole cultural equation in which love is an essential part.

Fava beans gestate in a pod lined with soft protective hairs. Inside each pod lies a definitive number of beans, generally between one and seven (Fig. 7). For the mystic mathematician, the fact that number sets would be created from singular objects aping a fusion of male and female genitals would make perfect sense: number could *only* be a result of the sexual act.

Following pages: 5. Sexuality and number in beans. The sexual act creates pure number, as exemplified by the metaphorical physiognomy of the lowly bean. **6-7.** Fava bean pods. Set of beans in pods exemplify the birth of number**.** The fava bean: an androgynous whole. The explicit depiction of male and female genitalia lay it open to mythological associations.

"Geometry is a mediator between form and matter. It can divide things and it provides proportion; it is something to be discovered and actually resides beneath the skin of the earth; it is not something you can really invent."

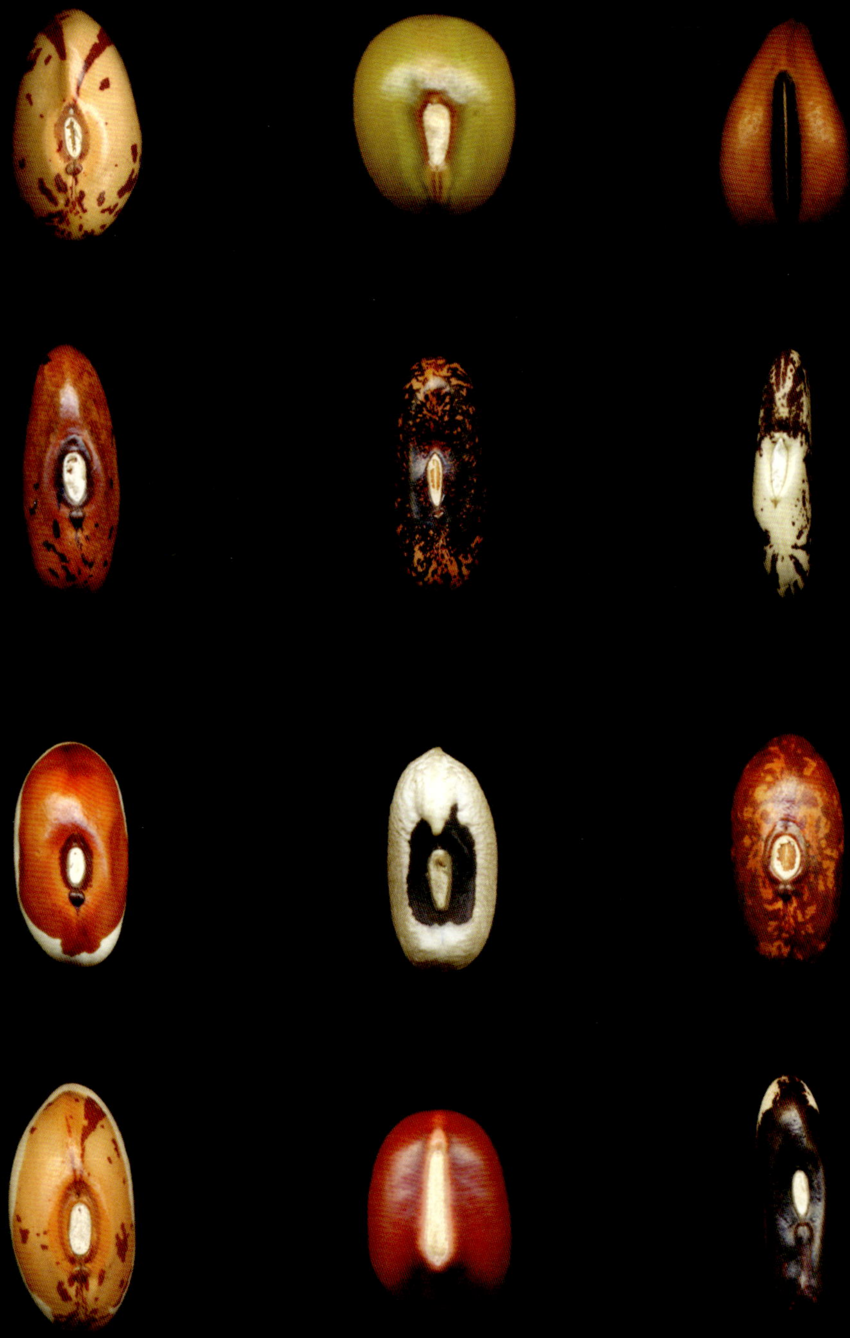

5

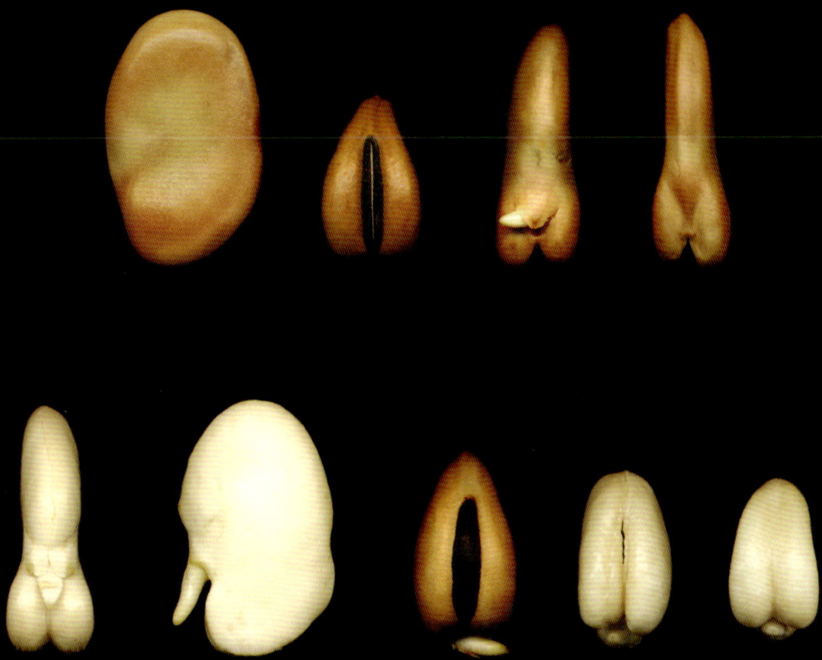

6

7

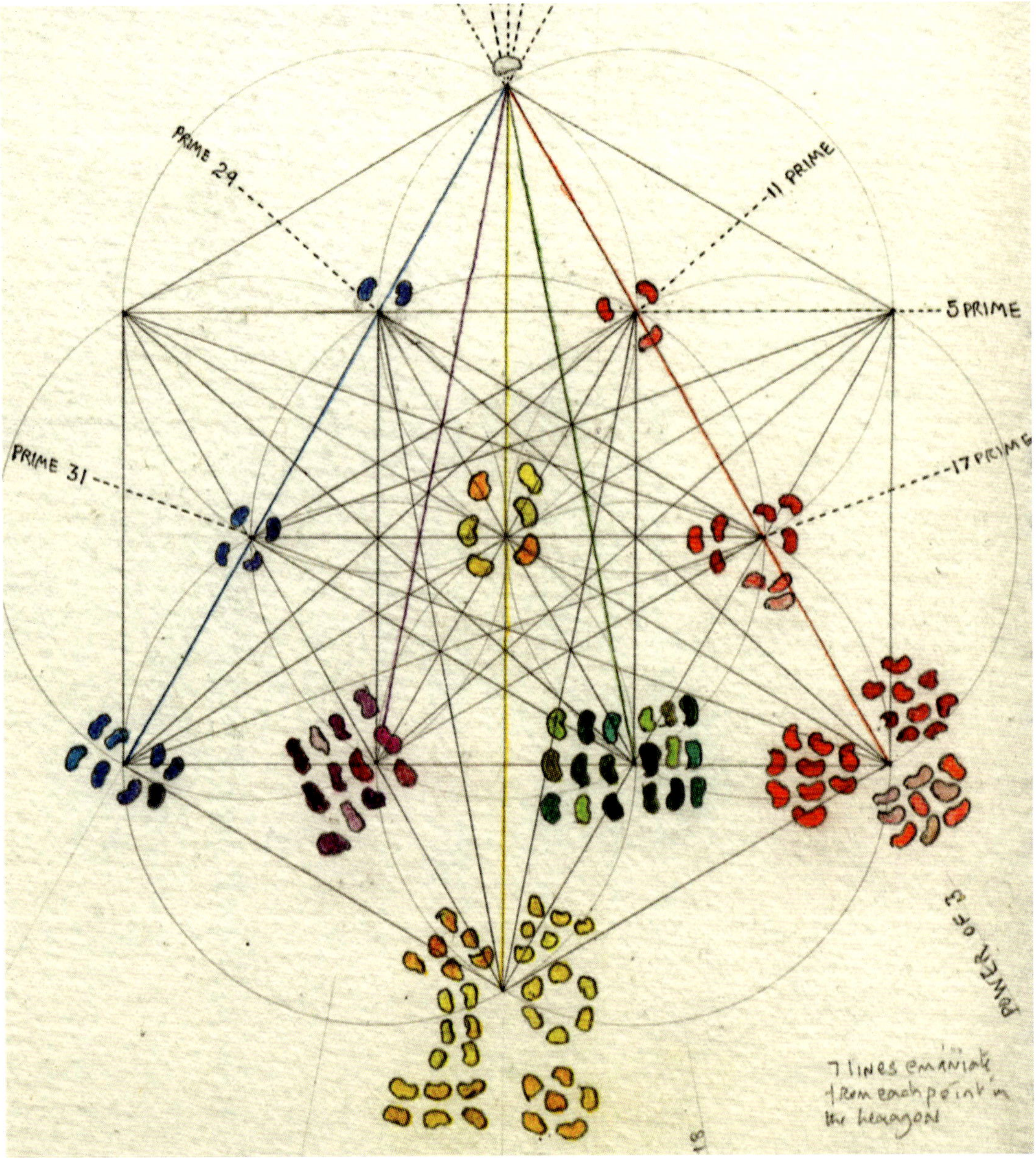

8

Plato, another great commentator on the qualities of number, uses the tectractys to demonstrate the *mixture*, within which resides proportion (Fig. 8). Proportion and measurement are not the same thing: proportion divides up a measured whole but there needs to be something material to measure, for proportion to be applied. Measurement is the one thing that the gods left off of their honey do list before they handed over the Earth to the humans. Prometheus stole fire, but how did humans obtain the length of units for measurement?

When performing geometric constructions on the beach with a couple of sticks and string, there comes a moment

9

10

8. The Tectractys. The Tectractys was Plato's method of exemplifying the arithmetic, geometric and harmonic means. Beans demonstrate the lively relationships within and between numbers. **9.** Drawing on the beach. The fixed length of a circle's radius enables a cornucopia of geometric constructions. Without that measured length, nothing happens. **10.** Creating an ellipse. A circle knocked out of kilter forms an ellipse, making ineffable gradations of form that are righted by anamorphic viewing.

TILE FAMILIES ROOT; TRUCHET; (LUNDA) KUFIC; VERSI; MEZIN. TILES+CUBE NETS.

11

12

13

when the length of the string is unambiguously defined. Measurement comes to be in the generating line, and within the generating line spills a wonderment of differentiation (Figs. 9,10).

Earlier, Evan Douglis showed a tiling system, the Kufic tiles, made out of two different tiles, one positive and the other negative, one black and the other white (Fig. 11). The modules composing any tiling system provide the units within a measured whole, but what is the nature of that whole, the thing to be measured? To reduce the world to blackness and whiteness is the Holy Grail for the geometer, emotionally it is draining to work on, but thrilling nevertheless. Pairs of Kufic tiles can create a multitude of wholesome designs, but they can also be used to make fields of swastikas, a taboo form in Euro-American design. (Fig. 13) A practice of tiling inevitably reveals the four limb spiral, aka swastika: it is the quintessential form describing the body, for both have four articulated limbs linked to a torso. On one hand measurement appears to mete out inches on a rule, but on the other hand it encompasses the richness of cultural wherewithal. Measurement is tricky business.

There are moments before measure. To exemplify this, I have created a taxonomy of over two hundred labyrinths drawn on paper. If a labyrinth is understood to be a winding path of a fixed length that eventually leads you to the center, surely a moment exists beforehand where all is an unfathomable abyss, without measurement. That abyss, here a disc of yellow ochre, is populated by rings of movement, which flex their being and test the inside and outside edges before being geometricized. (Fig. 14)

At the other end of the spectrum is the Chartres labyrinth, designed as a liturgy to reenact the journey to deliver Christ from Hell on Easter Day (Fig. 15). For the rest of the year pilgrims would shuffle 2000 steps, reenacting the tortuous journey to Jerusalem, feeling the measure of their body through their knees.

I am interested in manifesting space without spending money. What it is like to make architecture without any expenditure whatsoever, without any kind of material signification?

11. A family of tile systems. The Kufic Tile belongs to a family of modules that can create a multitude of both geometric and figurative designs. **12.** The 'Kufic tile' in three dimensions: a powerful module that can perform much with a simple geometry. **13.** A wall of four limbed spirals. Kufic Cubes, exhibited in the DAAP Building, University of Cincinnati, confront the taboo of the unmentionable swastika.

"The hubris of incremental measurement, the walk from A to B, is that when we get to B we think that something might be found. We look for Paradise but instead find Paradise Lost. In the desire to Go, Get It! we find that our fingers have been burned. For me, this is the sensation of measurement; it is the moment when your fingers are burned."

A prospective client heard that I designed labyrinths and wanted to spend big money to make one for his organization. I took him to a Chicago beach and began to trace a path from memory by walking in prepared sand. Once done, we looked at it and I said, "Here it is. Forget the marble and fancy hedges, just hire someone to rake out a bed of sand and teach others by leading them in a meandering walk." Naturally I did not get the job, but upon seeing what his own footprints could do in the sand he began to shed a tear.

Measure is something that you feel intuitively. I don't know how else to put it. In New Harmony, where I now live, I sometimes walk into the dew in front of the great three dimensional labyrinth: Richard Meier's *"New Harmony Athenaeum"*. When the walk is done I feel right, for something got measured within (Fig.16). A measured walk need not only be a labyrinth, it could also be an 80 mile walk through the rolling landscape of southern Indiana. A young man, on probation and out of work, wanted a job and so I asked him if he was willing to walk 80 miles for a week's wages. He replied, "Can I take my Pit Bull?" and off he went. His journey became a bar for him, against which other things could be measured (Fig.17).

Spending a few years thinking about the notion of measurement in the studio provides a code, a pattern, which you can take with you everywhere. I would like a practice with no building; I guess I've done that to date anyway, but to declare a practice of architecture without building would be something else entirely.

Geometry is the mediator between Form and Matter, terms used in the Catholic Church to differentiate between the Word and the Body. Geometry can divide things and

14

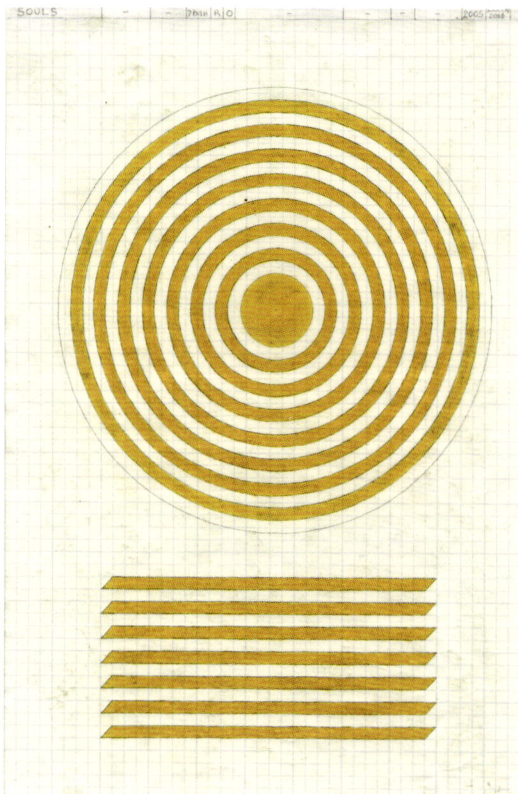

15

14-17. A family of tile systems. The Kufic Tile belongs to a family of modules that can create a multitude of both geometric and figurative designs.

provides proportion; it is something to be discovered and actually resides beneath the skin of the earth; it is not something you can invent. Measure, on the other hand, is something that humans are left alone to invent, collectively we have to figure this one out and find a good reliable measure, something that relates to the stuff we surround ourselves in.

The temple of Jerusalem had its Cubits and its Royal cubits, of slightly different length depending upon what was being measured. Leonardo's spread-eagle man had a pair of geometric centers: one upon the belly button and the other squared upon the penis. Nowhere is there a record of the measured distance between them, of what would constitute the measure of us all. For that we can visit Durer's copious drawings of every sort of human dimension, his wonderful sheets of faces and arms and limbs; he averaged them out to make a sort of proto-robotic perfect measured man, in turn morphing into the portraits of Adam and Eve, which was what he was aiming at. He conjectured a measure for God, in the image of Man, in the image of God.

Napoleon set new measures for time, distance and weight, with varying success. The ten day week only lasted a couple of years as the peasants saw through his ruse to get them to work nine days before taking Sunday off. So again, some of these constructs hit a place where they won't work. Apropos of what Alberto Perez Gomez has been describing, there are qualities that you can't put any system to; humans just won't work nine days straight without a break. Napoleon gave birth to the kilometer, 10,000 of them spaced about a quarter circle of the planet and 40,000 of them in a full circumnavigation. Taking a tape measure to the round belly of Mother Earth is reasonable enough, but why 40,000

16

17

FOUR LABYRINTH FAMILIES: BATTLEMENT, STAGGER BATTLEMENT, MEANDER, SWASTIKA.

16

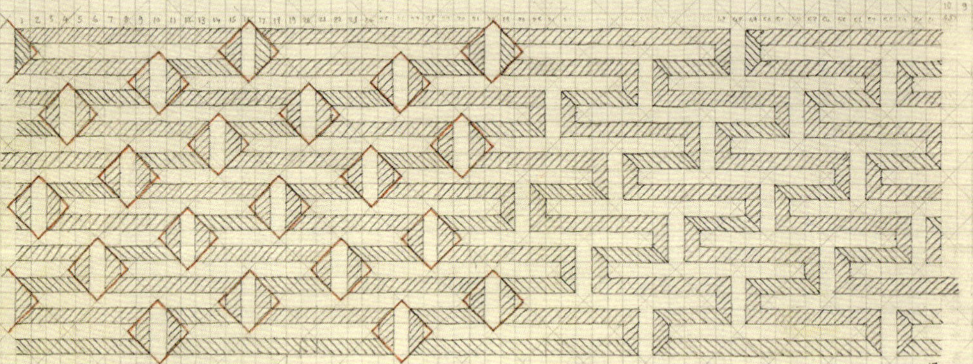

17

This is nothing more than a staggered battlement

The LAbyRINTH STORYS.

1600 BC LAB, BULL+ACROBATS (OCD 810.)

1. LABYRINTH: DOUBLE AXE Theseus + Minataur

ILIAD 18.590. DAIDALOS Builds dancing floor FOR ARIADNE. The DANCE was some kind like the potters wheel, or "they would form rows, and run crossing each other. Depicted on Daidalos shield made for Achilles.

METAMORPHOSIS, OVID VIII. 136-183.
Daedalus designs + constructs the maze for the Minataur, with twisting paths that double back like the River Meander. Bull killed by Theseus, Aegeus son. Every 9 years, 7 Boys + 7 GIRLS sent to feed Minataur. ARIADNE, KING MINOS' Daughter, gives THESEUS gold thread and Ball of pitch.

PLUTARCH LIVES: Theseus XV-XXII
ON THESEUS RETURN, STOPS AT DELOS + PERFORMS THE

2. CRANE DANCE "consisting of certain measured turnings + returnings, imitative of the windings and twistings of the LABYRINTH" around the Ceratonian ALTAR, made of Horns from left of HEAD.

AENEID / VIRGIL BOOK 6. ON The DOOR OF THE TEMPLE, DAEDALUS show the story OF DEATH OF ANDROGEOS + Athenian penalty of 7 youths for Minataur — the Bull man, result of KING MINOS adulterous wife PASIPHAE Mating with Bull.

2. The TROJAN games
3. AENEAD Book 5. 3 companies of horses, 3 leaders, 12 boys + 12 Drill masters. ADVANCE + RETREATING intermingled alternate circles, like THE LABYRINTH IN CRETE. The GAME is called TROY, created by ASCANIUS, SON OF AENEAS. See The ETRUSCAN WINE JUG 625 BC - The GAME OF TROY. (THE TRAGLIATELLA PITCHER)

CHRISTIANS SWAP City of TROY WITH city of JERICHO THEN SWAP JERICO with JERUSALEM, the celestial city.

The thread of Ariadne translates into a rope for holding onto in DANCE.

The meanders, found in continuity on vases, make the DANCE WORK, SWASTICA labyrinth Also.

2. Theseus' crane dance at Delos was for Apollo.

1) The STORY OF Theseus + the LABRINTH composed from accounts in ILLIAD, AENEAD, METAMORPHASIS and PLUTARCHS LIVES. (HOMER, Virgil, Ovid)

PASIPHAE, the wife of KING MINOS OF CRETE, gives BIRTH TO THE MINATAUR, a Bull Man resulting from an adulterous affair she had had with a white Bull. Shamed, King MINOS orders DAEDALUS TO Build a LABYRINTHINE PRISON for the MINATAUR, being an EXPERT After having already LAID OUT a LABYRINTH the DANCE FLOOR for MINOS' DAughter ARIADNE, which is depicted on the shield he had made for Achilles.

To Feed the Minataur, King Minos exacted a tribute of 7 virgins and 7 young men every nine years from King Aegeus, in Recompense for the Athenians having killed King MINOS' SON ANDROGEOS after he was the victor at the Panathenaic games.

The third delivery of sacrificial youths included Theseus, king Aegeus' son, who instantly fell in Love with ARIADNE, King MINOS' Daughter, when he arrived in Knossos, Crete. Daedalus provided Ariadne with golden thread and a ball of Pitch which she gave to Theseus as he entered the Labyrinth with his 13 colleagues. He unspooled the thread and then threw the pitch into the minataurs mouth at which point he stabbed the beast with his sword.

Theseus followed the golden thread back out of the Labyrinth and upon his success consummates his love with Ariadne. They then set out for Athens, stopping at Delos to perform the Labyrinthine CRANE dance around the horned Ceratonian altar in thanks to Apollo (or Venus?). A second stop is made at NAXOS during a storm to let off ARIADNE to safeguard her pregnancy, where she died in childbirth. Theseus went on to Attica, but forgot to exchange the black sail with a red sail given to the captain as a sign that Theseus had succeeded in slaying the Minataur and was safe.

Upon seeing the Black sail, his father, King Aegeus hurled himself off a Rock into the sea.

PLINY NATURAL HISTORY X.36.19.85 distinguishes between unicursal and multicursal Labyrinths L78.

3) The GAME OF TROY a horse back mock battle enacted by 3 SQUADRONS OF 12 riders as six pairs. Described by Virgil in AENEAD in BOOK 5. The game is created by AENEAS to commemorate the death of his FATHER ANCHISES.

3) The CRANE DANCE The GERANOS, PLUTARCH. Theseus XV-XXII. See ABOVE.

4) DAIDALOS LABYRINTH for a DANCING FLOOR for ARIADNE, set + depicted on Achilles shield. ILIAD 18.590.

CHRISTIANITY ADOPTS The Theseus + MINATAUR story

Theseus, Aeneas, Moses, David, Jason and Hercules are substituted by the messiah, ARIADNE'S thread becomes CHRIST leading us through life.

Christ the Saviour goes down into hell and Rescues ADAM and the elect from Purgatory. The journey is reenacted at Easter in a MAZE DANCE recreating the HARROWING of Hell by Jesus as he descends into Hell on the Third DAY. He makes a recursive journey of reversal and renewal from Limbo: the Dance has the Dean and clergy going in + out of the Labyrinth, whilst throwing the leather PILOTA BALL, Theseus' Ball of Pitch, the rising sun and the harmony of spheres all rolled into ONE, and holding on to an Ariadnean ribbon thread.

ON THE EASTER DAY DANCE the world events of escape from the bodily world are gathered and compressed. ADAM IS BORN, ABRAHAM sacrifices a sheep for ISAAC, the Israelites depart Egypt and Christ saves the Damned. Like the Lamb sacrificed for ISAAC, the messiah is sacrificed for Humanity.

Because of the reciprocal nature of christ being the Alpha and omega, the first and the last, the beginning and the End, the concept of a recursive Labyrinth is a perfect metaphor. Christ ends the temporal life and begins the spiritual life. AND CHRIST SHUTTLES between the inseperable and reciprocal natures of GOD + SATAN. The Labyrinth is both in Bono and in Malo. Sometimes its goal is celestial and at other times hellish - Mankind between. The Labyrinth is also a realm of sin or an enactment of the 40 year, 40 day solitude in the Desert, or a 7 fold encirclement of Jericho or a terrestrial journey to Earthly Jerusalem or a Celestial Journey to Heavenly Jerusalem. Meanwhile Catholic Pilgrims collectively inch their way around the orbits on their knees, and the solitary protestant Pilgrim is the WANDERING SOUL OF Humanity.

WWW.LABYRINTHPROJECT.COM (ST LOUIS L.P)
ROBERT FERRE is the DIRECTOR OF THE ST LOUIS LABYRINTH PROJECT ST. LOUIS MISSOURI.
JEFF SAWARD is the EDITOR OF CAERDROIA The JOURNAL OF MAZES + LABYRINTHS.
THROUGH THE LABYRINTH. HERMANN KERN, 1982+2000
The Idea of the Labyrinth. P.R. DOOB 1990
MAZES + LABYRINTHS W.H. MATTHEWS 1922

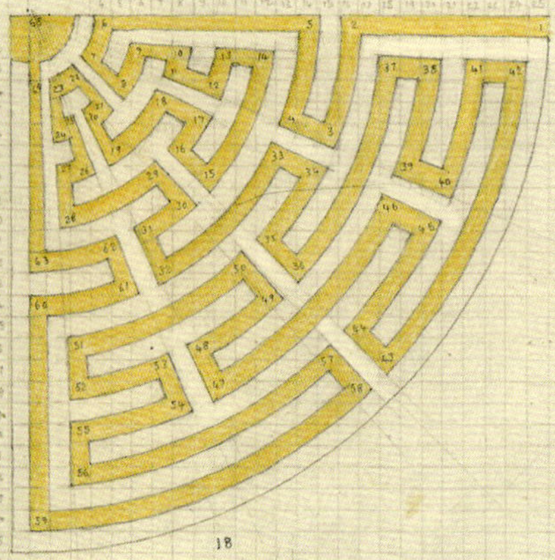

18

19

FRANCE

CHARTRES 1215-1221
294 meters 34C PATH 8c

The PENITANT PILGRIM M
OF The LABYRINTH ON H
Whilst reciting the Praye
AT SENS 2000 STEPS + 7
SENS LABYRINTH 1180s
ENTRANCE + exit differ - C
30 feet in DIAMETER. 2

REIMS 1290 34 feet D
OCTAGONAL, ARCHITECTS/
Depicted

AMIENS 1288 12.16 me
OCTAGONAL. 2nd Larges
CHARTRES Type.

ST QUENTIN 1495 18
ONE OF 2 LARGE LABYR
INTACT. OCTAGONAL. S
AXIS. Maybe a copy of

ST OMER 1350 1
SQUARE OF 49 STONES (4

ITALY

12th century 3.6M NOT w

20 STAGGER BATTLEMENT, CHARTRES 1/4, 2 BUNDLE, 141 LOOP, 11 CIRCUIT, IN + OUT

units that break down to a mind boggling forty million millimeters? What was he thinking of?

The plot thickens with Jay Kappraff's new study of the Parthenon's base measure in *"The System of Proportions of the Parthenon and its Meaning"* that bears an uncanny 5 decimal point resemblance to the meter. Were he in the know, the title of Dan Brown's next book might be "*The Napoleo–Pereclean Code*".

Measuring time has been equally tricky: a day's length is always changing and the length of the year is equally unreliable. The atomic clock helps out a little, measuring the zillions of vibrations of a particular atom – at one time the smallest thing we can measure with an instrument, but it's a measure that sits awkwardly upon the patched–up wobbly solar/lunar system.

God, Earth, Atoms, Flocks of Birds and the length of the Emperor's foot all have their problems; nothing seems to work when it comes to measurement, for it is a constantly changing thing. That is the point: despite its desire to be rock hard and stable, measurement may be confident in a measure for today but it switches allegiance to something tomorrow. Humankind is fickle when it comes to nailing down a standard unit of measurement. Whether the past is visited, or a trip is made into the digital future, one thing is certain: measurement remains fugitive. Thank goodness, for within that space the ineffable is left to its own devices.

19

20

Facing page: 18. Chartres labyrinth Pilgrims would shuffle 2000 steps, reenacting the tortuous journey to Jerusalem, feeing the measure of their body through their knees. **19.** A labyrinth made of dew. A labyrinth can be drawn from memory, the body measuring it out in a field of dew, only to be burned off by mid-morning. **20.** Southern Indiana Weedscape. A walker can unwind a labyrinth, and set off on a path across the landscape, leaving the measured coils behind, yet having them nearby, imprinted on the mind.

ALLUSIONS, ANALOGIES AND THE UNPRESENTABLE

Lebbeus Woods

In this group of optimists, I am the alien. For me the 'ineffable' means the 'unspeakable' – that which cannot be said – so I can understand why people would not want to speak or even think about it. The ineffable is momentous and profoundly disturbing, always. Nevertheless, it is the topic the organizers have set out to explore, so I am going to talk about the unspeakable, in a brief time, because how much can one say?

Let's start with the bad news – *the ineffable cannot be designed*. We are addressing a group of designers, presumably, and people interested in design. Telling them that the ineffable – which is sometimes called 'the beauty beyond expression' – is beyond the reach of their skills and talents, can only be upsetting. I will go as far as to say that designing is the enemy of the ineffable. As soon as we design, we start to control, we start to set up the defining boundaries and limits and we squeeze out the ineffable, which is something that emerges when systems fail, when the limits are transgressed, and when things fall apart. We humans like to set up things so that we feel we are in control. Our controlled environment is arranged to reassure us that everything is OK. That is what our politicians do, tell us "Everything is OK, don't worry about Iraq, it's going to be OK – don't worry about pollution, we are going to take care of it." Architects are a part of that game, too. I am an architect, so I can speak to the architects. I think all of us are implicated.

Facing page: 1. Paul Lowe, "Families say goodbye to their relatives as they prepare for evacuation by the UN of the wounded and vulnerable from the besieged city."

I am really uncomfortable when I hear the upbeat talk of architects all the time, nothing but the upbeat talk. Our habits – the upbeat talk being one of them – our accustomed use of things, only serve to reassure us. We don't want to be discomforted, we don't want to have to move in a way that we are not used to moving. It's all about reassurance. But, in fact, it is only when we are shaken out of our habits that we are able to change and to grow.

The effect of design is largely to reinforce our habits and enhance our sense of safety within them. This very room is an example. I was here once before. And, I have to say it is really typical as a habitual set up, the usual arrangement of chairs, stage, the lectern. But what if we set it up differently, or if we stood in the streets, or if we didn't have a room at all? How would that affect our behavior and, more importantly, our thinking? What if we didn't have design to control and to influence what we say and do – could we still talk to each other, exchange ideas and feelings– could we still be human? When the habitual molds are broken, we are forced to ask these kinds of questions.

Normally, we give up our habits and change only when we are forced to. The changes can be caused by war, or flood, or personal calamity, and their severity determines how drastically we must adapt our thinking and actions. Designers normally polish up what we already know, but occasionally an architect can, by design, shake up our comfortable assumptions and actually build something that makes us say, "Hey wait, that's not architecture!"

I remember when I saw a photograph of Le Corbusier's Chapel at Ronchamp in 1957, just after it was completed (Fig. 2). I was 17 years old and a friend of mine was already in a school of architecture and came back one holiday and showed me a photo of it. "Look at that!' he said. *That* was the ugliest building I had ever seen. I couldn't believe people were calling it architecture. I was shaken. What makes it architecture and not just weirdness? I'm still not sure. But I am glad an architect can make a move like that, destabilizing me, making me uncomfortable, making me question what I think I know and believe. It is experiences like this through which the ineffable begins to leak and we can taste its bitterness.

The architect didn't design the ineffable, but he did set up the circumstances that enabled me to experience at least a bit of it. Of course, once the building sits there for a while, we get used to it, and maybe even say "What great architecture!" Thinking so, or just saying so, eventually becomes habitual.

Occasionally, artists, too, upset us with works that challenge the accepted limits of art. A Jackson Pollock painting from 1949 was made by dripping paint on a canvas, hardly the sort of control artists were supposed to have over their work (Fig.3). He was introducing chance and accident into painting, as the Surrealists had done, but to a far greater extent. He took spontaneity and 'the irrational' to a new limit. "This isn't painting, this isn't art"– typical comments at the time – were indicators that the 'shock of the new' has taken effect, and brought with it a whiff of the ineffable. But only a whiff, and only for a short time, because this painting is by now securely within the normal, having become habitual to us long ago. The ineffable is always of short duration, because of the great human capacity for adaptation.

A much stronger scent of the ineffable is seen in the photograph of a group of people obviously in distress (Fig.1). The photograph itself is not a self-conscious artwork, concerned with the limits of photography and the like, but a work of journalism, showing us a piece of a particular event. What it reports to us is not the event itself, but the faces of people witnessing it. Their expressions and

2

3

gestures touch us, even move us deeply, but only when we know more about the event. The people are shocked and dismayed. If they were reacting to a first glimpse of Ronchamp or the Pollock painting, we would perhaps understand their faces, but think their reactions overblown – unless they were devoted, conservative aesthetes. That would not move us very much.

But, clearly, they are not. What they are looking at is the destruction of the city where they live, Sarajevo in Bosnia in 1992 (Fig. 4). They are looking at the places where they have lived that have just been destroyed, by artillery and mortar fire. They are looking at their friends and neighbors

2. Le Corbusier, *Notre-Dame-du-Haut*, Chapel, exterior, Ronchamp, France, 1955. **3.** Jackson Pollock, *Number 4*, 1949. **4.** Paul Lowe, "Mostar was severely damaged during some of the heaviest fighting of the conflict, but it is slowly being rebuilt. These apartments were heavily damaged during the fighting, but are now restored."

lying dead in the street. Their sense of reality, their sense of the normality of life has been disrupted by violence. The violence has destroyed the familiar for them, what they relied on, how they identified themselves, who they were, what they did every day. Theirs are the faces of the ineffable.

A wounded woman is being rescued in a street under attack (Fig. 6). There is an urgent sense of panic, of terror. In such moments, the ineffable fully breaks out and it is unspeakable. The photograph only makes us aware of its existence, being second hand. You had to be there as Paul Lowe, a very courageous photographer, whom I met there in '93, was – to know the ineffable's full dimensions. "Is this the end? What is life worth, if everything that matters is destroyed?" Blind instinct takes over, and we are far beyond the realm of the habitual and any forms of comfort.

War is an extreme of destructive violence, but so are the 'natural' disasters. In New Orleans, the violence of Katrina's extreme wind and flood destroyed people's worlds as effectively as war. Normal rooms are absurdly rearranged, becoming parodies of the everyday (Fig. 5). Compared with a wholesale destruction of buildings the damage seems small, but the fabric of the everyday is more subtle and fragile than we think. The sofa is still there, but no one can any longer sit or lie on it. The 'sanctity of the home' has been violated, and it matters little that it was by accident and not by intention. Some terrible event has occurred and the ineffable has leaked through into reality, leaving us with the dread that our existence is really very tenuous and not assured at all.

Painful ironies abound. The new buildings tipped – over by an earthquake in Taiwan fell because architects and engineers left the ground floors as open as possible for shopping malls, weakening them with disregard for the threat from powerful lateral earth forces active in a seismic zone (Figs. 8,9). Who is to blame here – nature, or the architects and engineers? From the viewpoint of the inhabitants caught in this catastrophe, it hardly matters. The ineffable cannot be designed, but design can certainly invite it in.

The list goes on. The 'urban clearance' of German and Japanese cities designed during World War II by British and American war planners unleashed hell on earth, and also an entire world of ineffability where 'the shock of the

4

5

"If we want to be free, we can't avoid the inevitable."

5. Robert Polidori, *6013 St. Anthony Avenue, New Orleans, Louisiana*, 2006. **Following pages: 6.** Paul Lowe, "United Nations peacekeeping soldiers from Egypt help an injured woman running from the scene of an explosion in the city centre."

new' was at once a sound of doom and the prelude to the construction of a post-war world (Fig. 7). People affected simply had to 'adjust' their everyday habits, and 'adapt.' Is it necessary to bomb cities flat in order to build them anew? Obviously not. But some form of destruction of the old is necessary, and that produces for many the trauma of change. Is, then, the ineffable also the inevitable?

Before answering, I'll extend my list of sources of the ineffable by one more: the destruction of the World Trade Center on September 11, 2001 (Figs. 10, 11). Until then, America had prided itself on its major cities never having been violently attacked by a foreign enemy. We had never suffered the sort of destruction experienced by Europeans and Asians in World War II, save for some homegrown exceptions like the Civil War (called by historians the first modern war, in part because cities became targets) and the bombing of the Federal Building in Oklahoma City. But now, major American cities were attacked, and our whole idea of reality was twisted.

The destruction was limited, but the fact that it was caused by foreigners, using American airliners as weapons, qualified the attack as a national calamity. The sense of loss was overwhelming. Loss of so many lives, loss of physical symbols of American power, loss of the sense of invulnerability,

"I will go as far as to say that designing is the enemy of the ineffable. As soon as we design, we start to control, we start to set up the defining boundaries and limits and we squeeze out the ineffable, which is something that emerges when systems fail, when the limits are transgressed, and when things fall apart."

8

9

Facing page: 7. Destruction of Dresden, 1945. **8.** A building lay collapsed in Taipei County. **9.** Rescue workers search for survivors at collapsed building in Taipei.

loss of innocence, however misplaced it had been, loss of America's privileged place in the world. A profound sense of loss is the main effect of our experience of the ineffable.

Coming back to the faces photographed in Sarajevo, we might be able to see that they don't belong to some people somewhere else. They are our faces. These faces portray unspeakable loss, as do the photos of the collapsing towers, and their ruins. But there is also something else.

Loss is inevitable in the story of each person. Losing your wallet, losing your job, losing your home, your family, your city, your life – the degree of loss escalates from the inconvenient to the inconceivable, and with it the experience of the ineffable. Loss, however, is necessary in order for us to change, not only in our habits, but also in our understandings and beliefs. As long as we cling comfortably to what we are and know, we cannot learn, or create. If design is to be a creative act, it must take on the tough situations in our lives. It must offer more than comfort and entertainment. In short, it must confront the unspeakable and undesignable and become an instrument for expanding our limits, as individuals and communities, at once embracing and transcending them.

Americans love to talk about freedom. We want to be free, we want our children to be free, and we are willing to kill and die for it. When I hear this talk, I often wonder if people understand that loss is the price we pay for freedom. At one romantic extreme, the old song line, "freedom's just another word for nothin' left to lose" – referring to vagabonds and the homeless, but also to searching and restless wanderers in mind and spirit – sums it up: we are most free – to recreate ourselves and the world around us – when we have lost those comforting things that define and limit us. At a more realistic level, we would do well to have only what we need to go forward, remembering that, if we want to be free, we cannot avoid the inevitable. Thank you.

10

10. Second in a series of four photos---The south tower of the World Trade Center begins to collapse following a terrorist attack on the New York landmark, Tuesday, Sept. 11, 2001. **Facing page: 11.** Rescue workers conduct search and rescue attempts, descending deep into the rubble of the World Trade Center. New York, NY (Sept. 14, 2001).

IN THE SHOES OF LE CORBUSIER

José Oubrerie

Before going further, I would like to say something because we were discussing the notion of tradition, history, heritage and all that. In fact, this relates to me. As you know or don't know, initially this was a project of Le Corbusier's with whom I was working from the beginning, alone, since it was not big enough for several people in the studio. I have been confronted with this problem of heritage: some people ask me about authenticity, and say that you have all the plans etc… as if that is somehow enough. But nothing of this is true.

Jacques Derrida summed it up nicely in a book called *For What Tomorrow… in dialogue with Elisabeth Roudinesco:* "It is true, whether it's a question of life or work or thought, that I have always recognized myself in the figure of the heir – and more and more so, in a way that is more and more deliberate, and often happy. By insistently confronting this concept or this figure of the legatee, I came to think that, far from the secure comfort that we rather too quickly associate with this word, *the heir must always respond to a sort of double injunction, a contradictory assignation: It is necessary first of all to know and to know how to reaffirm what comes "before us," which we therefore receive even before choosing, and to behave in this respect as a free subject. Yes, it is necessary [il faut] (and this it is necessary is inscribed directly on and within the received heritage), it is necessary to do everything to appropriate a past even though we know that it remains fundamentally unsuitable,* whether it is a question of philosophical memory or the precedence of a language, a culture, and a filiation in general. What does it mean to reaffirm? It means not simply accepting this heritage but launching it again otherwise and keeping it alive. Not choosing it (since what characterizes an heritage is first of all that one does not choose it; it is what violently elects us), but choosing to keep it alive.

It would be necessary therefore to begin from this formal and apparent contradiction between the passivity of reception and the decision to say "yes," then to select, to filter, to interpret, and therefore to transform; not to leave intact or unharmed, not to leave safe the very thing one claims to respect before all else. And after all. Not to leave it safe: to save it, perhaps, yet again, for a time, but without the illusion of a final salvation." [1]

I think that describes exactly the problem I encountered. There is both tradition and invention in our life, and here, for me, in the making of this building, two different elements are present, in a kind of dialectical relationship between safety and adventure altogether, again, emblematic of my engagement in this project.

Facing page: 1. Le Corbusier having a photo record made of a broken blood vessel at his return from his trip to Brasilia's embassy site.

I also want to address the notion of the Ineffable. As you know the expression was invented or put in place by Le Corbusier's "Espace Indicible" and I agree with what Lebbeus said about this kind of description of ourselves in front of some unpredictable event (I was robbed in front of the Prado in Madrid of my wallet containing all my credit cards, passport and green card and I can tell you that the feeling of loss, of sudden vulnerability is very strong, despite the admiration you can have, at the same time, for the audacity and the dexterity of the robber).

This final sense of ineffable, of astonishment achieved by design, is what we attempted to do at Firminy, and it is only when the construction is finished that the real "miracle" happens or not.

I have authored an article called *Architecture Before Geometry* which traces in fact the slow construction of such an effect and even today, using all the possibilities of computation, every architectural project is for me first a mental construction, a construction of feelings: a project does not exist, it is an invention, it is an artifact; it is a dialogue between you and a succession of models, of sketches, of drawings: in fact, a succession of descriptions of something still in great part unknown and it has no reality, I mean these diverse representations by themselves do not represent the project. So what you have at the end is something which can hopefully create astonishment and emotion: the first things that you can create when you enter a building – like if you go to James Turrell's mountain and you arrive through a long tunnel and suddenly see the sky, it's a fantastic thing. These are kinds of Ineffable.

In fact, at first, you can see Firminy as an assemblage of numbers. What I mean is that while measurement, dimension, are critical in projecting the building you are not sure of any success before you build it…you experience it. In other words you can design everything you want but, before being put in real conditions to be able to evaluate what you have done and where you are as the construction process reveals new opportunities that you have to catch, to take advantage of: it is like making a sculpture in clay, after successive alternances between sketches and building it up and discovering constantly what it "wants to be." For example, in Ronchamp certain solutions were never designed before the construction was well advanced; or later in Boston where Jose Luis Sert was building the Visual Art Center for Le Corbusier and sometimes despaired because he had something with no solution and Le Corbusier was saying "OK, it will come." I had the same problems at some point in Firminy when I was asked what is going to happen in some place, what were we going to do? I would answer: right now I don't know, I cannot tell you, I have no idea and I will not do anything before I have got some time, and then, some time later I would get up in my bed and say: here's what we should do. So it works like painting a painting. And I think that for me this is what architecture is.

Perhaps that is why I do not have that much work; nobody wants to build this way: it costs time and money.

Perhaps there is something we can salvage in our condition of architects in the new situation of today which has been created by the digitalization available to us now. In the 1970s I was participating in France in the making of computer programs for architecture but then I was sent to visit Negroponte in MIT and I thought that what they were doing was absolutely fantastic and that we were far behind. Even in this project we used the computer; we used simulation, drawing and 3D, and at least from a professional point of view, for example, as you will see, we have been directly participating in the production of drawings with the contractors, so getting involved in a new way in the "production" sequence. A little bit like Michelangelo who knew and practiced stone cutting was involved in creating the materiality of his projects, sculptures or buildings. I have been building a house in Kentucky piece by piece and each element successively built created new conditions which required new responses and a new attitude towards the project and without this flexibility or otherwise, Miller House would never had been done as finished.

So I won't explain the building to you; I am just going to show you a series of images. This is in Firminy, a small city near Saint-Etienne which is close to Lyon and the monastery of La Tourette. It's a strange adventure because I started the project in 1960 with Le Corbusier who died in 1965. I started to build a part of it in '72 and '79, but the clients ran out of money and the project stopped for years. To protect it, it became a historical monument in 1996.

When I re-started in 2003, I could not touch it because it was a historical monument. It was a reserved area for a special category: the "architects of historical monuments;" the weight of the Beaux-Arts tradition. When they finished cleaning up the building I was allowed to make an "addition to a "historical monument" that I had built myself and that you could see unfinished, a kind of "monster" in Firminy, in the company of several other buildings of Le Corbusier's on the site.

So I completed the Church after 43 years. Nobody can say what it would have been if Le Corbusier had been alive, and as I said once: "I put my feet in the shoes of Le Corbusier: I hope the size was exact."

2

3

"The first thing you can create is astonishment when you enter a building. Like if you go to James Turrell's mountain and you arrive and suddenly see the sky, it's a fantastic thing. These are kinds of Ineffable."

2. Left to right: José Oubrerie, Eugene Claudius-Petit, Le Corbusier, RP Cocagnac and Abbe-Tardy. **3.** Left to right: Alain Taves, Guillermo Julian de la Fuente, Le Corbusier and José Oubrerie.

Note:

1. Jacques Derrida and Elisabeth Roudinesco, *For What Tomorrow: A Dialogue* (Stanford, CA: Stanford University Press, 2004), 3-4.

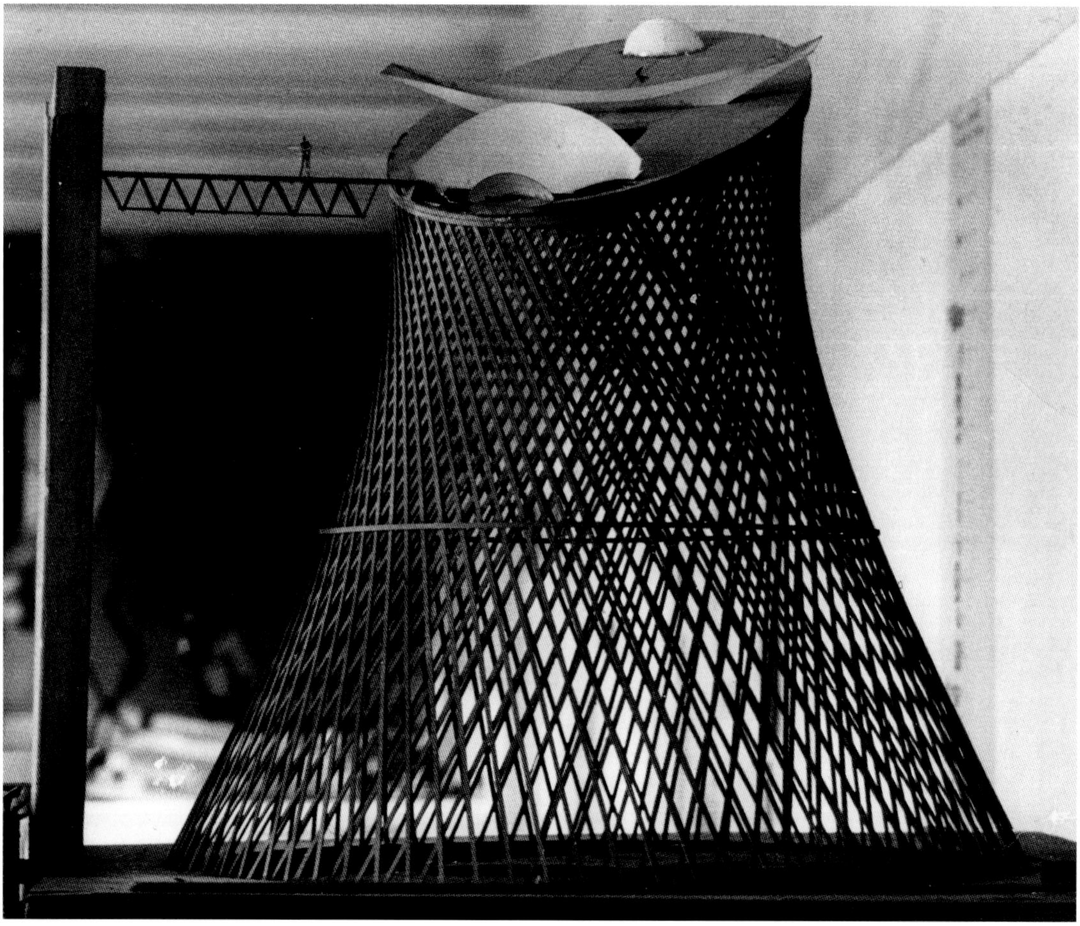

4

5

6

4. Le Corbusier, Maquette du Palais de l'Assemblée à Chandigarh dans l'Atelier de Le Corbusier, 35 rue de Sèvres. Photographie. FLC L4(13)33. **5-6.** José Oubrerie, Sketches, 1982 for IAUS 14. **7.** Conception, Le Corbusier architecte, José Oubrerie assistant (1960-65). Réalisation, José Oubrerie architecte (1968-2007). *Eglise Saint Pierre*, Firminy. Plan. FLC 16523. **8.** Le Corbusier, *Verre à pied, cafetière, pipe et bilboquet*. Dessin. FLC 1635.

7

8

10

11

12

9-19. Atelier José Oubrerie, Architect, *Eglise Saint Pierre*, Firminy. **Facing page: 9.** Model, 1972. **10.** 'The bouchon' the top of the shell. **11.** Church view from west. **12.** Cannons and Fentes de lumiere, exterior view. **Following pages: 13.** The "rib" east side detail. **14.** Peripheral "Fentes de lumiere".

15

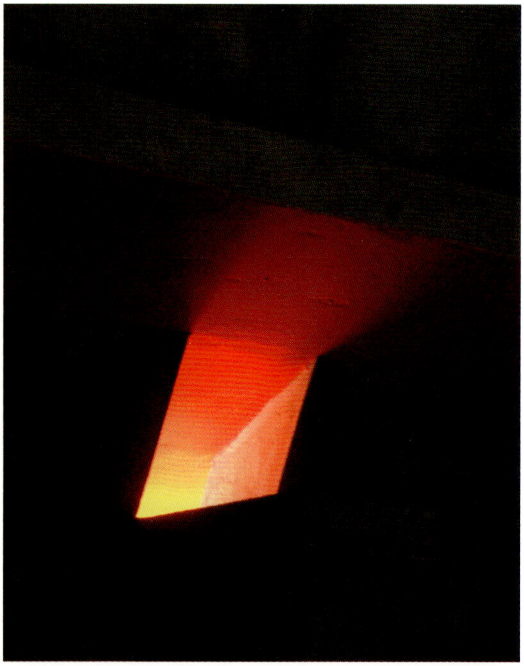

16

17

15-18. Light devices: "Cannons and fentes de lumieres," interior views. **17.** View from Southeast corner. **Facing page: 18.** Interior effects they produce. **Following pages: 19.** View of the stadium and church from "Maison des Jeunes."

TANGIBLE MEDIA/ INTANGIBLE MATTER

Meejin Yoon and Eric Höweler

When thinking about the title of the conference, "Ineffable", and the title of this lecture "Tangible Media Intangible Matter", we were interested in terms that would confound our accepted understandings of Media and Matter. The notion of Media is something elusive and uncontrollable and other, while the notion of Matter is something solid, inert, and knowable. Rendering Media tangible through its deployment in urban space while utilizing Matter in ways that produce atmospheric effects that seem to dematerialize their physicality – are some of our objectives.

The first image is from an exhibition we did on our work. The image is not a seamless image, but an image that is emphatically *seam - full*; it's an image of a project that was printed on thousands of round adhesive labels. The image we had placed on the wall individually as a pixelated image, an explicitly low resolution image, which we call "ONE dpi."(Fig. 1) So much of architectural imaging seeks to create a seamless illusionary space that is entirely seductive, yet completely elusive, that we felt that it would be interesting to highlight the gaps, or seams in the images. The low res qualities of the image disrupt the illusory space of representation and are suggestive of a kind of tactility of the image.

Facing page: 1. The "Light Stream" part of Low Rez/ Hi Fi creates a transparent screen of suspended pixels, that broadcast a layered feed of image and text. **2.** An infrared sensor mounted to a micro-controller detects the "intruder" and triggers the quills.

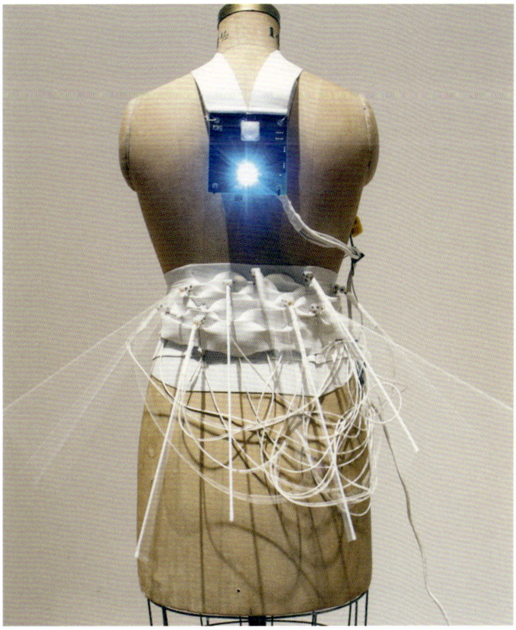

2

In her essay on Walter Benjamin, entitled "*Aesthetics and Anesthetics*," Susan Buck-Morss discusses the fact that the word "aesthetics" shares a root with "anesthetics." [1] In Greek Aisthetikos refers to the act of sensation, to the ability to feel or perceive. Aesthetics has its origins in a kind of tactility, just as the anesthetic condition refers to a kind of numbness. For Buck-Morss, the anesthetic is a defining characteristic of Modernity, and the contemporary, brought about by capital, by congestion, and by the proliferation of images. The notion of tangible or intangible is suggestive, and we hope to show projects that might get at the notion of a new kind of tactility: a new "graspability."

I will present a few projects that deal with the notion of public space. Unlike Benjamin's public spaces, which were so important to the history of Modernity, the public space of today is completely transformed by technologies, by images, but also by a post 9/11 condition in which the notion of public is radically transformed. Benjamin himself famously talked about architecture as experienced in a state of distraction and that interests us; this notion of distraction and attention, and architecture as trying to participate or intervene in that new sensorium.

This is a project designed by my partner Meejin Yoon called the *Defensible Dress* (Figs. 2-3). It was inspired by the porcupine and the blow fish. The *Defensible Dress* deals with the notion of personal space and the definition of public and private space. It tries to map out a territory around the body. We developed a garment equipped with mechanical quills that are technologically enabled. The dress combines a micro-controller with an infrared sensor that activates a series of these quills. The quills are activated when a foreign body intrudes into the personal space of the wearer, causing the quills to lift up. Our first prototype used a servo motor to rotate the quills into position. The final version actually uses a smart material called Nitinol. As a shape memory alloy, it contracts when an electrical charge runs through the wire. The fact that the dress works through material transformation is important, as this is something that we continue to study– the relation-

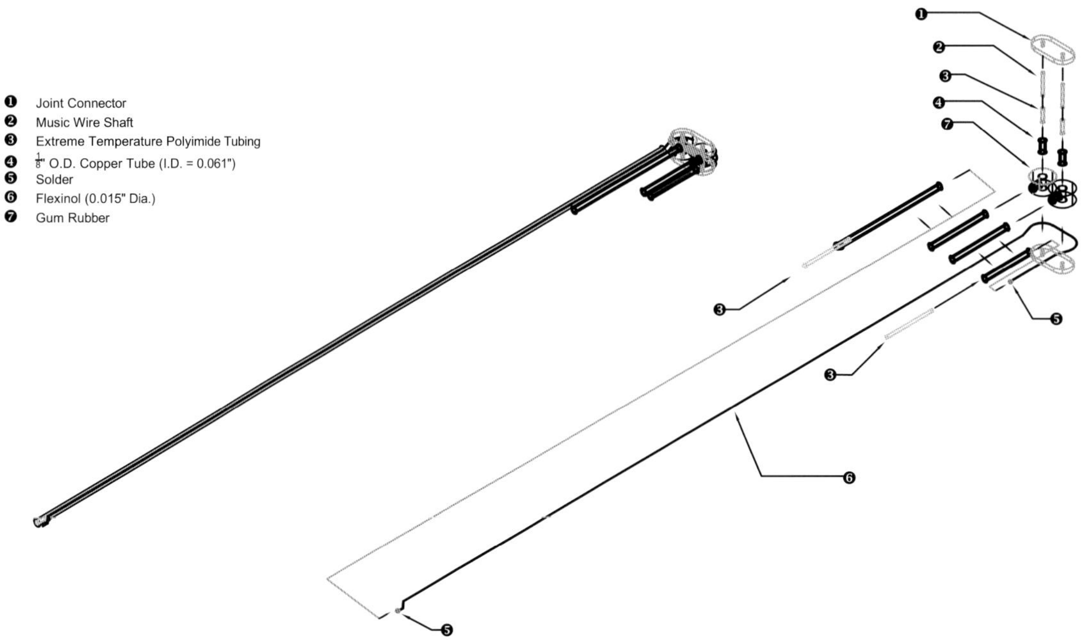

Above: 3. The components of the Defensible Dress, include a shape memory alloy, Nitenol, running through a copper tube. When an electrical charge runs through the Nitenol wire, the wire contracts, and the "quill" is raised. **4.** White Noise /White Light, an interactive light and sound installation, invites the user to interact with the field of fiber optic "stalks." **5.** When triggered, the site is illuminated in a swaying field of light and the sound of white noise.

ship of material changes (in this case, the movement of the body and the movement of the quills) through electronic mediators in ways that articulate the spaces we inhabit.

We produced this dress as a kind of collaborative conceptual project. We worked with electrical engineers – using the tools of the engineer, as well as the tools of the tailor or seamstress, to create an architecture that engages these different disciplines. By starting with the intention of defining personal space, generally, we produced a piece of very intimate architecture.

The electronic components that were used for the *Defensible Dress* were also used for a project that we did for the Athens 2004 Olympics (Figs. 4-8). In this project we proposed a public space installation with the intention of enabling the user to feel or touch the city, or be touched by the city. The project was very simple: we constructed a field of light and sound that recorded your movement as you walked through it.

4

5

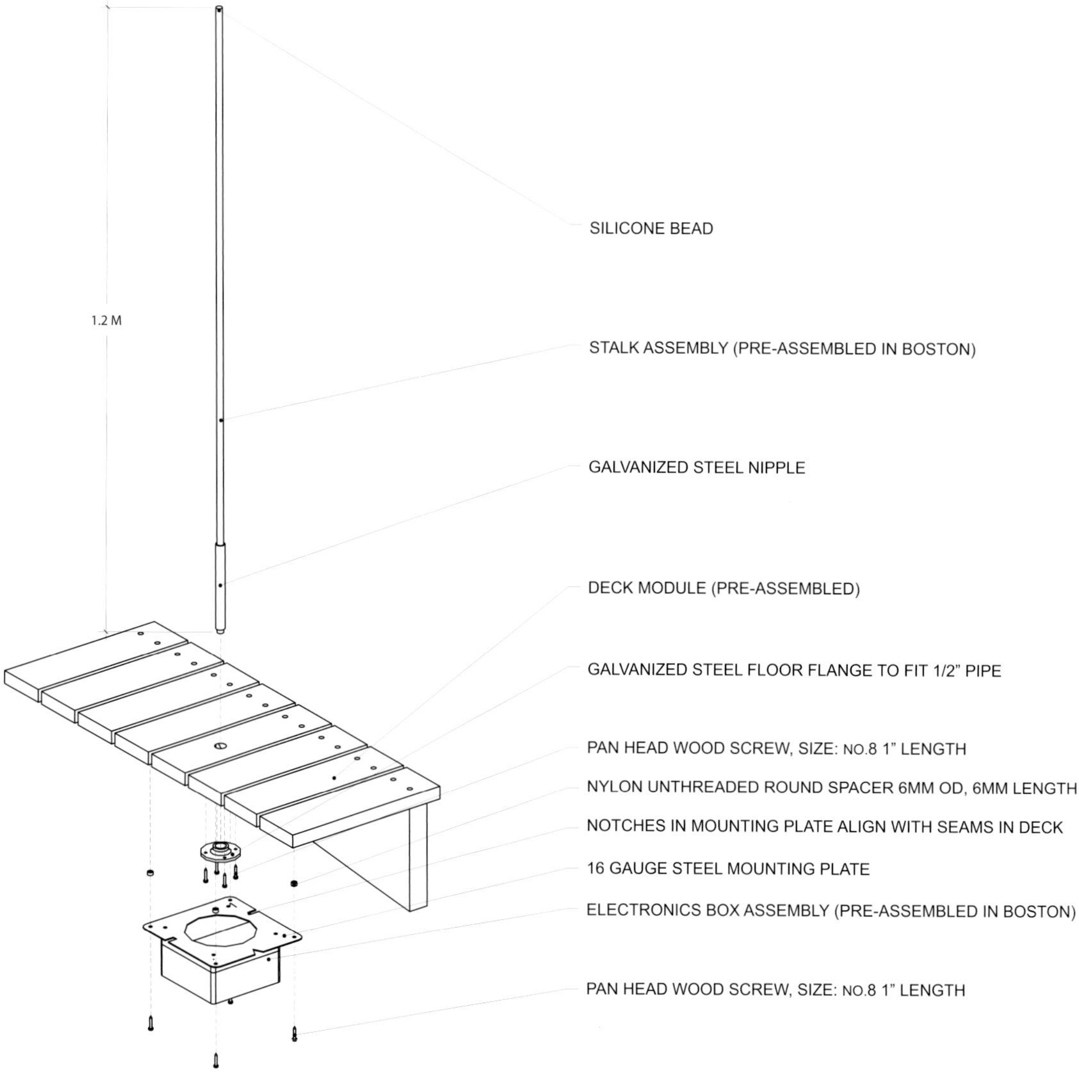

Above: 6. The field consists of a raised wooden deck platform, below which waterproof electronic housings are mounted. A fiber optic "stalk" in a polycarbonate tube is attached to the deck and mounted over the electronic components. **7.** A side view of the microcontroller and outdoor speaker. **8.** A top view of the speaker and circuit board. The microcontroller contains an infrared sensor and an LED light. **9.** The "Light Stream" part of Low Rez/Hi Fi broadcasts information, even as it is overlaid with real time images from a surveillance video camera. **Following pages: 10.** The "Sound Grove" part of the Low Rez / Hi Fi project creates a musical instrument as a spatial field.

The field itself was constructed out of a series of fiber optic strands that utilized an infrared sensor similar to the one used by the *Defensible Dress.* The fibers were lit at a very low level. A body's presence would trigger the sensor, causing the fibers to brighten. Emitting a white noise and a white light in response to a body, the field creates a tracing of the body as it moves. This was a way to measure the way a user moves through the city and the way that the city would feel you or touch you. The video shows bodies moving through a field defining a space in the city as trace or a wake of light and sound.

The images show the components that were used to produce the field of effects. It consists of a wooden deck, built in modules and shipped to Athens. Underneath the deck was a waterproof housing which contained the circuit board, the infrared sensor, the LED light, and the outdoor speaker. The fiber optic strand was attached to the housing and projected up through the wooden deck. We built prototypes at MIT, where we also did a lot of the assembly of the circuit boards.

7

8

9

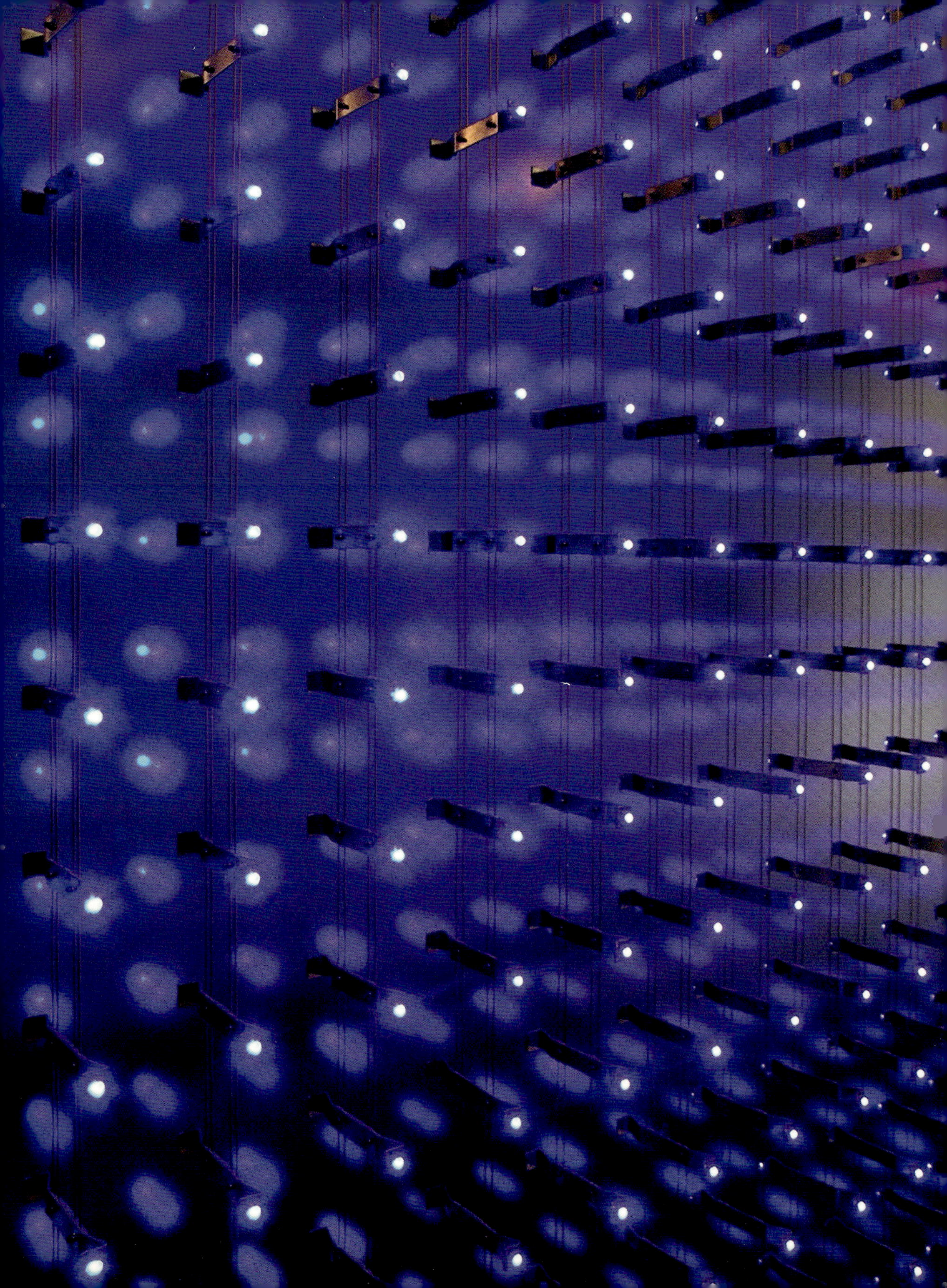

This is one of the first projects that we were able to realize, even in a temporary way, for an intervention within a city, which creates a new space within the city, and that space was actually produced through light and sound, it has no materiality. Because it relies on the user to engage it, the space is entirely situational. When it is empty it is almost immaterial, absent.

White Noise White Light led to the next project, which we completed in Washington DC. It is a permanent project for an existing office building. We were asked by the client/owner to produce an intervention in the public realm that marks the limit of the lobby and occupies the interfaces between the sidewalk and the city, the lobby and the office building (Figs. 9-12). *Low Rez Hi Fi* consists of two parts: to the left is the *Hi Fi*, a sound garden with touch-sensitive poles that produce musical notes; to the right is the *Low Rez*. The *Low Rez* is the screen which "slides" from the inside out, dislodging a piece of the screen into the public realm. The idea for the *Low Rez* part was motivated by an impulse similar to the one that drove *White Noise White Light*. We wanted to produce a kind of field condition in the screen so that it would register your body's movement as you encountered it. This is accomplished with a surveillance camera that was already there, and a live feed from

"We intervened within the public realm with an architecture that is not in the traditional sense physical material; but one that actually deploys infrastructures or behaviors that are fluid and intangible and produces things that are unchoreographed or unpredictable."

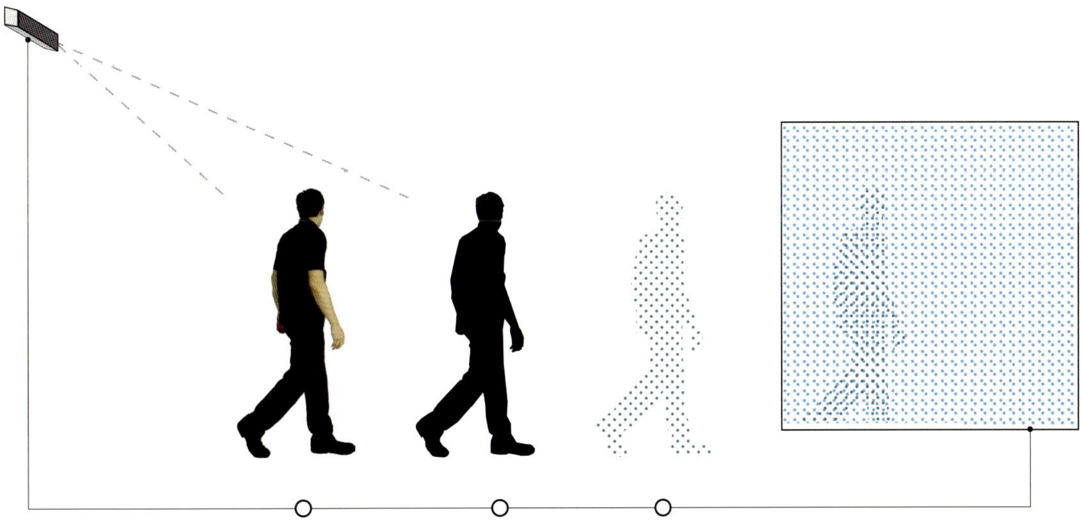

12

Facing page: 11. Individual pixels in Low Rez / Hi Fi, are suspended in a grid 2 inches apart, producing a highly transparent low resolution screen. **12.** The "digital shadow" feeds the pixel net with real time images from the camera's field of vision.

the camera to the screen (Fig. 12). We call it a digital shadow. The background image is a series of ones and zeros which is the building address, 1110 Vermont Avenue. We were able to propose this project as a building signage exercise, but it is really a public space intervention.

The video shows Meejin interacting with her digital shadow. We developed the screen ourselves because we wanted it to be completely transparent to encourage interaction from both sides. To do this we developed a custom two-sided pixel armature, with LED lights on both sides (Fig. 11). It's a completely addressable prototype which is taking data from the computer screen. The prototyping phase (which we did with Parallel Development out of Brooklyn) took about a year for research and development. We built several prototypes for testing. The final configuration suspends the pixels on 4 wires, which act to support the pixels, supply the power, and also the signal.

The images show the project installed (Figs. 9,10). The digital shadow provides the passer-by with the opportunity to intervene within the screen and alter the official content of the building address, with a live projection; it is a playful way to write with your body over the scrolling content on the screen. The images show a zoom-in on the pixels in a glass vitrine. The pixels are suspended between the glass, which is very transparent, so that you can actually see other bodies behind it and through it.

The second part of the project is called *Hi Fi*; it's touch-sensitive, using capacity sensing to produce a new kind of inhabitable musical instrument. *Hi Fi* is composed of twenty poles, which defines a cube of space in the public realm that invites a body into it. Each pole has four segments and each segment sounds a different note, so you play the instrument by deploying your body in space. Watching people interact with it, it is interesting to see people do

13

13. Roof plan of the "Loop" proposal for PS1's courtyard. **14.** A single cell made of three sheets of polypropylene plastic provides a sense of lightness and enclosure.

things which they wouldn't normally do. Public spaces are distinct from private spaces, and they are characterized by a set of behavioral codes. One behaves differently in the street, than in one's own home. This project aims to invite different behavioral codes in the public realm.

One can intervene within the public realm with an architecture that is not in the traditional sense physically material, but rather, deploying infrastructures or behaviors that are sort of fluid and intangible – an architecture of things that are unone'schoreographed or unpredictable.

The last project is a proposal for the PS1 MoMA's Young Architects competition (Figs. 13-17). It is a perfect program, because the brief asks for a space for play. The installation in the PS1 courtyard is an infrastructure for fun. We looked at their requirements and we asked ourselves, "how can we fill the courtyard with something which would enable these kinds of behaviors?" Rather than produce an object, we tried to produce a field condition or matrix that could occupy the whole courtyard in a three-dimensional way. We utilized the voronoi, which is a mathematical principle for subdividing space. Traditionally it is processed two-dimensionally, but we developed a method for producing a voronoi as a three-dimensional cellular condition. We took the courtyard and located certain points within it, then ran a script to produce a three-dimensional voronoi which in turn produced a volume of cells. From the cells we constructed a series of vertices or planes, and from those planes we extracted curvilinear lines. These produced rings or loops that we projected towards the center. The images show the final proposal, which is a dense curvilinear lattice that occupies the edges of the voronoi cells.

As a design process, we began by filling this space casting – with an idea about a material that was solid and po-

14

rous. We developed a series of loops that were studies in paper. We were building models out of paper, folding and bending to create these geometries which we then tried to simulate in the computer through computer modeling (Fig. 15). We found that it was actually quite difficult to do digitally what the paper could do so easily by itself the way the material itself was computing. We eventually figured out how to model it and how to use the computer models to deform it. Then computer models were created for producing these representations, but we thought, given the scope of the competition, we actually had to prove its constructability to make it a valid proposal. So in terms of our design process, we were always working back and forth between the material and the digital, or perhaps between the representational and the instrumental.

The images show the roof plan and the program distribution in the plan (Figs. 13,16,17). We produced representations of how that space would be used including areas for slippery wet fun, showering spaces, bouncy sorts of spaces, trampolines, and so on. We produced a series of spaces you could sit on as well as climb into. Images of the process show the back and forth between the computer model and the physical models: building a 3D model in Rhino, unrolling it, assembling a physical model, and then figuring out how to realize that in a full-scale proposition.

At the full scale, we looked at some different materials. In this case we chose polypropylene, which is a material that has an inherent flexibility, or bounce. We built these loops in the MIT shop (Fig. 14). By holding it gently you get a kind of buoyant deformation of the material. Working with fabricators we found that the material is heat formable, and weldable. We studied the joints and connections, and eventually produced a series of full scale of prototypes. Some of the parts were heat molded in a large oven around these CNC-milled wooden molds. We strapped them together to produce some full scale furniture pieces. Out of two sheets we produced this mini-cellular shape to prove that this concept of the inhabitable lattice was not so far-fetched and that it could have a kind of material realization. After we were told we didn't win the competition we kept developing the furniture pieces, making loop chairs which are very spatial and accommodate bodies in different ways.

To conclude: how do we talk about practice within the contemporary, if we understand the anesthetic as a symptom of the contemporary? We believe that tactility is a way of addressing the numbness which sometimes threatens to overwhelm the contemporary. As practitioners, we have new tools, which expand our notion of what is possible, but we have also found that it is most productive to work back and forth between the analog and the digital. We find in our own process that even if you are working with a computational script or digital process, there is always the impulse to insert one's hand. I think that in fact it's more than an impulse, that the presence of the hand and the manual within the digital is something we can't escape. In these projects, we hope to show instances of a kind of "graspability" of the present.

15. Working back and forth, between the physical desktop and the computer desktop. Materials that produced geometry through bending are re-modeled in the computer, then unrolled, printed and cut out of new materials. **16.** Water elements integrated into the lattice provide spaces for dipping and floating. **Following pages: 17.** The dense lattice of loop surfaces creates a single environment that encourages lounging and climbing, while producing shade.

Notes:

1. Susan Buck-Morss, "*Aesthetics and Anaesthetics: Walter Benjamin's Artwork Essay Reconsidered,*" October 62 (Autumn, 1992): 3-41.

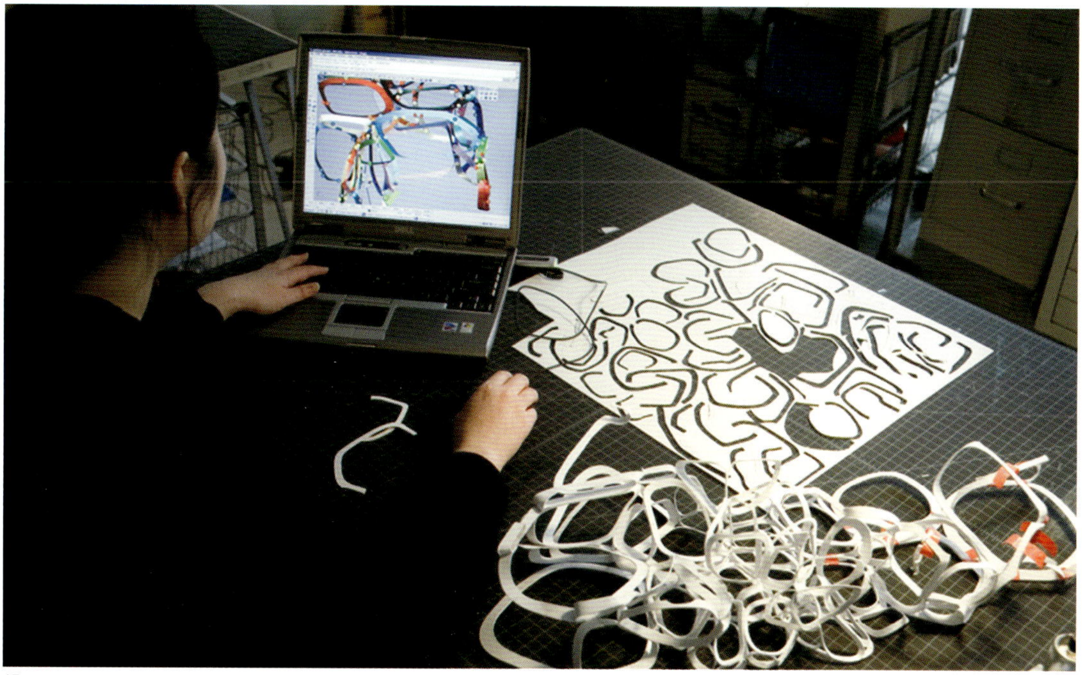

15

16

Panel Three

DISCUSSION

Moderated by Ashley Schafer

Panelists: Evan Douglis · Ben Nicholson · Lebbeus Woods · José Oubrerie · Meejin Yoon & Eric Howeler

AS: I would like to get beyond the earlier antagonism being set out against the computational, and say that this panel as a whole seemed to do a good job showing us projects and ideas that get beyond that antagonism. I noted other terms that people were using that might be referring to a similar set of logics and also moving beyond them. Evan used the phrase "logic based systems", Ben Nicholson referred to "organizational structures", Lebbeus Woods used the phrase "systems out of control", Jose referred to "unpredictability and the assemblage of numbers" and Eric referred to "digital processes, scripts and mathematical principles". I was impressed with all of the phrases, which in one way or another, began to address some of the concepts that were discussed earlier, but all of them met with a material reality. The actual destruction of cities that Lebbeus talked about, Ben's mazes, Jose's church, Evan's installations, and Eric and Meejin's electronic projects as well. I should just ask you whether you think that's a fair way to move the discussion along.

LW: To me, the issue is the human being, obviously. What I am missing from a number of presentations is the presence of the human, the human mind and the human soul. Human beings seem to be reduced to, in many of the projects, not just yours, Eric, a kind of mannequin that is operating some system or caught in some system. The whole conference on the Ineffable suggested to me the human dimension; because there is no ineffable system; it doesn't exist. There is no system to produce the ineffable, ineffable meaning that which makes us in a sense most aware of what it is to be human. None of the systems produces that, none of the paradigms, algorithms, computational methods, nothing. That's what I am missing from this and maybe someone can tell me where I'm wrong.

AS: Lebbeus, wouldn't you say that your drawings of the cities, the vector diagrams of System Wien, for example, are missing the human?

LW: No, because the human beings were in the space. They went into the space, they occupied the space, they made the space. It is all about energy, human energy, hands that make things. So it's very old fashioned. Even though it might have looked somewhat digital, in reality it was made of wires and screws into the floor; it wasn't produced digitally. It was produced by hand. That is not my issue though. My issue is that we live in a time that is so fraught with difficulties and designers are too often simply glossing over the real social condition of us, even at this table, even though we are privileged. We are part of the privileged class; we are getting paid to come here and offer our opinions. Most of the human race is slaving for little money and no glory whatsoever. We have to remember that architecture and design are disciplines that roll into human beings, not just to come up with new ways to make things. Maybe new ways of making things will benefit human beings. That is what we hope, I'm sure that every one at the table hopes that. But in themselves, they're meaningless. That's all.

ED: Lebbeus, it seems to me that there was an explicit desire on your part to propose that the Ineffable is a paradoxical situation that certainly can not be obtained, like the uncanny. I fully respect that and I would be in complete agreement that the kind of radical emergence of something poignant in architecture isn't something that you seek, it appears; and it appears after many, many, many years of hard work, and a kind of obsessive and relentless dedication towards one's practice. If the term is a trap, then so be it.

LW: The Ineffable?

ED: Yes. If for some architects the means of production in a material practice is about utilizing certain technologies to develop their work, I don't think there is anyone in this room that would take the position that they are producing the "Ineffable". The other part of your comment has to do with a kind of social contract, and I think there are many ways to get there; some people choose to be more direct, and others move at it obliquely. I would also argue that for the most part everyone in this room lives in this kind of strangely beautiful schizophrenic existence between teaching and practicing in a way. The reason why I raise the question of being an educator is because I do think that in fact it's a much more direct avenue and arena in terms of immediacy to find the kind of ethic you are speaking to.

BN: The issue you brought up that the Ineffable is something that comes to you when you are out of control of yourself. I am not so sure about that. Design and Ineffable are not in counterpoint because to create is to always hope that at some point in a moment of production, it will happen. It seems to be rather the same conversation that happened earlier on in the day where there was this sense that it came from elsewhere and there was another group who really wanted the machine to make this creature and that it would become alive. I truly believe that the process of design is one that has the optimism to hope that you may be lucky enough once in your life or a million times that you could orchestrate with all good will something that you don't understand with as much grace as something coming to you. The pictures you showed us today were really beautiful. There is no question about it. But the darkness of them, I am not so sure the Ineffable is only manufactured or brought about by that kind of darkness.

LW: Yes I emphasized that. Indeed, I did. But I did start with Ronchamp and with the Pollock painting because occasionally art can take us, transport us or upset our world in such a way so that we suddenly realize that we are suspended over an abyss, we're suspended over an abyss. We just think we stand on solid ground, but we are suspended over an abyss and that abyss is something that we don't like to recognize.

BN: That abyss becomes very tender with time though and you can look at something like the Ronchamp building and it was uncomfortable when it was built as many great works are, but then over time they suddenly appear like an old friend. All of the beauty that I'm alluding to exists in the same object but from the distance of time. So the Ineffable is in both places, a place of great haunting provocation and one of enormous comfort; and it is the same object that will bring it about.

LW: Let me just say that I think that the Ineffable is not for all of us. Do we really want the Ineffable if we have to be so discomforted? Maybe we should just go with our comforts and pleasures. There was a whole school of Greek philosophy, several of them, the Epicureans, for one, who just said "Enjoy! Forget all this heavy duty Sophistry, all this life and death stuff, just enjoy life" and then you go wherever you go. There are those who live that way and there are those who feel that void under their feet, that abyss that they're standing on, that they're just floating over by some miraculous means. So it is not for everyone. I don't think Ineffable is something that you can market or say "Hey everyone, get with the Ineffable. Let's go."

JO: I am more optimistic. I think that the Ineffable can happen but when we are at the moment of building we don't know if it will or not. What I know as a human being and an architect is the difficulty of making things and if you want to do something, it requires a lot of time and a lot of trial and error; wandering. Sometimes it can be instantaneous, you have an idea and "bing" it is simply fantastic but still on paper, as drawing. The elaboration of the type of architecture in which I was involved requires a lot of experimentation. You have to be able to appreciate if it's going to produce the effect that you want, you make physical models but you may even have to build a full size one. Of course you have a result at a certain moment when it is built; it is here in front of you, now real, and now out of our control and the question becomes: will people react to it? That is maybe the way in which I am still involved with my past, with the way we were working when we did not have laptops and printers and so forth...when we could imagine for example more complex geometries but could not really build it easily (think about the complexity of the making of the Philips Pavilion!) Today computation has invaded our lives and that means we should explore the new possibilities given to us. We started using T–squares, went to the MayLine...I am not going to stay with it all my life, and we have seen in this conference numerous beautiful results of that new way of working to materialize our dreams. For me that is what the bridge of Michael Silver does, you know respecting Venice, respecting the beauty of Venice by disappearing and coming back and forth, or Eric's lights. ... Yes the important thing is that in our work, with my old way or the new ones you have to produce poetics, you try to make it, if not, why make things? Architecture? After Wolf Prix went to Firminy he sent me an email to say that it was the most moving building he has ever seen, as Greg Lynn also told me recently. And even Leon Krier got shocked by it! And as I said in my title "I put my feet in the shoes of Le Corbusier, I hope I had the right size"

Audience: An historical footnote because of course I believe in history. It is interesting, this discussion of the ineffable. It is resonant with an early Greek appreciation of the fundamental effect of architecture. They understood it in terms of thaumata which means to convey wonder. Wonder unfolds into both fear and admiration, which is really its poetic moment. So, maybe the bar is very high and maybe we are OK with pleasure, but in my opinion, if we understand the primary tradition of architecture, it is really about thaumata – and maybe the ineffable. In fact, Vitruvius calls this central quality venustas, the quality of Venus, mostly translated as beauty in the tradition but that in its intended association has more to do with the destabilizing and wonderful effects of love. It is not beauty in a kind of hygienic sense, maybe something that you would understand as composition, aesthetic beauty or pleasure. The issue is always this ambivalence, we are fearful of that moment of revelation which is the poetic moment that also reveals our mortality. I don't understand why one should shy away from it. I do think we all need it. Maybe we don't want it, but we need it.

JO: 99 % of the architecture in the United States and of other countries is not made by architects.

Audience: If I remember in my reading of the Modulor, there is the notion of a body of numbers and systems which come together in the blue and red series. However, within the modular, there are constant references to lyricism which means that in order to achieve the ineffable, there needs to be singing as I remember Peter Eisenman saying , "it doesn't sing", in other words, you can have a measurement system, but within that, there is a tonality and there is a lyricism which then brings it into the realm of emotion. And in music there is the adoption of affections. So when you walk into a space, does it move you or is it just dead. Is it mere numbers or is it what Benjamin talked about; the loss of aura and how do you get that aura? It has to be beyond numbers, it has to be the spirit of man rising to the skies. And it's through lyricism as Bernstein said in his unanswered question, we are in this condition because of the fall of hermeneutics, the fall also of tectonics, in which we start with the cry, which is what Lebbeus I think you were talking about. And then a question is which of these projects then fall on the side of mere numbers, and which of the projects fall on the side of aura?

JO: For me to make a project it is first a mental construction, it's not one where you start by putting numbers on paper but by trying to represent in a succession of sketches what you imagine. And slowly it becomes more and more precise. So geometry comes in use when the project takes shape, this research of the number, when you have to go from the irrational to the rational which becomes ultimately expressed in numbers; in dimensions because we have to be rational to build, but it is the most difficult moment, the moment when the premises of the project can be lost; And yes at this time modular proportion can be effective or it cannot. Don't forget that the Modulor that which Le Corbusier invented came about only when the golden section alone would not work effectively, it had to be married with anthropomorphic dimensions and it worked for him pretty well.

Audience: Part of what I think was of real value and is admirable was the light that José showed with those holes, and the fact that the holes actually end; the light creates the complexity of the ineffable, the ineffable is actually the light. And then there is something moving between those faces and the classic enigma of two faces looking at each other, there is something that is quite infinite and unmeasurable. So in a way, I don't mean this as flatly as it sounds, but I think I would ask Ben, to me the fact that you draw those labyrinths by hand and with an enormous exchange between two faces, your face and the face of the labyrinth, there is a kind of reciprocity, there is a drawing and all of that. To me that says something deeply about the ineffable and maybe it has a little bit to do with this ship debate, you know the big titanic vs. the Polynesian sailboats and I think just wrestling with the fact that if you did the 1000 variations of the labyrinth in a week, you wouldn't be doing the same thing; something else would be going on, and so you draw them for a reason, I'm sure.

BN: Well the way that I draw them is that I draw them as if I were walking, I now figured out a way to use a very blunt pencil, I never sharpen any pencil ever. It's just a way to expose the material. It goes with me as I go around the project. In the end it's cheaper than going to north Africa to visit all the Roman projects and all over Italy and France. I just sit there and it takes me, you know, an extra day or something to draw like that. But what happens is that when it's drawn, it feels to me as if I had visited it in North Africa. And now I get up every 20 minutes and exercise because I can't draw it any other way. And it shows in the work. The new ones, I wish I could have brought the new one because finally I have broken through the nature of the yellow pencil. And it's been amazing. It's just like a stupid drawing. But it's happened.

Audience: To me that is the essence of the question: that you are in an experience of reciprocity while you are thinking.

BN: I tried computers about 10 years ago, but the noise, the color and the fact that I'd have to be in a dark room, the lack of variation of light...; it was too much for me, and still is too much for me. I can't even use a light bulb, let alone... I have to have the light. Natural light, changing every minute otherwise there is no authenticity for me. The building that you've made is a process of a drawing that I made and computers can't do that yet. When they can, I'll check them out.

LW: I started off my presentation saying "You can't design the ineffable, you can't design beauty, and you can't design meaning." These are not things you can design, ... you've got to give up or lose control at some point. And I think the ability to give up control with the right point in the right way is the art of it. But, it's like the Pollock painting that I mentioned, it's just paint dripping out of a can, but of course he is swinging the can, he sort of knows the can but it's still the can that is doing part of the thing. The problem is that designers are too obsessed with controlling every damn thing. They won't let go of any of it because they have an end result in mind. When they have an end result in mind, then it's all over. You can make an object quite amazing. But it's just a dead thing.

BN: I think it's an issue of, I wouldn't call it letting go but rather releasing, it's not even releasing control but getting yourself into a place where it really doesn't matter if you succeed or fail, and you just relax into your work, and it's terribly difficult to get to that stage and it may happen a few times in your life or forever. I don't know, but you can't even aim for it, it just comes to you, but you have to know about it, you have to be aware of it.

ED: But it's extremely important to talk about material practices in the context of having a kind of predisposition to behave in a certain way and privilege certain kinds of effects. Lebbeus showed this incredible Pollock. It still resonates as we go into the 21st century in terms of the value of controlled chance. I would just like to kind of return to David's comments with Ben in the context of putting the body almost in the position of the pencil. For instance, it seems to me that we should take note of the fact that Ben is very conscious of slowing time down in order to get into a kind of critical interiority. I think his full scale drawings are absolutely brilliant and the kind of simultaneity of being there and not being there, is sublime because he was speaking in his presentation about not wanting and I'm going to paraphrase here, not necessarily wanting to make the thing or not wanting to use the capital and all the kind of mess that comes with that practice to make architecture but to do it with an economy of means and I thought his labyrinths on the ground were absolutely conceptually precise because they were able to regulate the choreography of the body and the horse and at the same time they live in the realm of the drawing. I do disagree with Ben and it's kind of an unfortunate reading of the computer, I think, but in the context of having this obsessive fascination about a typological system, you would think if there were any tool out there that one could appropriate to speed the world up in order to take the intelligence and the kind of vast creativity of an author like Ben Nicholson to assess all those iterations, this would be the machine.

Audience: But it's not about iteration; its about your heart rate, why you are drawing.

ED: I don't even think of the computer as a vast data collection machine; that's the least interesting part of it. It seems to me that it participates in a kind of collaborative way to deal with the unexpected. And for those who are unable to see that I can only tell you that you are caught in a lament because all tools are capable of being reconfigured intellectually and conceptually based on the agenda of the author. Period. So if the world moves too fast in order to address the kind of specificity of value then you slow the world down and if it means using these kinds of accelerated monsters then you find a creative way to intervene to assume control.

Audience: I think that this discussion kind of proves the point that both of you are trying to make in a way in that, for Ben the computer produces pain, for Evan it produces pleasure. I'm sure those things flip for both of you but I think that the point of it for architecture, whether we're calling it the ineffable or anything, is that kind of emergent property that Kate and I were trying to hint at this morning that exceeds process, that exceeds the object that in José's words causes astonishment. And I think that astonishment can take a lot of forms and we can be astonished that Ben would sit there for days with an unsharpened pencil just as we can be astonished by Eric that he would make those little tiny things. I think that architecture is constantly playing with these games of pleasure and pain and I think that is where Alberto's point from this morning, about architecture being about love, being about emotion, being about exceeding cognition to kind of reach that ineffable realm comes from. And I think for me, it's funny that the argument seems to be about the same thing.

BH: We have to stop but I have to thank the speakers today. Lebbeus mentioned that they were being paid to give their opinion but in fact it was not enough, not nearly enough. And honestly this was enormously generous on the part of everyone here today not only the speakers but also the audience who stuck it out and had faith in this project; which is a testament to how interesting the conversation was. I want to mention one thing in response to what Lebbeus showed today in the photographs. I was astonished in looking at those images, especially one particularly devastating one of the World Trade Center collapse. I could have sworn I was looking at one of his drawings. I wanted to mention that because in some way Lebbeus challenged us all this evening by not showing his own work and I really respect that. What is fascinating to me about it is that I got a sense of what you have been trying to convey in all of your work just by looking at that image which I found really amazing, so I thank you for that. I just want to conclude by once again extending a really warm thank you to everyone who participated today and I don't know if it's worth transcribing a conference on the ineffable but we are going to give it a try and hopefully you will be able to see it somewhere soon and access it, so thank you.

Contributors

Maria Berman

Is an architect living and working in New York City. She is cofounder and principal of Berman/Horn Studio, a firm specializing in residential and hospitality projects in the United States. The firm incorporates the design of lighting and furniture into an interdisciplinary practice that combines an interest in architecture with interior design. Their work has been published in books and periodicals such as *Taschen's New York*, *the New York Times*, *New York Magazine*, *Architectural Record*, and the *Architect's Newspaper*. She also writes for several art publications and has exhibited work in New York City galleries.

Maria has taught at Parsons School of Design and Pratt Institute and is currently an adjunct professor at the City College of New York, Bernard and Anne Spitzer the field of design Maria trained and practiced as an art conservator at major NYC museums including the Museum of Modern Art and the Cooper-Hewitt National Design Museum. She holds undergraduate and masters degrees from the University of Chicago and New York University Institute of Fine Arts and received her M Arch from Columbia University Graduate School of Architecture, Planning and Preservation.

Karl S. Chu

Originally from Mandalay, Karl Chu is principal of the architectural studio METAXY. He is a professor at Pratt Institute, Brooklyn, NY, and was the founding Director of the Institute for Genetic Architecture at the GSAPP, Columbia University, New York. He is also a Co-director of the Biodigital Architecture Program at ESARQ, Universitat Internacional de Catalunya, Barcelona. He introduced genetic architecture into the discipline of architecture the early nineties. He is involved in the research and development of genetic architecture along with developing a philosophical ontology on the architecture of possible worlds. He has taught, lectured, published and exhibited internationally.

Evan Douglis

Evan Douglis is the principal of Evan Douglis Studio; an internationally renowned architecture and interdisciplinary design firm committed to the practice of digital alchemy. The firm's unique cutting edge research into computer-aided digital design and fabrication technology as applied to a range of diverse gallery installations, product design, commercial projects, urban redevelopment schemes and prefabricated modular building components has elicited international acclaim.

Douglis is currently the new Dean of the School of Architecture at Rensselaer Polytechnic Institute. Prior to this appointment he was the Chair of the Undergraduate department at the School of Architecture at Pratt Institute, an Associate Assistant Professor and the Director of the Architecture Galleries at Columbia University, and a Visiting Instructor at The Irwin S. Chanin School of Architecture at the Cooper Union. He has taught at various programs in the US and abroad including; The International University in Cataluyna, Barcelona, Spain, Hubei Fine Arts Institute in Wuhan, China, SCI-Arc Southern California Institute of Architecture, and The Central Academy of Fine Arts in Beijing, China. In 2008 he was awarded a Distinguished Professorship from The City College of New York. Recognized for his innovative approach to design Douglis' awards include: a NYFA fellowship, a Design Vanguard profile by *Architectural Record*, an *I.D. Magazine* Honorable Mention, a FEIDAD Design Merit Award, a finalist nomination for the North American James Beard Foundation Restaurant Design Awards, a selected fellow in the EKWC European Ceramic Work Centre's Brick Project Residency Program, an ACADIA Award for Emerging Digital Practice and more recently a Presidential Citation from The Cooper Union.

His work has been exhibited at the SAM Swiss Architecture Museum, ARCHILAB in Orléans, France, the MOCA Museum at the Pacific Design Center in Los Angeles, Artist Space in New York and the Rotterdam and London Biennales. His Helioscope project is in the permanent architecture collection at the FRAC Centre in Orleans, France. His work has been included in the publications: *Sign as Surface*, *INDEX Architecture*, *The State of Architecture at the Beginning of the 21st Century*, *the ARCHILAB Exhibition Catalog: Naked City*, and the Phaidon publication entitled *10 x10_2*, *Distinguishing Digital Architecture*, the SAM catalog *Re-Sampling Ornament*, the *AD issues*; Protoarchitecture: Analogue and Digital Hybrids and Programming Cultures: Design, Science and Software, *FURNISH: Furniture and Interior Design for the 21st Century, Architecture Now 5* by Taschen Publishers and *Digital Architecture Now: a Global Survey of Emerging Talent*. His recent book *Autogenic Structures* published by Taylor & Francis was released in 2008. Douglis received his B.Arch from The Cooper Union and his M. Arch from the GSD at Harvard University.

Yael Erel

Yael Erel graduated with honors from The Cooper Union School of Architecture, where she received the Irma Giustino Weiss Prize for creative achievement. She is a registered architect in New York and Israel. In 2006, she co-founded YEStudio–lightexture, a New York based collaboration with lighting designer Avner Ben Natan. Their work focuses on the interplay of architecture, art and light through building projects, lighting installations and the design and fabrication of light fixtures. Prior to founding YEStudio, Erel worked with the award-winning architect Diane Lewis and ROART Inc. Her work has been published in *Metropolis Magazine*, *artnow* Magazine, *Architect Magazine* and exhibited at the Krakow Biennial, Pratt Institute and in installations throughout New York City. Erel is currently a visiting architecture critic at Harvard GSD. She taught Architecture Design Studio at Columbia University and The Cooper Union and is an Adjunct Associate Professor at Pratt Institute where she has been teaching Architecture since 2004.

Todd Gannon

Todd Gannon is a registered architect and writer based in Los Angeles. He currently teaches at SCI–Arc, UCLA, and Otis College, and was a member of the faculty at Ohio State's Knowlton School of Architecture from 1999-2004. As series editor of Source Books in Architecture, he produced monographs on the work of Morphosis, Bernard Tschumi, UN Studio, Steven Holl, Mack Scogin/Merrill Elam, Zaha Hadid, Peter Eisenman, and on the MoMA exhibition "Light Construction." His latest book, released in July 2009, is *Pendulum Plane/Oyler Wu Collaborative*. His essays have appeared in *Log, Loud Paper, Dialogue*, and elsewhere, and he has lectured at institutions across the United States and in Europe. He serves on the board of directors for the LA Forum, currently directing the group's publication efforts. His work has been recognized and supported by the Graham Foundation for Advanced Studies in the Arts, the National Endowment for the Arts, the American Institute of Architects, the Los Angeles Department of Cultural Affairs, The Ohio State University, and UCLA. A graduate of Ohio State (BS Arch, 1995; M Arch, 1997) and a doctoral candidate at UCLA, he is currently at work on a dissertation focused on the recalibration of architecture and technology in postwar Britain.

David Gersten

Is a professor of architecture and head of the first year design studio in the Irwin S. Chanin School of Architecture at the Cooper Union, where he also teaches a seminar entitled "A Material Imagination of the Social Contract." Gersten has served as Associate Dean of the School of Architecture and has taught every level of the school's five year design sequence, as well as seminars in the Faculty of Humanities and Social Sciences. Gersten has taught studios and seminars throughout Europe and the Americas, including the City College of New York, Universidad Politecnica de Valencia in Spain, the Universidad Catolica de Cordoba in Argentina and the Universidad Andina Simon Bolivar in Bolivia. He currently teaches a seminar in the Graduate Studies division of the Rhode Island School of Design (RISD). A graduate of The Cooper Union, Gersten has also pursued studies in phenomenology at the New School for Social Research as well as Islamic studies at the Jewish Theological Seminary. Working with literature as a central force in architecture, he has created a community of literary/architectural structures; each is drawn, built and written in more than 100 short stories. His work has appeared in international exhibitions, including the XIII Architecture Biennial in Santiago, Chile; the VII Architecture Biennial in La Paz, Bolivia; and the o.a.r. Filial sibiu–valcea in Sibiu, Romania, as well as in solo exhibitions at the Cooper Union, RISD and the University of Virginia. Professor Gersten has written and lectured extensively on a wide range of issues including: The Global capital markets, ethics, technology and social justice as well as the literary and poetic dimensions of art and architecture. Gersten's work is held in the collection of the Canadian Centre of Architecture and has been featured in publications such as *'Res: Anthropology and Aesthetics'*, Harvard's *'Critical Digital'* publication, the literary journal *'Boulevard,'* RISD's *'Design Principles'* and *'Globalizacion, Comunicacion, Arquitectura'* Chile. He is currently finalizing a book of his complete drawings and writings to be published by Editions Firmin–Didot, Paris.

N. Katherine Hayles

Is a Professor of Literature and Information Science, Information Studies at Duke University. She writes and teaches on the relationship of science, technology, and literature in the late 20th and 21st centuries. Her book "*How We Became Posthuman: Virtual Bodies in Cybernetics, Literature, and Informatics*" won the Rene Wellek Prize for the Best Book in Literary Theory for 1998-99, and her book "*Writing Machines*" won the Suzanne Langer Award for Outstanding Scholarship. Other recent books include "*My Mother Was a Computer: Digital Subjects and Literary Texts*" and "*Electronic Literature: New Horizons for the Literary.*" She is currently at work on a book entitled "*How We Think: The Transforming Power of Digital Technologies.*"

Brad Horn

Brad Horn received his Bachelor of Architecture from The Cooper Union, his Master of Architecture from Columbia University and is a licensed architect in the State of New York. He is cofounder and principal of Berman/Horn Studio, a firm specializing in residential and hospitality projects in the United States. The firm incorporates the design of lighting and furniture into an interdisciplinary practice that combines an interest in architecture with interior design. Horn's writing and work have been published internationally in journals and books including *Architectural Record, 3: Lux Letters, The Architect's Newspaper, Taschen's New York, Frieze Magazine, Journal of Architecture and Computation Culture, the New York Times, New York Magazine, the AN Blog and Autogenic Structures* from Taylor and Francis Press. He has published peer-reviewed papers and chaired panels on the subjects of computation and design pedagogy and has taught design at The Cooper Union, Harvard University,Pratt Institute, and Columbia University. Horn has been awarded numerous grants including those from the Graham, LEF, and Solow Foundations for research conducted at The City College of New York Bernard and Anne Spitzer School of Architecture, where he is currently Director of the Master of Architecture Program.

Höweler + Yoon Architecture / My Studio

Höweler + Yoon Architecture/MY Studio is a multidisciplinary practice, operating in the space between architecture, art, and landscape. They believe in an embodied experience of architecture, seeing media as material and its effects as palpable elements of architectural speculation. While their work lies at the intersection of the conceptual and the corporeal, they are committed to both the practice of and prospects for architecture. Engaged in projects of all scales, they are interested in the material realities and material effects of their work. From concept to construct they are determined to realize the built idea and to test projects through the dynamic interaction between the construct and the larger public. HYA/MYS' multi-disciplinary projects include architecture, planning, interiors, installations, furniture, concept clothing and artist books. They embrace all scales as an opportunity to engage design research to investigate the relationships between form/performance, interactivity/media, and inhabitation/event. In addition to current architecture production methods, they are engaged in design-build of interactive installations and fabrication of custom electronics. Current projects include Chengdu Skycourt, Building 2345, Rhomboid House, Outside-In Loft, Low Rez Hi Fi, White Noise White Light, Loop and 3 Degrees of Felt. Recently awarded the Architecture League's Emerging Voices award for 2007 and *Architectural Record*'s Design Vanguard for 2007, their recent interactive architecture / landscape projects are featured in the 2006 National Design Triennial at the Institute of Contemporary Art in Boston. Their work has been included in exhibitions ranging from the Skin + Bones Exhibition at the Los Angeles Museum of Contemporary Art (2006), the PS1 Young Architects Program finalist exhibition at the Museum of Modern Art in New York (2006, 2009), Unravel Fashion Show at Sigraph 2006, and Confines at the Instituto Valenciano de Arte Moderno, in Valencia (2009). Their work has been published and reviewed in *Architect Magazine, Architectural Record, Domus, The Village Voice, Interior Design Magazine, Architectural Lighting and I.D. Magazine, The New York Times, The Boston Globe, The Financial Times* and published in the following books: *Young Architects Americas* (DAAB 2007), *Material Process: Young Architects 4* (Princeton Architectural Press 2003). Their monograph, "*Expanded Practice*" was recently published by Princeton Architectural Press in 2009.

Ed Keller

Is a designer, professor, writer, and musician/multimedia artist. He is an Associate Professor at Parsons the New School for Design, in the School of Design Strategies. Ed teaches graduate design studios and seminars studying the overlap of cinema, architecture, locative media, and digital game design. He has taught at SCIArc, as founder/coordinator of MediaSCAPES and fulltime faculty [2004-09]; Columbia University GSAPP [1998-2009]; FIU Miami, Paul L. Cejas Eminent Scholars Endowed Chair [2007]; and at UPenn, Pratt, RPI, Bennington, and Parsons [1996-2006]. In 2000-01, he was acting director of the Columbia University GSAPP Advanced Architectural Design MS degree. Ed is a founder with Carla Leitao of AUM Studio, an award winning architecture and new media firm. AUM Studio's work has been shown at Experimenta [Lisbon, 2009], the MAK Center [Vienna and Los Angeles 2006], New Blood [Lisboa Architect's Guild 2006], TELIC Gallery [LA 2006], Crossing Disciplines [Pratt] 2005], and Beijing Biennale [NY Hotspot 2004]. Ed's work has been exhibited at the PixelGallery [Toronto 2003], The Kitchen [NY 1999], iMage Architettura in Movimento [Firenze 1997] and ISEA [Art Institute of Chicago, 1997]. His essays on culture, technology, film, and architecture have been published in books including *Four Lines* [Merz/Solitude], *Beyond Form* [Lusitania], *The State of Architecture in the 21st Century* [CBA], and *Beyond Postmodernism* [Routledge]. His writing and work has been published in journals including *PRAXIS, AD, Film Philosophy, Leonardo Online, ZAPP, Ottagono, Space, Scroope, Architecture, ArchRecord2, Parpaings, Precis, ANY, Metropolis, Wired, AD, Metamorfosi, Ottagono, Construir,* and *Architectura e Vida*.

Ben Nicholson

Was born in Britain and educated at the Architectural Association, Cooper Union and Cranbrook Academy. He is currently working as an Associate Professor of architecture at SAIC in Chicago. He recently moved to New Harmony, a small town on the Wabash River in Indiana. He was the Bannister Fletcher Visiting Professor at the Bartlett, and has been the Guest Professor at SCI–Arc, the Royal Danish Academy and the University of Edinburgh. He was a Fellow at the Chicago Institute for Architecture and Urbanism and has received grants from the Graham Foundation. Design work includes Appliance House (MIT 1990) and *Thinking The Unthinkable House* (1997, CD–Rom from renaissancesociety.com). As part of a long standing interest in American culture, he contributed to Bitomsky's documentary film B–52 (2001). His book *The World: Who Wants It?* (BDP 2004), a satire on western culture, was included in the American Pavilion of the 2002 Venice Biennale and a follow up text, *New Harmony: The Hands Can't Do What the Mind Can't See* (2006, Archeworks) muses on the vigor of small town life and speculates upon its possibilities. He took part in the exhibition Architecture by Numbers at the Whitney Museum at Altria which is developing into a book entitled *Horror Vacui: The Desire to Fill Space*, and discusses the nature of number, geometry and the structure of applications, the results of which were included in the exhibition *Leonardo da Vinci: Man.Inventor. Genius* at the Museum of Science and Industry, Chicago (2006). Currently he is concluding a five year project of hand drawing over two hundred monocursal labyrinths, which were exhibited at the 2008 Venice Biennale of Architecture, and has recently co-edited the book *Forms of Spirituality: Modern Architecture and Landscape in New Harmony.*

José Oubrerie

Is a professor at the Austin Knowlton School of Architecture and a registered architect in France. He has maintained a balanced career of teaching and practice. He has taught at the Unite Pedagogique #8 in Paris and was a visiting lecturer at The Cooper Union, New York Institute of Technology, Columbia University GSAPP, and was both professor and Dean of the College of Architecture of the University of Kentucky. Oubrerie's architectural accomplishments include the Miller House in Kentucky, the French Cultural Center in Damascus, Syria, the reconstruction of the Espirit Nouveau Pavilion in Bologna, along with several other residences, building projects, and competitions. Having been a collaborator with Le Corbusier from 1958 to 1965, Oubrerie was notably in charge of the Firminy Church project, which he built from 1970 to 2006. He has lectured extensively in the U.S. and abroad, has written on architecture, and has been widely exhibited. Most recently, Oubrerie's work on the Firminy Church was exhibited in the show "Architecture Interruptus" at the Wexner Center for the Visual Arts at Ohio State University, with a catalogue featuring an essay by Jeffrey Kipnis. In late 2009 the Firminy Church along with the Miller House will be the subject of an exhibition at The City College of New York Bernard and Anne Spitzer School of Architecture.

Alberto Pérez–Gómez

Was born in Mexico City in 1949, where he studied architecture and practiced. He did postgraduate work at Cornell University, and was awarded an M.A. and a Ph.D. by the University of Essex (England). He has taught at universities in Mexico, Houston, Syracuse, Toronto, and at London's Architectural Association. In 1983 he became Director of Carleton University's School of Architecture. He has lectured extensively around the world and is the author of numerous articles published in major periodicals and books. He is also co-editor of a well–known series of journals entitled *CHORA: Intervals in the Philosophy of Architecture.* In January 1987 he was appointed Bronfman Professor of Architectural History at McGill University, where he chairs the History and Theory division, and is currently Director of Post - Professional (Master's and Doctoral) Programs. His book *Architecture and the Crisis of Modern Science* (MIT Press, 1983) won the Hitchcock Award in 1984. Later books include the erotic narrative theory *Polyphilo* or *The Dark Forest Revisited* (1992), *Architectural Representation and the Perspective Hinge* (co–authored with Louise Pelletier, 1997), which traces the history and theory of modern European architectural representation, and most recently, *Built upon Love: Architectural Longing after Ethics and Aesthetics* (2006). In his most recent book, Dr. Pérez–Gómez examines points of convergence between ethics and poetics in architectural history and philosophy, and draws important conclusions for contemporary practice.

George Ranalli

George Ranalli has been Dean of the Bernard and Anne Spitzer School of Architecture at City College since 1999. He was born in New York City. He received his Bachelor of Architecture from Pratt Institute in 1972 and Master of Architecture from the Graduate School of Design at Harvard University in 1974. From 1976-1999 he was Professor of Architecture at Yale University, and in 1988-1989 he was the William Henry Bishop Chaired Professor in Architectural Design. Mr. Ranalli recently completed his fourth monograph, *Saratoga*, devoted to his Saratoga Avenue Community Center for the New York City Housing Authority. That project has been widely praised, notably in a May 13, 2009 article by Ada Louise Huxtable in the *Wall Street Journal*. His architectural and design work has been published internationally in numerous journals including *Domus, A+U, Progressive Architecture, L" Architettura, G.A. Houses, Architectural Digest, Architecture D'Aujourd'hui, Architectural Design*, and *Lotus*. His work has been exhibited and collected at the Cooper-Hewitt Museum, Sperone-Westwater Gallery, the Museum of Contemporary Art in Chicago, the Museum of Finnish Architecture, Centre Pompidou in France, Deutsches Architekturmuseum in Frankfurt, the XVII Triennale Di Milano in Italy, the Denver Art Museum, the Indianapolis Museum of Art, the Metropolitan Museum of Art and a one man exhibit at Artists Space Gallery in New York 1998. He designed the exhibition Frank Lloyd Wright: Designs for an American Landscape, 1922-1932 for the Whitney Museum of Art in 1997 and designed the installation for the exhibition of work of Carlo Scarpa, in 1999 at the Canadian Centre for Architecture Montreal, Canada.

Yehuda Emmanuel Safran

Studied Art, Architecture and Philosophy at Saint Martin's School of Art, the Royal College of Art and University College, London. He taught at the Architectural Association, Goldsmith's College, London University, as well as fine art and theory at the LAN Van Eyck Academy, Maastricht, Holland. He was a fellow of the Chicago Institute of Architecture and Urbanism and Visiting Professor at the School of Architecture, University of Illinois in Chicago as well as at RISDI Providence, Rhode Island and Cornell University. He has published essays on many aspects of the theory and practice of art, architecture and film – in *Domus, Sight and Sound, Lotus, A+U, AA File, Springer, Artpress, Prototypo, Metalocus* and *9H* etc. With Steven Holl and others he was editor of *32 Bejing/New York*. His book *Mies van der Rohe*, was published by Blau in Lisbon and Gustavo Gilli in Barcelona (2000). He curated, inter alia, the Arts Council of Great Britain touring exhibition 'The Architecture of Adolf Loos' and the 'Fredrick Kiesler' show at the Architecture Association. He was a trustee of the 9H Gallery and a founding member of the Architecture Foundation in London and a member of the College International de Philosophie, Paris. Currently he lives and works in Paris and New York, is Visiting Professor at the Graduate Institute of Architecture at Nanjing University, China; Consultant to Steven Holl Architects, and teaches architecture and theory at the Graduate School of Architecture, Planning and Preservation at Columbia University in New York City and at Pratt Institute.

Ashley Schafer

Ashley Schafer is co-founder and co-editor of the journal, *PRAXIS*. Under her direction, the journal has received critical acclaim as well as numerous awards and honors, including an ID award for the cover design, and was twice awarded the largest grant in design from the National Endowment for the Arts. A writer, designer, and practicing architect, Schafer is currently an associate professor and Head of Architecture at the Ohio State University Knowlton School of Architecture. She previously held an appointment as associate professor at Harvard University Graduate School of Design and at Tulane University in New Orleans, Louisiana. Schafer holds a BS Arch from the University of Virginia and her M Arch from Columbia University Graduate School of Architecture, Planning and Preservation.

Mike Silver

Holds a Masters of Building Design from Columbia University, and was both a LeFevre_ 29 research fellow for The Knowlton School of Architecture in Columbus Ohio and a Sanders Fellow at the University of Michigan. He is the former Director of Digital Media at the Yale School of Architecture and has taught at Harvard's Graduate School of Design. Mike Silver is also the author of numerous books and articles on technology and design including *"Pamphlet Architecture #19 Reading / Drawing / Building, AD's _Mapping in the Age of Digital Media_* and his new release by Wiley and Sons, entitled *_Programming Cultures_*. Mr. Silver currently directs a multidisciplinary design laboratory based in New York.

In collaboration with mathematicians, computer scientists, and engineers his office has worked at a variety of scales and has extensive experience in the design of furnishings, consumer products, web sites and buildings. Today, Mr. Silver continues his research in the field of digital mapping, advanced composite manufacturing and software engineering. His current work explores technologies like L.I.D.A.R., numerically controlled fiber-placement technology and high throughput computer modeling. As an experimental collaborative Mr. Silver's firm is deeply committed to the precise alignment of advanced technology, academic research and building design. His work has been exhibited at the New Museum of Contemporary Art, in Manhattan, the IDC in Nagoya Japan, the National Building Museum in Washington, D.C., the Architectural League in New York and the Cooper–Hewitt National Design Museum. He currently teaches design at the school of Architecture at Cornell University where he also directs the department of digital media.

Jason Oliver Vollen

Jason Oliver Vollen is a Registered Architect and Associate Professor in the Built Ecologies Graduate Program at Rensselaer Polytechnic Institute and researcher at CASE, Center for Architecture Science and Ecology, a multi institutional research collaboration co-hosted by Rensselaer and Skidmore Owings & Merrill. Prior to joining RPI, Vollen was an Assistant Professor at the University of Arizona working in the Emerging Material Technologies Research Group. His research is focused on emerging material technologies, specifically, the development and integration of energy performative structural ceramics as a building envelope, dynamic systems and environmental simulation, and digital fabrication. Vollen is a principal with Binary design, a collaborative practice focusing on energy effective architecture and emerging material processes. He has worked with Matter Architecture Practice in New York and as a project manager, designer, and fabricator with the Cranbrook Architecture Office.

Lebbeus Woods

(1940) Is an architect and theoretician whose work focuses on experimentation and critical transformations of buildings, cities, and landscapes. His notable projects include Centricity, Berlin Free-Zone, Sarajevo and Havana reconstruction projects, Terrain, as well as installations in New York, Paris, and Vienna. Monographs on his work include *Anarchitecture: architecture is a political act, Radical Reconstruction, The Storm* and *The Fall*, and *System Wien*. His works are in public collections including the Museum of Modern Art, The Whitney Museum of American Art, the Carnegie Museum of Art, the Austrian Museum of Applied Arts, and the Getty Research Institute for the Arts and Humanities in Los Angeles. He is the recipient of an American Institute of Architects Honors Award, the Chrysler Award for Innovation in Design, and the American Academy of Arts and Letters Award for Architecture. He has been a visiting professor at The Bartlett in London, SCI–ARC, Columbia University and Harvard University. He is presently Professor of Architecture at The Cooper Union in New York City.

Image Credits

18-27. 246-247. Courtesy of Mike Silver.

28, 31, 34-35, 37. Courtesy of David Gersten.

38, 43. © Micha Ullman. Courtesy of Galerie Cora Hölzl.

44. Abaris Books.

48. © 2010 Artists Rights Society (ARS), New York / ADAGP, Paris / F. L. C.
Photo credit: Scott Gilchrist / stock.archivision.com.

52-53. Credit: Ian Kaminski.

55. Masaccio (Maso di San Giovanni) (1401-1428). *Expulsion from Paradise*.
Brancacci Chapel, S. Maria del Carmine, Florence, Italy.
Photo credit: Scala / Art Resource, NY.

56. Peter Paul Rubens (1577-1640). *Prometheus Bound*, begun c. 1611-12, completed by 1618 (The eagle was painted by Frans Snyders). Oil on canvas, 95 1/2 x 82 1/2 inches (242.6 x 209.5cm). Purchased with the W. P. Wilstach Fund, 1950.
Philadelphia Museum of Art, Philadelphia, Pennsylvania, U.S.A.
Photo credit: The Philadelphia Museum of Art / Art Resource, NY.

58, 68-71. Courtesy of Arakawa and Madeline Gins.

60, 62-67. © the Archigram Archives.

80. Courtesy of Universal City Studios LLLP.

83. © Wolfgang Kumm/dpa/Corbis.

84. Hans Namuth (1915-1990) © Hans Namuth Ltd. *Jackson Pollock*. Gelatin silver print on paper, 1950. 37.6 cm x 35.1 cm.
National Portrait Gallery, Smithsonian Institution, Washington, DC, U.S.A.
Photo credit: National Portrait Gallery, Smithsonian Institution / Art Resource, NY.

86-90. THE EXORCIST © Warner Bros. Inc. and Hoya Productions, Inc. All Rights Reserved.

92. Image 10. From Luciano Floridi, "Semantic Conceptions of Information."
Stanford Encyclopedia of Philosophy, 2005. http://plato.stanford.edu/entries/information-semantic/

91, 92. Image 11, 94-95. © 2010 Artists Rights Society (ARS), New York / SIAE, Rome. Federico Fellini Renewal Copyright 1991 Corinth Films, Inc.

96. Credit: Kelly Winn and Matt Gindlesparger.

100-101. Courtesy of Jason Vollen. Photo taken by Kelly Winn.

103. Testa & Weiser (2001-04).

104. Credit: Kelly Winn.

105-107. Credit: Jason Vollen, Kelly Winn, Jed Laver.

108. Courtesy of the MIT Press, reprinted from *Anthony Vidler, Claude-Nicolas Ledoux: architecture and social reform at the end of the Ancien Regime* (Cambridge, MA: MIT Press, 1990), p. 254.

110. Image 2. Soprintendenza Speciale per il Patrimonio Storico Artistico ed Etnoantropologico e per il Polo Museale della Città di Firenze - Gabinetto Fotografico.

110. Images 3, 4. Bibliothèque nationale de France.

110. Image 5. Henri Labrouste (1801-1875). "Temple of Hera I ("Portique"), Paestum. Restoration. Section and Perspective" in Arther Drexler, *Architecture of the Ecole des Beaux Arts* (New York: MoMA, 1977), p. 362.
The Museum of Modern Art, New York, NY, U.S.A.
Digital image © The Museum of Modern Art/Licensed by SCALA / Art Resource, NY.

110. Image 6, 111. Image 7. Photo credit: Scott Gilchrist / stock.archivision.com.

111. Image 8. Photo credit: stock.archivision.com.

111. Image 9. Bibliothèque-musée de l'Opéra.

112. Images 10-12. By courtesy of the Trustees of Sir John Soane's Museum.
Image 10. Photo credit: Martin Charles.

113. Images 13, 14. WAGNER : WERK Museum Postsparkasse.

114. Image 15. Frank Lloyd Wright (1867-1959) © 2010 Frank Lloyd Wright Foundation, Scottsdale, AZ / Artists Rights Society (ARS), NY. *Aline Barnsdall Residence, "Hollyhock House,"* Los Angeles, CA 1920. (Photograph of a lost drawing.)
The Frank Lloyd Wright Foundation, Scottsdale, Arizona, U.S.A.
© The Frank Lloyd Wright Foundation, AZ / Art Resource, NY.

114. Image 16. © 2010 Frank Lloyd Wright Foundation, Scottsdale, AZ / Artists Rights Society (ARS), NY.
Image: © Tim Street-Porter/Beateworks/Corbis.

115. Hugh Ferriss (1889-1962). "Overhead Traffic Ways" in Jean Ferriss Leich, *Architectural Visions: The Drawings of Hugh Ferriss* (New York: Whitney Library of Design, 1980), p. 44.
The Museum of Modern Art, New York, NY, U.S.A.
Digital Image © The Museum of Modern Art/Licensed by SCALA / Art Resource, NY.

116. Image 18. © ABIR ABDULLAH/epa/Corbis.

116. Images 19, 20. Louis I. Kahn Collection, University of Pennsylvania and the Pennsylvania Historical and Museum Commission.

117. Photo: Courtesy of George Ranalli.

118. Aldo Rossi (1931-1997) © Eredi Aldo Rossi. Courtesy Fondazione Aldo Rossi. *Cemetery of San Cataldo*, Modena, Italy, Plan. 1971. Ink, color ink and graphite on tracing paper, 23 1/2 x 29 3/4" (59.7 x 75.6 cm). Gift of the Howard Gilman Foundation. (1282.2000)
The Museum of Modern Art, New York, NY, U.S.A.

Digital Image © The Museum of Modern Art/Licensed by SCALA / Art Resource, NY.

119-121. © Paul Warchol.

122, 127-128, 131, 134-135. Courtesy of Karl Chu.

138. Courtesy of Jeanee Hammet.

140-141. Courtesy of Dan Brietner, diagramed by Yael Erel.

142. Image 6. Austrian National Library, Picture Archive, Cod. 2554, fol. lv.

142. Image 7. (Set of 5 images) © Claude Edelmann / Photo Researchers, Inc.

143. Courtesy of Patrick Collins.

144-145. Courtesy of Patrick Collins, diagramed by Yael Erel.

146. Courtesy of James Orielly.

156. Courtesy of George Potter, http://www.kufic.info.

158. Image 2. (Set of 3 images) © Sterling and Francine Clark Art Institute, Williamstown, Massachussetts, U.S.A.
Photo credit: Michael Agee.

158. Image 3. © CORBIS.

158. Images 4, 5. Courtesy of micro*scope (http://microscope.mbl.edu)

159. Courtesy of Felice Frankel. From *ENVISIONING SCIENCE: THE DESIGN AND CRAFT OF THE SCIENCE IMAGE,* published by The MIT Press.

160. Image 7. Andrea Pozzo (1642-1709). *The Glorification of St.Ignatius*, ceiling fresco, 1691-99.
S. Ignazio, Rome, Italy.
Photo credit: Scala / Art Resource, NY.

160. Image 8, 161. Image 9. M.C. Escher's "Gravity" and "Smaller and Smaller".
© 2009 The M.C. Escher Company-Holland. All rights reserved. www.mcescher.com.

161. Images 10, 11. Reprinted with permission of the author Tamás F. Farkas.

162. Image 12. *EXTREME TEXTILES* by Matilda McQuaid. Copyright 2005 by PRINCETON ARCHITECTURAL PRESS, INC.. Reproduced with permission of PRINCETON ARCHITECTURAL PRESS, INC. in the format Other book via Copyright Clearance Center.

162. Image 13. Courtesy of Acorn Cardiovascular, Inc.

162. Image 14. Courtesy of Ellis Developments, Ltd.
4-5, 163, 164, 166-167, 169-173, 244-245. Courtesy of Evan Douglis.

176. Image 2. Courtesy of the Law Offices of Countryman & McDaniel at www.CargoLaw.com.

174, 176. Images 3, 4. 178-182, 184-187. Courtesy of Ben Nicholson.

188, 191. Image 4, 192-193. © Paul Lowe/Panos Pictures.

190. Image 2. Le Corbusier (Charles-Edouard Jeanneret, 1887-1965) © 2010 Artists Rights Society (ARS), New York / ADAGP, Paris / FLC. *Notre-Dame-du-Haut*, Chapel, 1955. Exterior. Chapelle de Notre-Dame du Haut, Ronchamp, France.
Photo credit: Vanni / Art Resource, NY.

190. Image 3. Jackson Pollock (1912-1956) © 2010 The Pollock-Krasner Foundation / Artists Rights Society (ARS), New York. *Number 4*. 1949. Oil, enamel and aluminum paint with pebbles on cut canvas, on composition board. 90.2 x 87.3 cm (35 1/2 x 34 3/8 in.) The Katharine Ordway Collection. 1980.12.6.
Yale University Art Gallery, New Haven, Connecticut, U.S.A.
Photo credit: Yale University Art Gallery / Art Resource, NY.

191. Image 5. Photo credit: Robert Polidori.

194. Images 7, 8. © Reuters/CORBIS.

195. © Hulton-Deutsch Collection/CORBIS.

196. AP Photo/Amy Sancetta.

197. U.S. Navy Photo by Photographer's Mate 2nd Class Jim Watson. (RELEASED)

198. Courtesy of Ann Pendleton-Jullian.
Photo credit: Guillermo Jullian de la Fuente.

201. Image 2. Photo credit: Jean Capellades.

201. Image 3. Photo credit: Roggio Andreini.

202. Image 4, 203. Image 8. © 2010 Artists Rights Society (ARS), New York / ADAGP, Paris / FLC.

202. Images 5, 6. Courtesy of José Oubrerie.

202. Image 7. Photo credit: College of Architecture University of Kentucky: Exhibition José Oubrerie 1982.

2-3, 204-211. Saint-Pierre de Firminy-Vert: Conception Le Corbusier Architect, José Oubrerie assistant (1960-65) Realization José Oubrerie Architect (1970-2006) Photos courtesy of Luis Burriel Bielza, Architect, Madrid, PhD. Cum Laude dissertation entitled: "Saint-Pierre of Firminy-Vert: the building as an objet-à-réactionémouvante".

212-223, 225-227. Courtesy of Höweler + Yoon Architecture/MY Studio.

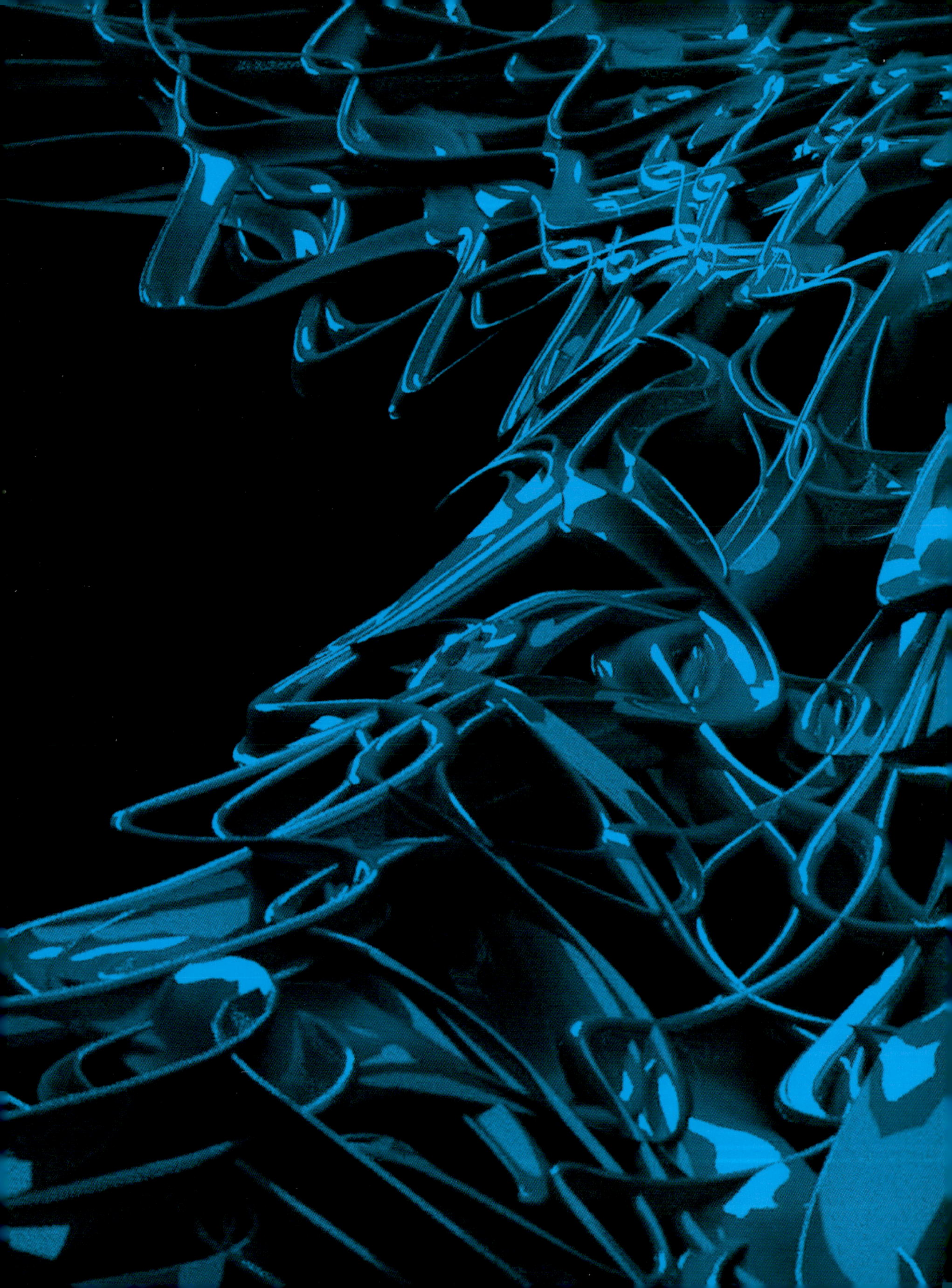

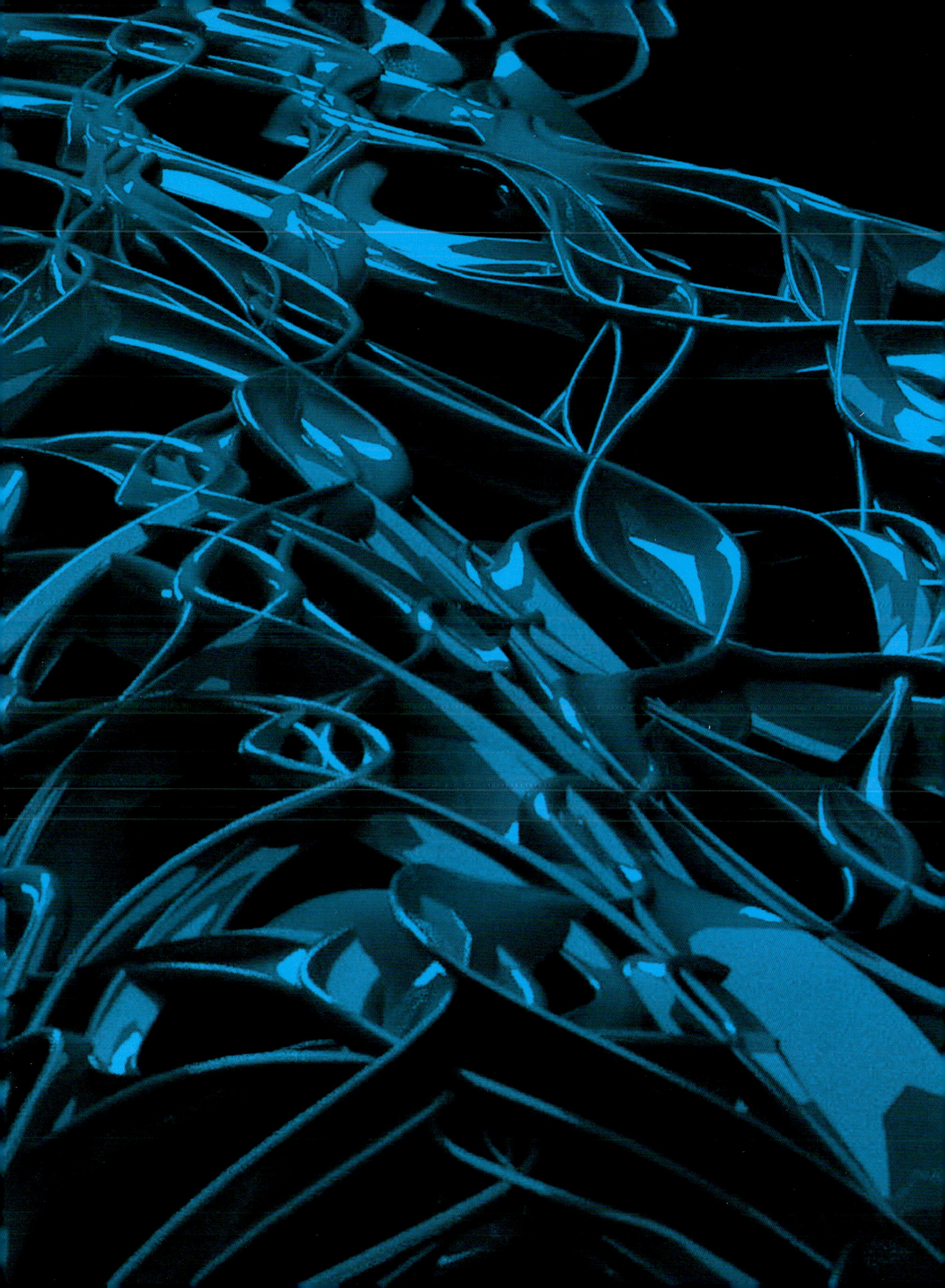

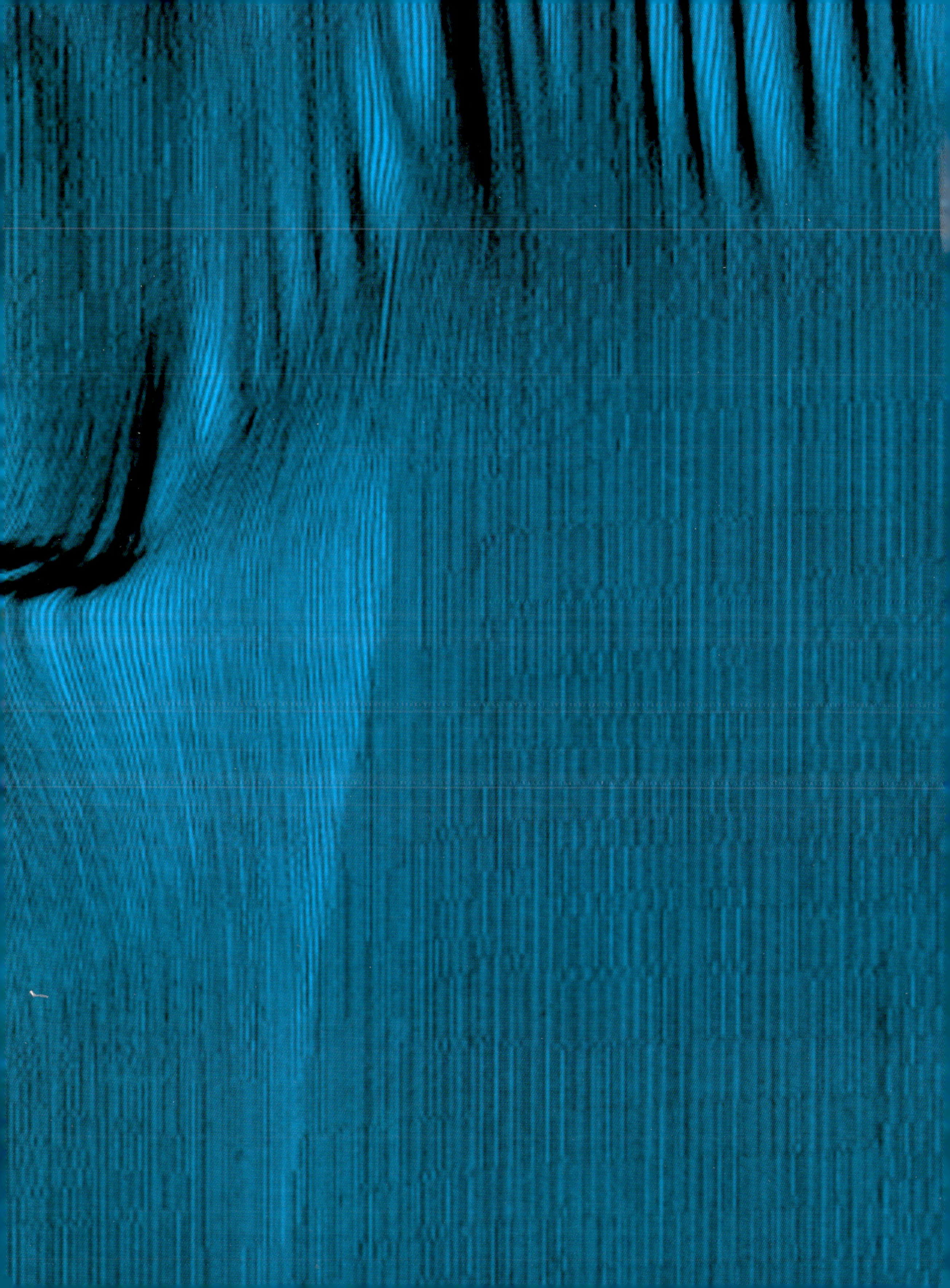

"Every effort has been made to trace the original copyright holders of all photos published herein. If any mistakes have been made please notify us of your concerns and corrections will be made."

Book Credits
Creative Direction by Leo Malinow
Graphic Design by Alejandra Román, Yanina Arabena, and Rosa Santos
Copy Editing by Kit Maude

Oscar Riera Ojeda Publishers

USA

143 South 2nd Street, Suite 208
Philadelphia PA 19106-3073, USA
T: +1 215 238 1333 | F: +1 215 238 1103

www.oscarrieraojeda.com
info@oscarrieraojeda.com

China

Park A, Fang Da Cheng
Longjing Bei Huan Avenue, Nanshan District,
Shenzhen 518055, China
T: +86 755 8336 6138 | F: +86 755 8321 9630

ISBN 978-988-15125-5-0

Printed in China